# Table of Contents

Name _____

# Batter Up!

What did Bobby yell to the batter?

**Directions:** To find out, say the name of each picture. On the line, write the letter that you hear at the beginning of each picture.

H i t     a

h o m e     r u n !

Name _____

# Bats and Balls

**Directions:** Look at the baseball words below. Use the letters from the word box to make new words. **Hint:** Some letters can be used for both sets of words.

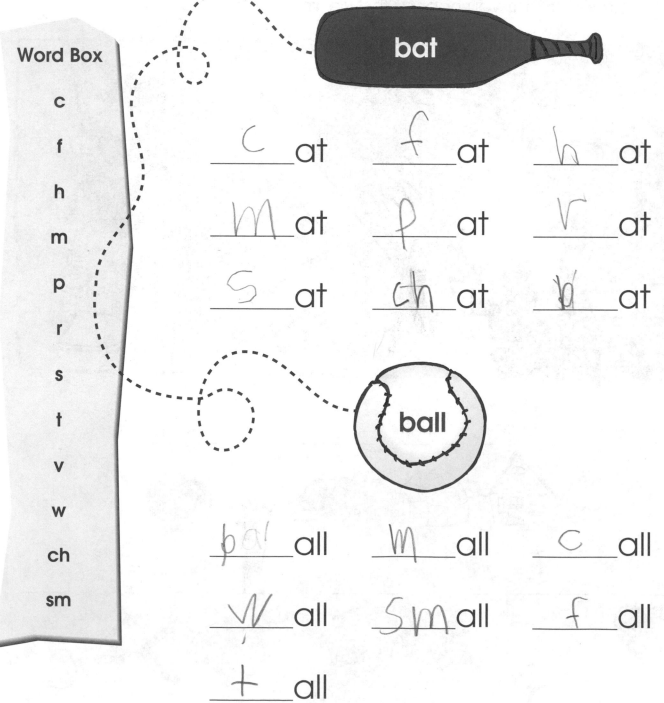

**Word Box**

c
f
h
m
p
r
s
t
v
w
ch
sm

bat

___c__at     ___f__at     ___h__at

___m__at     ___p__at     ___r__at

___s__at     ___ch__at     ___b__at

ball

___ball__all     ___m__all     ___c__all

___w__all     ___sm__all     ___f__all

___t__all

Name _____

# What Does That Spell?

**Directions:** Write the letters from the word box to make new words. Some letters can be used for both sets of words.

| f | b | c | n | p | sk | s | t | fl |

**win**

_f_ f in     _w_ in

_sk_ in     _t_ in

_fl_ in     _p_ in

**game**

_t_ ame     _n_ ame

_n_ ame     _fl_ ame

_f_ ame     _sk_ ame

Name _____

# Sounds the Same

Different words may begin with the same sound.

**Example: Box** and **boy** begin with the same sound.
**Cat** and **dog** do not.

**Directions:** Say each picture's name. Color the pictures in the box if their names begin with the same sound.

# Tic-Tac-Toe

**Directions:** Find the three pictures in each game whose names begin with the same sound. Draw a line through them.

Name _____

# Beginning Consonants: b, c, d, f, g, h, j

**Directions:** Fill in the beginning consonant for each word.

**Example:** __c__ at

__b__ ox

__j__ acket

__g__ oat

__h__ ouse

__d__ og

__f__ ire

# Beginning Consonants: k, l, m, n, p, q, r

**Directions:** Write the letter that makes the beginning sound for each picture.

k     q     r     n

m     l     K     r

q     P     n     m

l     K     r     P

Name _____

# Beginning Consonants: k, l, m, n, p, q, r

**Directions:** Fill in the beginning consonant for each word.

**Example:** ___r___ ose

___m___ oney

___Q___ uilt

___L___ ion

___p___ an

___K___ ey

___n___ ose

Name _____

# Beginning Consonants: s, t, v, w, x, y, z

**Directions:** Write the letter under each picture that makes the beginning sound.

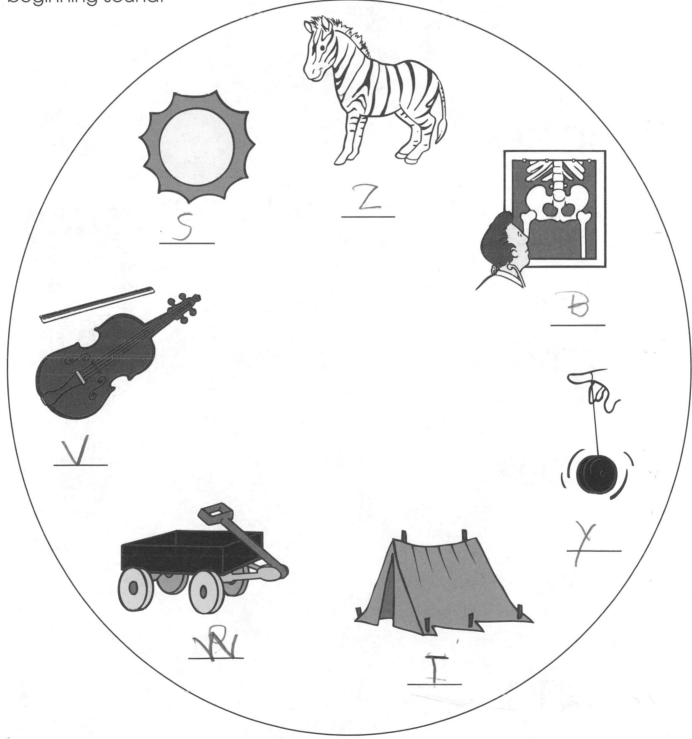

S

Z

B

V

X

W

T

Name _____

# Beginning Consonants: s, t, v, w, x, y, z

**Directions:** Fill in the beginning consonant for each word.

**Example:** __s__ ock

__Z__ ipper

__T__ able

__X__ ray

__V__ ase

__Y__ olk

__W__ and

Name _____

# Ending Consonants: b, d, f, g

**Directions:** Fill in the ending consonant for each word.

ma n _____

cu _____

roo _____

do _____

be _____

bi _____

# Ending Consonants: k, l, m, n, p, r

**Directions:** Fill in the ending consonant for each word.

nai __l__

ca __h__

gu __m__

ca __r__

truc __k__

ca __p__

pai __l__

Name _____

# Ending Consonants: s, t, x

**Directions:** Fill in the ending consonant for each word.

ca ____

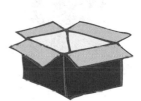

bo ____

bu ____

fo ____

boa ____

ma ____

Name _____

# Consonant Blends

**Consonant blends** are two or three consonant letters in a word whose sounds combine, or blend. **Examples: br, fr, gr, pr, tr**

**Directions:** Look at each picture. Say its name. Write the blend you hear at the beginning of each word.

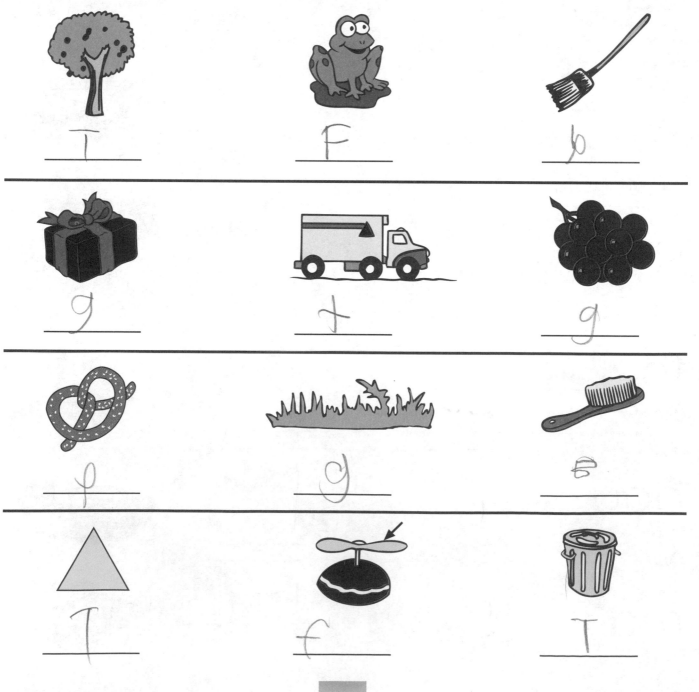

T _____    F _____    b _____

g _____    t _____    g _____

f _____    g _____    B _____

T _____    f _____    T _____

Name _____

# Blends: fl, br, pl, sk, sn

**Blends** are two consonants put together to form a single sound.

**Directions:** Look at the pictures and say their names. Write the letters for the beginning sound in each word.

# Blends: bl, sl, cr, cl

**Directions:** Look at the pictures and say their names. Write the letters for the beginning sound in each word.

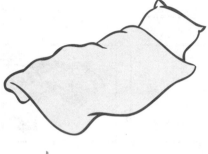

____cl____ own

____b____ anket

____cr____ ayon

____cl____ ock

____sl____ ide

____bl____ oud

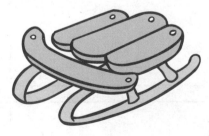

____sl____ ed

____cr____ ab

____cr____ ocodile

Name _____

# Consonant Blends

**Directions:** Write a word from the word box to answer each riddle.

| clock | glass | blow | climb | slipper |
|-------|-------|------|-------|---------|
| sleep | gloves | clap | blocks | flashlight |

1. You need me when the lights go out.
   **What am I?** _____

2. People use me to tell the time.
   **What am I?** _____

3. You put me on your hands in the winter
   to keep them warm. **What am I?** _____

4. Cinderella lost one like me at midnight.
   **What am I?** _____

5. This is what you do with your hands when
   you are pleased. **What is it?** _____

6. You can do this with a whistle or with
   bubble gum. **What is it?** _____

7. These are what you might use to build a
   castle when you are playing.
   **What are they?** _____

8. You do this to get to the top of a hill.
   **What is it?** _____

9. This is what you use to drink water or milk.
   **What is it?** _____

10. You do this at night with your eyes closed.
    **What is it?** _____

Name _____

# Nothing But Net

**Directions:** Write the missing consonant blends.

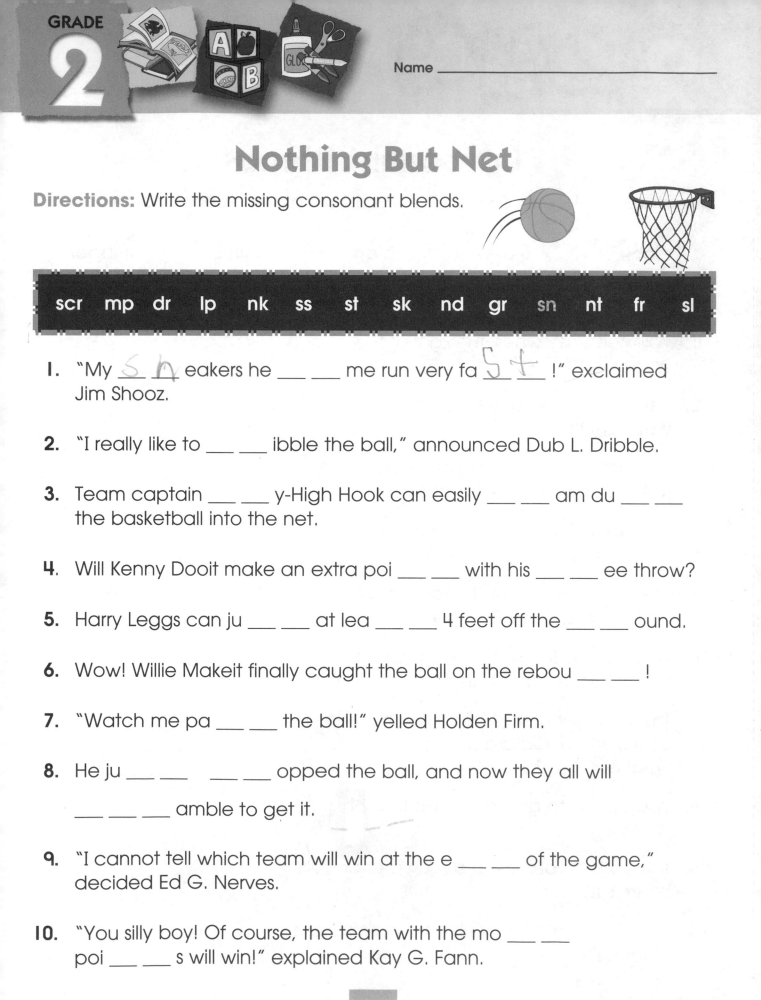

| scr | mp | dr | lp | nk | ss | st | sk | nd | gr | sn | nt | fr | sl |
|-----|-----|-----|-----|-----|-----|-----|-----|-----|-----|-----|-----|-----|-----|

1. "My s n eakers he ___ ___ me run very fa s t !" exclaimed Jim Shooz.

2. "I really like to ___ ___ ibble the ball," announced Dub L. Dribble.

3. Team captain ___ ___ y-High Hook can easily ___ ___ am du ___ ___ the basketball into the net.

4. Will Kenny Dooit make an extra poi ___ ___ with his ___ ___ ee throw?

5. Harry Leggs can ju ___ ___ at lea ___ ___ 4 feet off the ___ ___ ound.

6. Wow! Willie Makeit finally caught the ball on the rebou ___ ___ !

7. "Watch me pa ___ ___ the ball!" yelled Holden Firm.

8. He ju ___ ___  ___ ___ opped the ball, and now they all will

    ___ ___ ___ amble to get it.

9. "I cannot tell which team will win at the e ___ ___ of the game," decided Ed G. Nerves.

10. "You silly boy! Of course, the team with the mo ___ ___ poi ___ ___ s will win!" explained Kay G. Fann.

Name _____

# Consonant Digraph th

Some consonants work together to stand for a new sound. They are called **consonant digraphs**. Listen for the sound of consonant digraph **th** in **think**.

**th**ink

**Directions:** Print **th** under the pictures whose names begin with the sound of **th**. Color the **th** pictures.

th

ch

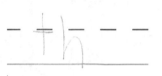

30

th

# Think About th

**Directions:** Say the name of each picture. Fill in the missing letter or letters.

think

h orn

thorn

10
t en

thumb

30
thirty

**Directions:** Find and circle these **th** words in the puzzle. The words may go **across** or **down**.

| think | thorn | thumb | thirty |
|-------|-------|-------|--------|

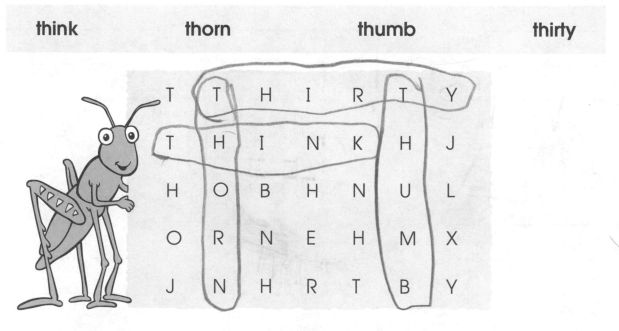

```
T  T  H  I  R  T  R  T  Y
T  T  H  I  N  K  H  J
H  O  B  H  N  U  L
O  R  N  E  H  M  X
J  N  H  R  T  B  Y
```

Name _____

# Consonant Digraph sh

Listen for the sound of consonant digraph **sh** in **sheep**.

**Directions:** Color the pictures whose names begin with the sound of **sh**.

**sh**eep

Name _____

# Change a Word

**Directions:** Make a new word by changing the beginning sound to **sh**. Write the new word on the line.

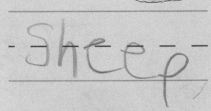
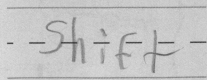

made - m
+ sh = shade

zip

_Ship_

tin

_Shin_

red

_Shed_

top

_Shop_

sell

_shell_

line

_Shine_

cape

_shape_

bake

_Shake_

beep

_Sheep_

lift

_Shift_

cave

_Shave_

feet

_Sheet_

# Consonant Digraph wh

**Directions:** Write **wh**, **th**, or **sh** to complete each word.

wh eel

wh ale

sh eep

th ink

wh eat

th orn

sh ip

th irty

wh ite

Name _____

# Wheel of Fortune

Listen for the sound of consonant digraph **wh** in **whale**.

**wh**ale

**Directions:** Color the pictures whose names begin with consonant digraph **wh**.

**wh**

30

Name _____

# Consonant Digraph ch

Listen for the sound of consonant digraph **ch** in **cherry**.

**ch**erry

**Directions:** Trace the cherry if the name of the picture begins with the **ch** sound. Use a red crayon.

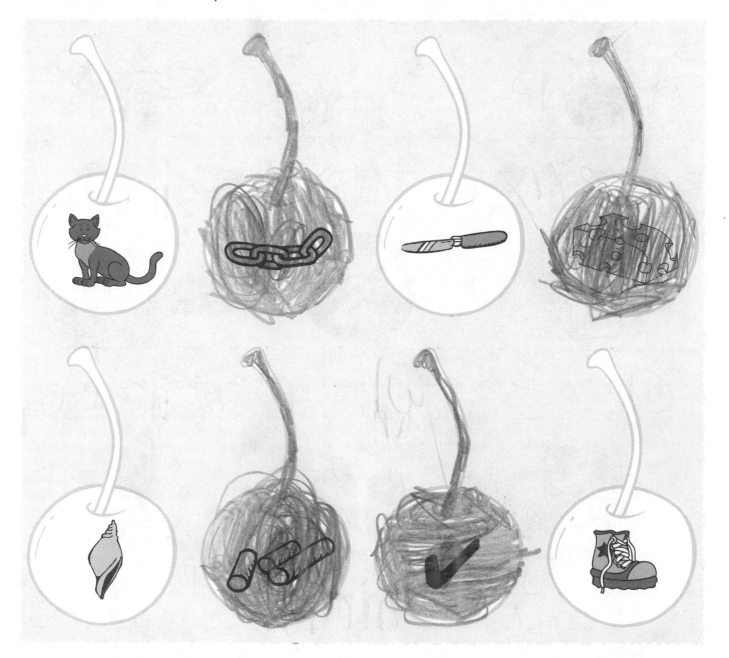

# Read and Write Digraphs

**Directions:** Write a word from the box to label each picture.

| chest | check | sheep |
| chimp | cherry | thirty |
| chain | cheese | wheel |

cherry

sheep

chain

chest

wheel

cheese

chimp

thirty

4wheel

# Consonant Digraph kn

Listen for the sound of consonant digraph **kn** in **knot**.
The **k** is silent.

**kn**ot

**Directions:** Color the pictures whose names begin with the **kn** sound.
Connect all the colored pictures from the knight to his horse.

# Knocking Around in Knickers

A long time ago, golfers wore knickers when they played. **Knickers** are short, loose trousers gathered just below the knee. **Kn** at the beginning of a word makes the same sound as **n**.

**Directions:** Look at each picture and write **kn** or **k** at the beginning to complete the words.

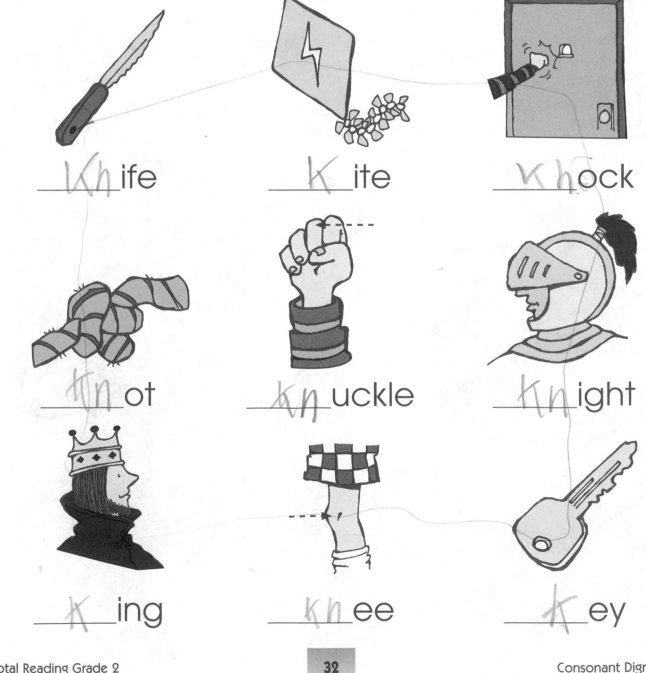

__Kn__ife     __K__ite     __K__nock

__kn__ot     __kn__uckle     __Kn__ight

__K__ing     __kn__ee     __K__ey

Name _____

# Consonant Digraph wr

Listen for the sound of consonant digraph **wr** in **wren**. The **w** is silent.

**wr**en

**Directions:** Write a word from the box to label each picture.
Color the pictures whose names begin with **wr**.

| web | wrist | wring | wrap | |
|-----|-------|-------|------|------|
| worm | write | wreath | wink | wrench |

wring

wrap

worm

wrist

wrench

web

wink

write

wreath

Name _____

# Ending Digraphs

Some words end with consonant digraphs. Listen for the ending digraphs in **duck**, **moth**, **dish**, and **branch**.

du**ck**     mo**th**     di**sh**     bran**ch**

**Directions:** Say the name of each picture. Circle the letters that stand for the ending sound.

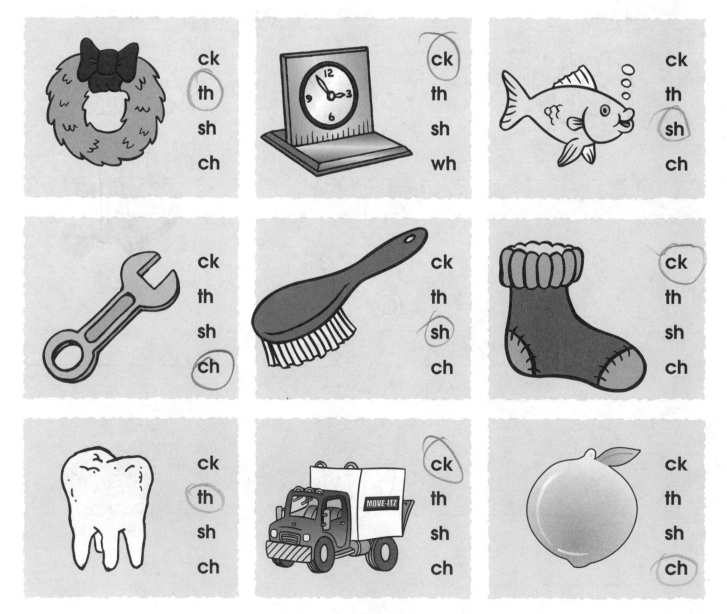

ck
(th)
sh
ch

(ck)
th
sh
wh

ck
th
(sh)
ch

ck
th
sh
(ch)

ck
th
(sh)
ch

(ck)
th
sh
ch

ck
(th)
sh
ch

(ck)
th
sh
ch

ck
th
sh
(ch)

Name _____

# Hear and Write Digraphs

**Directions:** The name of each picture below ends with **ck**, **th**, **sh**, or **ch**. Write each word on the lines below.

black     bench     splash

moth     peach     truck

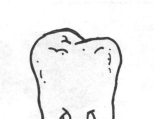

fish     tooth     paint

Name _____

# Missing Digraphs

**Directions:** Fill in the circle beside the missing digraph in each word.

Whale
- ● wh
- ○ wr
- ○ ch

peach
- ○ ck
- ○ th
- ● ch

Knife
- ● kn
- ○ ch
- ○ wr

Chimp
- ○ ck
- ○ kn
- ● ch

Shell
- ○ ch
- ● sh
- ○ ck

clock
- ● ck
- ○ ch
- ○ kn

write
- ○ kn
- ● wr
- ○ th

fish
- ○ ch
- ● sh
- ○ th

thorn
- ● th
- ○ wr
- ○ ch

Name _____

# Missing Digraphs

**Directions:** Fill in the circle beside the missing digraph in each word.

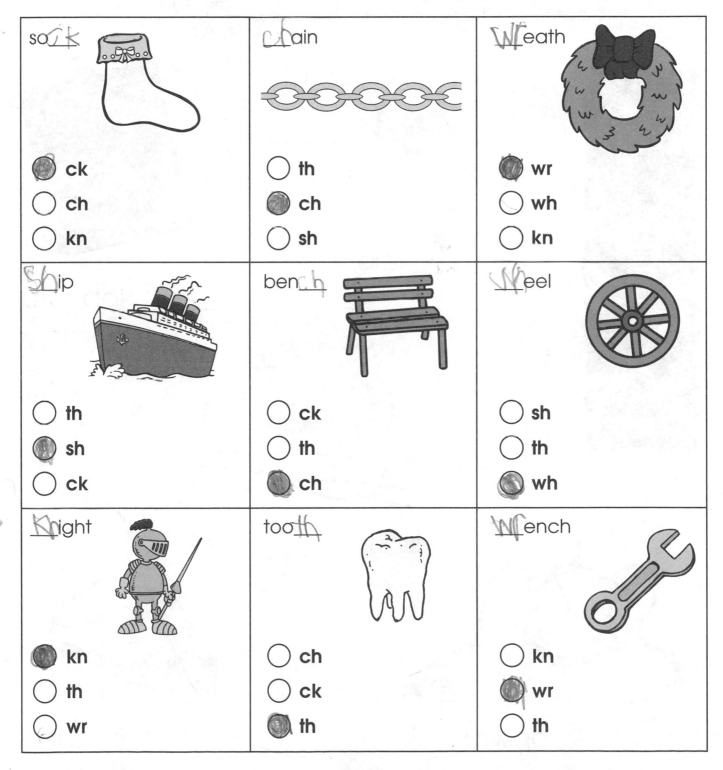

so_ck

- ● ck
- ○ ch
- ○ kn

ch ain

- ○ th
- ● ch
- ○ sh

Wreath

- ● wr
- ○ wh
- ○ kn

Ship

- ○ th
- ● sh
- ○ ck

ben ch

- ○ ck
- ○ th
- ● ch

Wheel

- ○ sh
- ○ th
- ● wh

Knight

- ● kn
- ○ th
- ○ wr

too th

- ○ ch
- ○ ck
- ● th

Wrench

- ○ kn
- ● wr
- ○ th

Name _____

# At the Pool

**Directions:** Write the correct letters from the word box to complete the word for each picture.

**Word Box**

wh

bl

sw

ci

st

ch

___Wh___ istle

___Cl___ ipboard

starting ___bl___ ock

___St___ opwat ___ch___

___Sw___ im cap

Name _____

# Silent Letters

Some words have letters you cannot hear at all, such as the **gh** in **night**, the **w** in **wrong**, the **l** in **walk**, the **k** in **knee**, the **b** in **climb**, and the **t** in **listen**.

**Directions:** Look at the words in the word box. Write the word under its picture. Underline the silent letters.

| knife | light | calf | wrench | lamb | eight |
|-------|-------|------|--------|------|-------|
| wrist | whistle | comb | thumb | knob | knee |

eight

wrist

knee

calf

lamb

knob

whistle

light

wrench

comb

thumb

knife

Name _____

# A Flying Saucer?

A **discus** is a flat circle made mostly of wood with a metal center and edge that looks a bit like a plate. A men's discus is about 9 inches across and weighs a little over 4 pounds. A women's discus is about 2 inches smaller and about 2 pounds lighter. The men's world record throw is 243 feet, but the women's world record is even greater—252 feet!

**Directions:** Read the word in each discus. Write its silent consonant in the center.

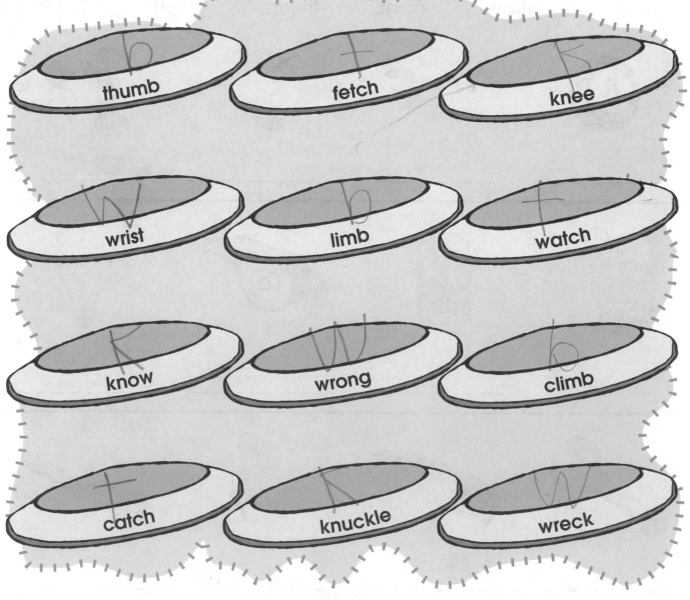

Name _____

# Hard and Soft c and g

**Directions:** Circle as many words in each word search as you can find. List them in the correct column. **Hint:** The words going up and down have the hard sound, and the words going across and backwards have the soft sound.

## g

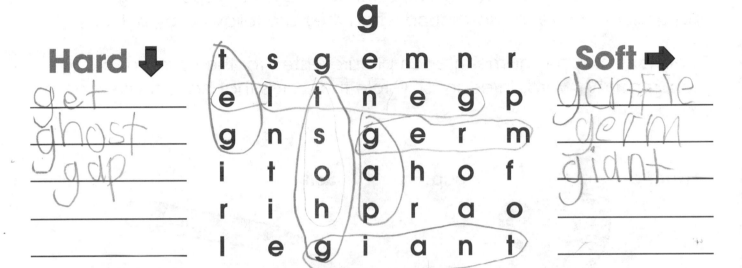

**Hard ⬇**
get
ghost
gap
_____
_____

**Soft ➡**
gentle
germ
giant
_____

```
t  s  g  e  m  n  r
e  l  t  n  e  g  p
g  n  s  g  e  r  m
i  t  o  a  h  o  f
r  i  h  p  r  a  o
l  e  g  i  a  n  t
```

Two words in the **c** word search go diagonally. They have both a hard and a soft **c** sound.

## c

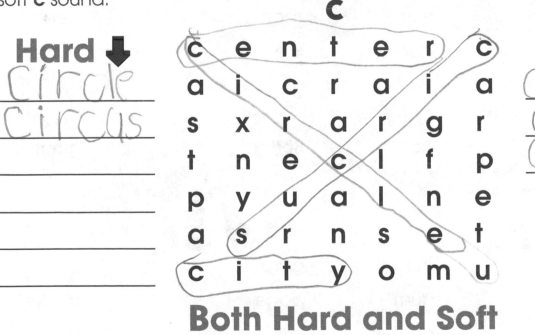

**Hard ⬇**
circle
circus
_____
_____
_____

**Soft ➡**
center
circle
circus

```
c  e  n  t  e  r  c
a  i  c  r  a  i  a
s  x  r  a  r  g  r
t  n  e  c  l  f  p
p  y  u  a  l  n  e
a  s  r  n  s  e  t
c  i  t  y  o  m  u
```

## Both Hard and Soft

_____    _____

Name _____

# Sounds of c and g

Consonants **c** and **g** each have two sounds. Listen for the soft **c** sound in **pencil**. Listen for the hard **c** sound in **cup**.

Listen for the soft **g** sound in **giant**. Listen for the hard **g** sound in **goat**. **C** and **g** usually have the soft sound when they are followed by **e**, **i**, or **y**.

**Directions:** Say the name of each picture. Listen for the sound of **c** or **g**. Then, read the words in each list. Circle the words that have that sound of **c** or **g**.

| **Hard c** | **cup** |
|---|---|
| car | race |
| city | rice |
| cone | can |

| **Soft c** | **pencil** |
|---|---|
| cage | cane |
| face | cent |
| ice | cube |

| **Hard g** | **goat** |
|---|---|
| good | magic |
| dragon | gum |
| stage | gentle |

| **Soft g** | **giant** |
|---|---|
| garden | gem |
| page | giraffe |
| gas | gorilla |

# Hard and Soft c and g

**Directions:** Underline the letter that follows the **c** or **g** in each word. Write **hard** if the word has the hard **c** or hard **g** sound. Write **soft** if the word has the soft **c** or soft **g** sound.

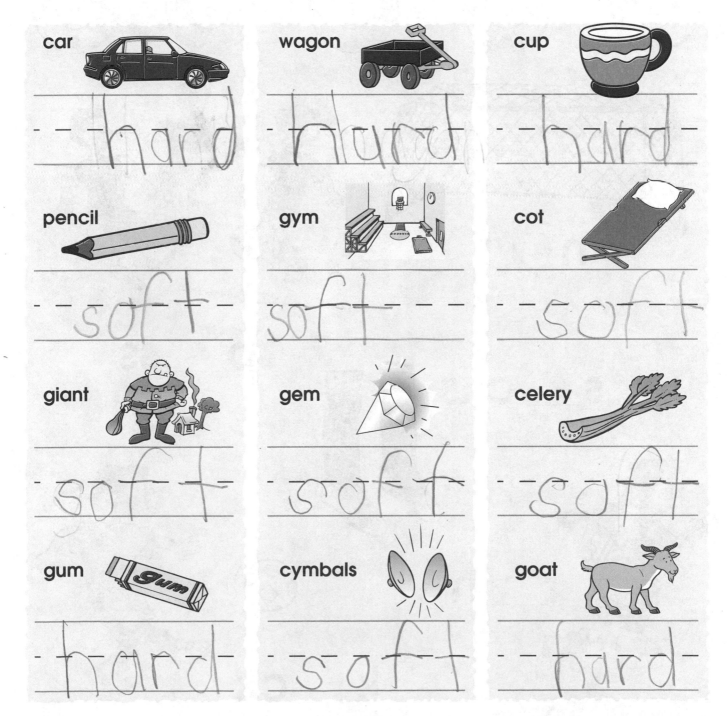

car — hard

wagon — hard

cup — hard

pencil — soft

gym — soft

cot — soft

giant — soft

gem — soft

celery — soft

gum — hard

cymbals — soft

goat — hard

Name _____

# Kick It In!

**Directions:** Write a vowel to complete each word below.

a    e    i    o    u

n_e_t

p_a_ss

s_o_cks

r_u_n

k_i_ck

# Super Silent e

Long vowel sounds have the same sound as their names. When a **Super Silent e** appears at the end of a word, you cannot hear it, but it makes the other vowel have a long sound. For example: **tub** has a **short** vowel sound, and **tube** has a **long** vowel sound.

**Directions:** Look at the following pictures. Decide if the word has a short or long vowel sound. Circle the correct word. Watch for the **Super Silent e**!

can   cane        tub   tube        rob   robe        rat   rate

pin   pine        cap   cape        not   note        pan   pane

slid   slide        dim   dime        tap   tape        cub   cube

Name _____

# Long Vowels

Long vowel sounds have the same sound as their names. When a **Super Silent e** comes at the end of a word, you cannot hear it, but it changes the short vowel sound to a long vowel sound.

**Examples:** rope, skate, bee, pie, cute

**Directions:** Say the name of the pictures. Listen for the long vowel sounds. Write the missing long vowel sound under each picture.

c _a_ ke          h _i_ ke          n _o_ se

___ pe          c _u_ be          gr _a_ pe

r _a_ ke          b _o_ ne          k _i_ te

          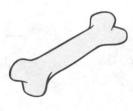

Name _____

# Review

**Directions:** Read the words in each box. Cross out the word that does **not** belong.

| long vowels | short vowels |
|---|---|
| (cube) | (man) |
| cup | pet |
| rake | fix |
| me | ice |

| long vowels | short vowels |
|---|---|
| (soap) | (cat) |
| seed | pin |
| read | rain |
| mat | frog |

**Directions:** Write **short** or **long** to label the words in each box.

| long vowels | Short vowels |
|---|---|
| (hose) | (frog) |
| take | hot |
| bead | sled |
| cube | lap |
| eat | block |
| see | sit |

Name _____

# Tricky ar

When **r** follows a vowel, it changes the vowel's sound.
Listen for the **ar** sound in **star**.

**Directions:** Color the pictures whose names have the **ar** sound.

 st**ar**

 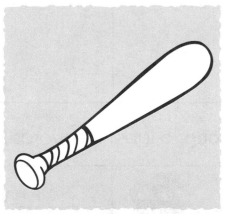 

**58**

# Write ar or or

Listen for the **or** sound in **horn**.

**Directions:** Write **ar** or **or** to complete each word.

horn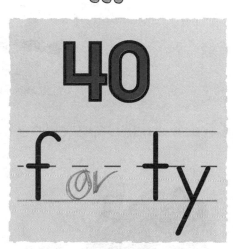

th o r n

c ar t

f or ty

st __ k

c or n

h ar p

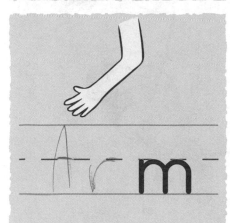

Ar m

st ar

p or ch

Name _____

# Mix and Match

The letters **ur**, **er**, and **ir** all have the same sound. Listen for the vowel sound in **surf**, **fern**, and **girl**.

s**ur**f

f**er**n

g**ir**l

**Directions:** Draw a line from each word in the circle to the picture it names.

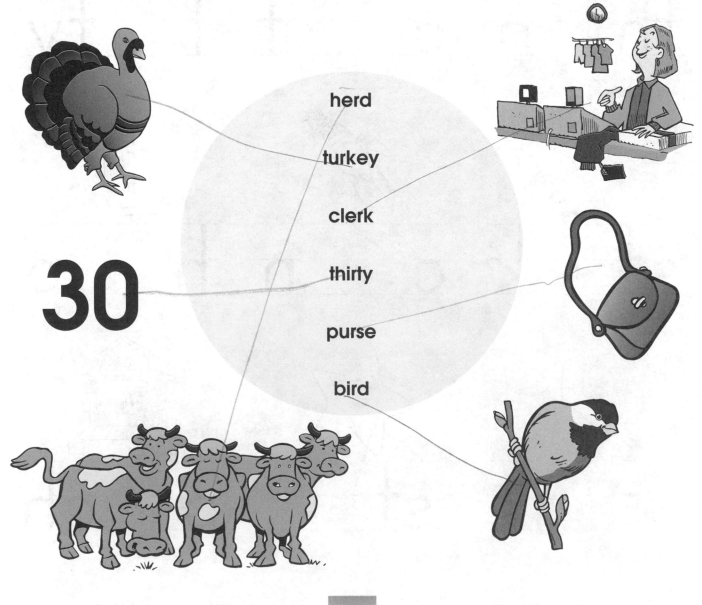

herd

turkey

clerk

thirty

purse

bird

30

# Write ur, er, and ir

**Directions:** Find a word from the box to name each picture. Write it on the line below the picture.

| turkey | clerk | dirt | fern | |
| girl | herd | purple | surf | thirty |

Name _____

# Vowel Pairs ai and ay

You know that the letters **a__e** usually stand for the long **a** sound. The vowel pairs **ai** and **ay** can stand for the long **a** sound, too. Listen for the long **a** sound in **train** and **hay**.

**Directions:** Say the name of each picture below. Look at the vowel pair that stands for the long **a** sound. Under each picture, write the words from the box that have the same long **a** vowel pair.

| | | | |
|---|---|---|---|
| cage | chain | gate | gray |
| mail | pay | snail | skate |
| play | snake | stay | tail |

cake        train        hay

cage      chain      gray

rake      stay      skate

make      pay      pay

take      snake      snake

# Vowel Pairs oa and ow

You know that the letters **o__e** and **oe** usually stand for the long **o** sound. The vowel pairs **oa** and **ow** can stand for the long **o** sound, too. Listen for the long **o** sound in **road** and **snow**.

**Directions:** Find and circle eight long **o** words. The words may go **across** or **down**. Beside each picture, write the words that use the same long **o** vowel pair.

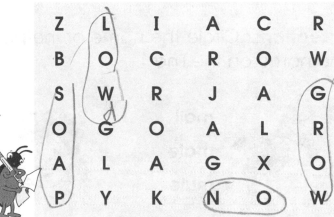

Z L I A C R
B O C R O W
S W R J A G
O G O A L R
A L A G X O
P Y K N O W

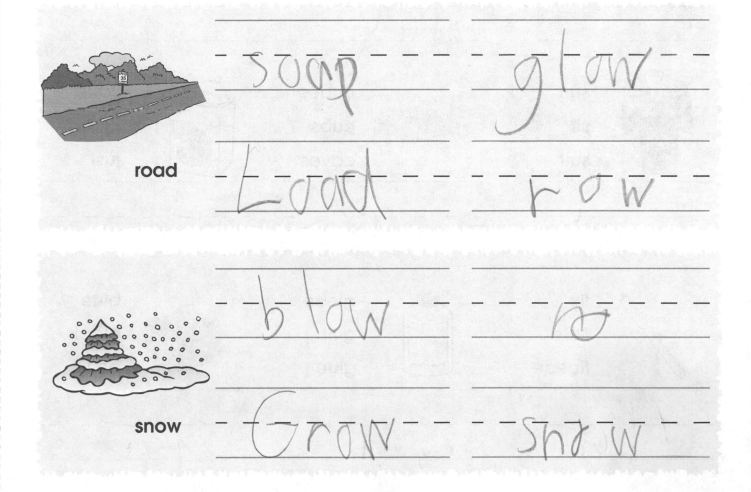

road

soap

load

glow

row

snow

blow

no

Grow

snow

Name _____

# Vowel Pair ui

You know that the letters **u__e** and **ue** usually stand for the long **u** sound. The vowel pair **ui** can stand for the long **u** sound, too. Listen for the long **u** sound in **cruise**.

**Directions:** Circle the name of the picture. Then, write the name on the line.

cru**ise**

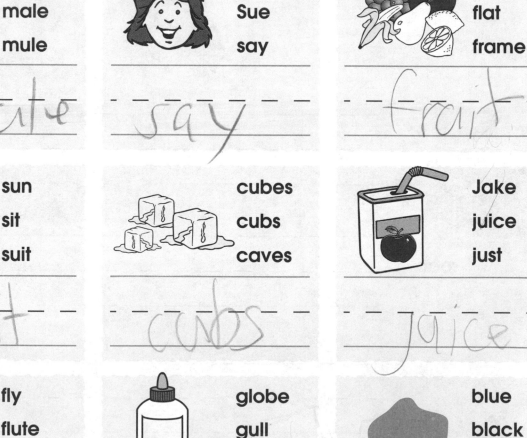

mall
male
mule

_mule_

sun
Sue
say

_say_

fruit
flat
frame

_fruit_

sun
sit
suit

_suit_

cubes
cubs
caves

_cubs_

Jake
juice
just

_juice_

fly
flute
fleece

_flute_

globe
gull
glue

_glue_

blue
black
ball

_blue_

Name _____

# Vowel Pair ie

You know that the letters **i__e** usually stand for the long **i** sound. The vowel pair **ie** can stand for the long **i** sound, too. Listen for the long **i** sound in **butterflies**.

**Directions:** Write **i__e** or **ie** to complete each word. Draw a picture for one **i__e** word and one **ie** word.

butterfl**ie**s

dime        tie        flies

five        knife        tried

pie        lie        kite

i__e picture

ie picture

Name _____

# Missing Vowel Pairs

**Directions:** Fill in the circle beside the missing vowel pair in each word.

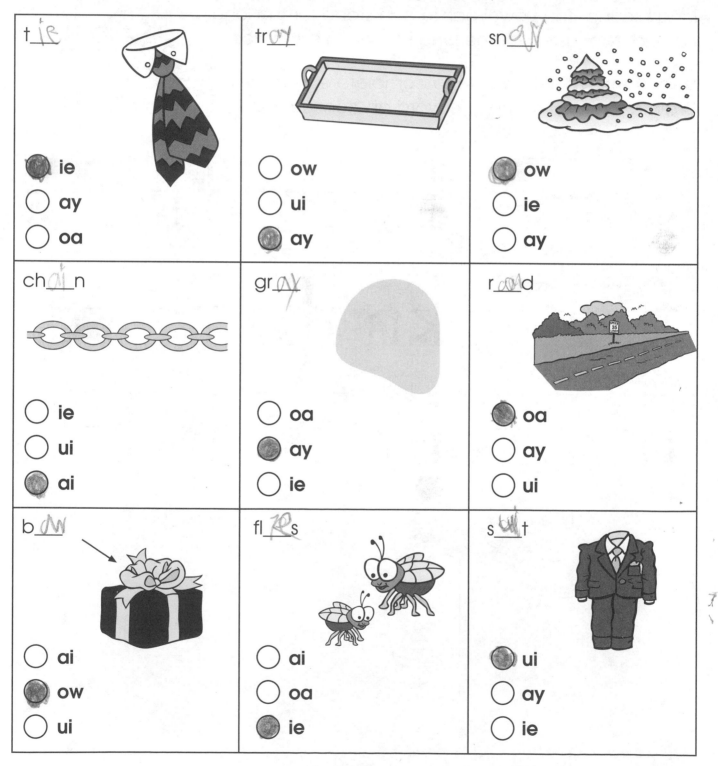

t _ie_

- ● ie
- ○ ay
- ○ oa

tr _oy_

- ○ ow
- ○ ui
- ● ay

sn _ow_

- ● ow
- ○ ie
- ○ ay

ch _ai_ n

- ○ ie
- ○ ui
- ● ai

gr _ay_

- ○ oa
- ● ay
- ○ ie

r _oa_ d

- ● oa
- ○ ay
- ○ ui

b _ow_

- ○ ai
- ● ow
- ○ ui

fl _ie_ s

- ○ ai
- ○ oa
- ● ie

s _ui_ t

- ● ui
- ○ ay
- ○ ie

Name _____

# Missing Vowel Pairs

**Directions:** Fill in the circle beside the missing vowel pair in each word.

h_ay_

○ ui
○ ow
● ay

tr_ai_n

○ oa
● ai
○ ie

s_oa_p

● oa
○ ai
○ ui

j_ui_ce

○ ai
● ui
○ ie

p_ie_

○ ui
○ oa
● ie

cr_ow_

○ ui
○ ay
● ow

g_oa_t

○ ai
● oa
○ ui

fr_ui_t

○ ai
○ ow
● ui

sn_ai_l

○ ow
● ai
○ ie

Name _____

# Vowel Pair ea

Some vowel pairs can stand for more than one sound. The vowel pair **ea** has the sound of long **e** in **team** and short **e** in **head**.

t**ea**m                     h**ea**d

**Directions:** Say the name of each picture. Listen for the sound that **ea** stands for. Circle **Long e** or **Short e**. Then, color the pictures whose names have the short **e** sound.

|  |  |  |
|---|---|---|
| (Long e)    Short e | Long e    (Short e) | (Long e)    Short e |
| Long e    (Short e) | Long e    (Short e) | (Long e)    Short e |
| Long e    (Short e) | (Long e)    Short e | Long e    (Short e) |

Name _____

# Vowel Pair oo

Listen for the difference between the sound of the vowel pair **oo** in **moon** and its sound in **book**.

moon   book

**Directions:** Say the name of the picture. Circle the picture of the moon or the book to show the sound of vowel pair **oo**.

Name _____

# Y as a Vowel

Y as a vowel can make two sounds. Y can make the long sound of **e** or the long sound of **i**.

**Directions:** Color the spaces:
**purple** – y sounds like **i**.
**yellow** – y sounds like **e**.

What is the picture? _____

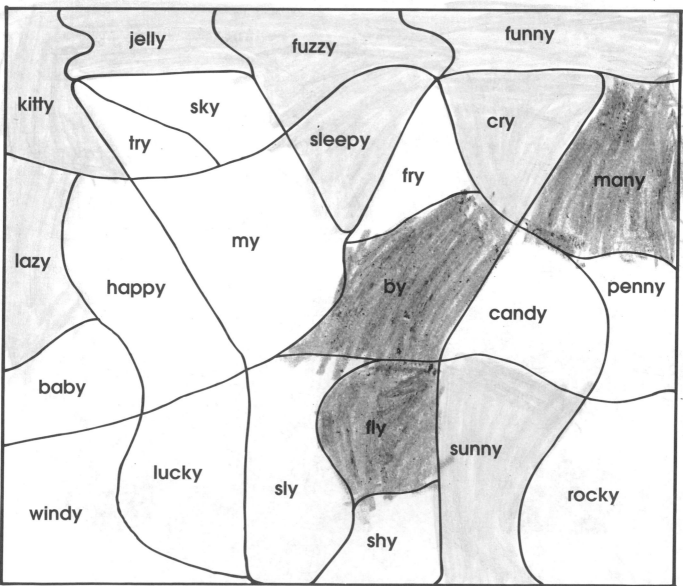

jelly

fuzzy

funny

kitty

sky

sleepy

cry

try

fry

many

my

lazy

happy

by

penny

candy

baby

fly

sunny

lucky

sly

rocky

windy

shy

Name _____

# A Fork in the Road

**Directions:** Write the words below on the correct "road."

| | | | | | |
|---|---|---|---|---|---|
| sky | jelly | try | kitty | fly | my |
| fry | cry | funny | dry | penny | |
| candy | by | sleepy | happy | lazy | baby |
| sly | fuzzy | shy | many | why | |

_____          _____

_____          _____

_____          _____

_____          _____

_____          _____

_____          _____

_____          _____

_____

_____

**Y** sounds like **long e**.          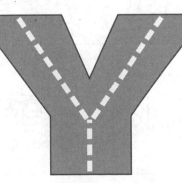          **Y** sounds like **long i**.

Name _____

# Short and Long a e i o u

**Directions:** Color the correct pictures in each box.

˘ means short vowel sound        ¯ means long vowel sound

| ă | blue | | |
| ā | orange | | | | |

| ĕ | red | | |
| ē | yellow | | | | |

| ĭ | green | | |
| ī | purple | | | | |

| ŏ | yellow | | |
| ō | blue | | | | |

| ŭ | green | | |
| ū | orange | | | | |

# Review

**Directions:** Read the story. Fill in the blanks with words from the word box.

| cookies | Joe | bowl | tooth | flour | eight |
|---------|-----|------|-------|-------|-------|
| spoon | eats | enjoys | round | boy | either |

Do you like to cook? I know a _____ named

_____ who loves to cook. When Joe has a sweet

_____, he makes _____. He puts

_____ and sugar in a _____ and

stirs it with a _____. Then, he adds the butter and eggs.

He makes cookies that are _____ or other shapes. He

likes them _____ way. Now is the part he

_____ the most: Joe _____ the cookies.

He might eat seven or _____ at a time!

# Compound Your Effort

A **compound word** is made from two shorter words. An example of a compound word is **sandbox**, made from **sand** and **box**.

**Directions:** Find one word in the word box that goes with each of the words below to make a compound word. Write the compound words on the lines. Cross out each word that you use.

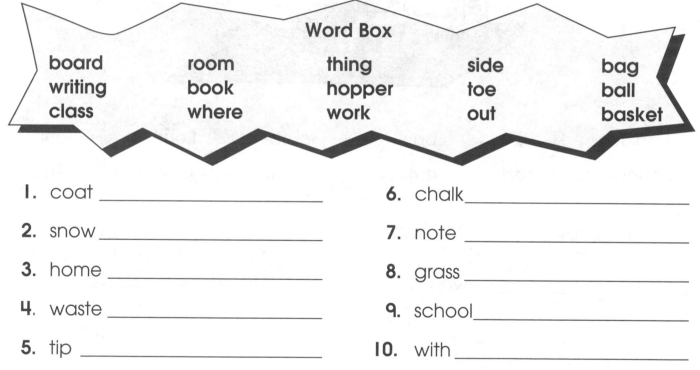

**Word Box**

| board | room | thing | side | bag |
| writing | book | hopper | toe | ball |
| class | where | work | out | basket |

1. coat _____

2. snow _____

3. home _____

4. waste _____

5. tip _____

6. chalk _____

7. note _____

8. grass _____

9. school _____

10. with _____

Look at the words in the word box that you did **not** use. Use those words to make your own compound words.

1. _____

2. _____

3. _____

4. _____

5. _____

Name _____

# Word Magic

Maggie Magician announced, "One plus one equals one!" The audience giggled. So, Maggie put two words into a hat and waved her magic wand. When she reached into the hat, Maggie pulled out one word and a plcture. "See," said Maggie, "I was right!"

**Directions:** Use the word box to help you write a compound word for each picture below.

| ball | door | rain | star | shirt | bell | fish | shoe | book | foot | basket |
|------|------|------|------|-------|------|------|------|------|------|--------|
| bow | lace | box | stool | light | sun | cup | mail | tail | cake | worm |

Name _____

# Mixing a Compound

sometimes    downtown    girlfriend

everybody    maybe    myself    lunchbox

baseball    outside    today

**Directions:** Write the correct compound word on the line. Then, use the numbered letters to solve the code.

1. Opposite of inside    __ __ __ __ __ __ __
                              1

2. Another word for *me*    __ __ __ __ __ __
                            2             3

3. A girl who is a friend   __ __ __ __ __ __ __ __ __ __
                4                  5

4. Not yesterday or tomorrow, but . . .   __ __ __ __ __
                                6

5. All of the people    __ __ __ __ __ __ __ __
                      7            8

6. A sport    __ __ __ __ __ __ __ __
                                  9

7. The main part of a town   __ __ __ __ __ __ __ __
                      10            11

8. Not always, just . . .   __ __ __ __ __ __ __ __ __
          12              13

9. A box for carrying your lunch   __ __ __ __ __ __ __ __
                          14

10. Perhaps or might   __ __ __ __ __
                              15

__ __ __ __ __ __ __ __ __ __ __ __ !
10  8  11  6  15  7  3  1  9    2  8  1

__ __ __ __ __ __ __ __
3  8  1  11  6  13  14  15

__ __ __ __ __ __ __ __ __ __ __ __ __ !
7  5  4  14  13  12  8  9  1  13  5  8  11

Name _____

# Prefix re

A **prefix** is a word part. It is added to the beginning of a base word to change the base word's meaning. The prefix **re** means "again."

**Example:**      **Refill** means "to fill again."

**Directions:** Look at the pictures. Read the base words. Add the prefix **re** to the base word to show that the action is being done again. Write your new word on the line.

read

_____

write

_____

paint

_____

use

_____

build

_____

pay

_____

Name _____

# Prefixes un and dis

The prefixes **un** and **dis** mean "not" or "the opposite of."

**Unlocked** means "not locked."

**Dismount** is the opposite of "mount."

**Directions:** Look at the pictures. Circle the word that tells about the picture. Then, write the word on the line.

tied

untied

like

dislike

happy

unhappy

obey

disobey

safe

unsafe

honest

dishonest

**80**

Name _____

# Suffixes ful, less, ness, ly

A **suffix** is a word part that is added at the end of a base word to change the base word's meaning. Look at the suffixes below.

The suffix **ful** means "full of." **Cheerful** means "full of cheer."

The suffix **less** means "without." **Cloudless** means "without clouds."

The suffix **ness** means "a state of being." **Darkness** means "being dark."

The suffix **ly** means "in this way." **Slowly** means "in a slow way."

**Directions:** Add the suffixes to the base words to make new words.

care + ful = _____

pain + less = _____

brave + ly = _____

sad + ly = _____

sick + ness = _____

Name _____

# Suffixes and Meanings

**Remember:** The suffix **ful** means "full of."

The suffix **less** means "without."

The suffix **ness** means "a state of being."

The suffix **ly** means "in this way."

The sun shines **brightly**.

**Directions:** Write the word that matches the meaning.

without pain

_____

— — — — — — — — — — —

_____

in a quick way

_____

— — — — — — — — — — —

_____

in a neat way

_____

— — — — — — — — — — —

_____

without fear

_____

— — — — — — — — — — —

_____

full of grace

_____

— — — — — — — — — — —

_____

the state of being soft

_____

— — — — — — — — — — —

_____

the state of being sick

_____

— — — — — — — — — — —

_____

in a glad way

_____

— — — — — — — — — — —

_____

# Suffixes er and est

Suffixes **er** and **est** can be used to compare. Use **er** when you compare two things. Use **est** when you compare more than two things.

**Example:** The puppy is small**er** than its mom.
This puppy is the small**est** puppy in the litter.

**Directions:** Add the suffixes to the base words to make words that compare.

| Base Word | + er | + est |
|---|---|---|
| 1. loud | louder | loudest |
| 2. old | | |
| 3. neat | | |
| 4. fast | | |
| 5. kind | | |
| 6. tall | | |

# Scale the Synonym Slope

**Synonyms** are words that have almost the same meaning. **Tired** and **sleepy** are synonyms. **Talk** and **speak** are synonyms.

**Directions:** Read the word. Find its synonym on the hill. Write the synonym on the line.

1. glad _____

2. little _____

3. begin _____

4. above _____

5. damp _____

6. large _____

wet

big

happy

over

small

start

# Synonym Match

**Directions:** Look at the pictures. Read the words in the box. Write two synonyms you could use to tell about each picture.

| rocks | start | road | begin | street | stones | sad | unhappy |

Name _____

# Almost the Same!

**Directions:** Write a word that has almost the same meaning as the **boldfaced** word. Use the word list for clues.

Hey, you're *large*!

And you're *big*!

| Word List | | |
|---|---|---|
| itchy | fortress | phantom |
| instructor | job | difficult |

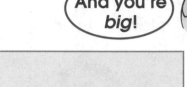

1. My **teacher** is very smart! _____

2. I don't like that sweater. It is too **scratchy**. _____

3. My teacher gave a very **hard** test in math. _____

4. The prince lived in a **castle**. _____

5. Everyone has a **task** to do in my house. _____

6. The **ghost** at the fun house was so scary! _____

Name _____

# Bored Belinda!

Belinda is bored with using the same words all the time. Help her figure out a new word for the **boldfaced** words in each sentence.

**Directions:** Read each sentence and then circle the correct new word below.

I hope my grandma will like this **gift**.

present          toaster

I always **laugh** when I watch my silly kitten.

chuckle          worry

My friend loves to **talk** on the telephone.

draw          chat

The little boy was **charming** to his grandparents.

delightful          naughty

Can you please **sew** this fabric together?

hitch          stitch

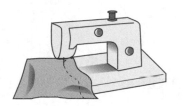

Name _____

# We Go Together!

**Directions:** Circle the two words in each line that have almost the same meaning.

1. gooey      sticky      hard

2. slow      hurry      rush

3. slope      hill      sled

4. stop      red      end

5. treat      pledge      promise

6. piece      bit      pie

7. excuse      easy      simple

8. complete      whole      pile

Name _____

# Amazing Antonyms

**Antonyms** are words that have opposite meanings. **Old** and **new** are antonyms. **Laugh** and **cry** are antonyms, too.

**Directions:** Below each word, write its antonym. Use words from the word box.

down
go
left
sad
dry

stop

happy

right

up

wet

Name _____

# Who's Afraid?

Help Frog and Toad escape from the snake.

**Directions:** Read the two words in each space. If the words are antonyms, color the space **green**. Do not color the other spaces.

go
stop

large
small

wide
narrow

dinner
supper

scared
afraid

brave
afraid

shut
close

happy
sad

dark
light

fall
rise

outside
inside

higher
lower

leap
jump

none
all

tremble
shake

fast
quick

happy
glad

stones
rocks

look
see

top
bottom

covers
blankets

friend
pal

down
up

shout
whisper

loud
soft

under
over

Toad's
House

Name _____

# Antonyms Are Opposites!

**Directions:** Look at the words on the balloons. Write an antonym to replace the word in the box for each sentence.

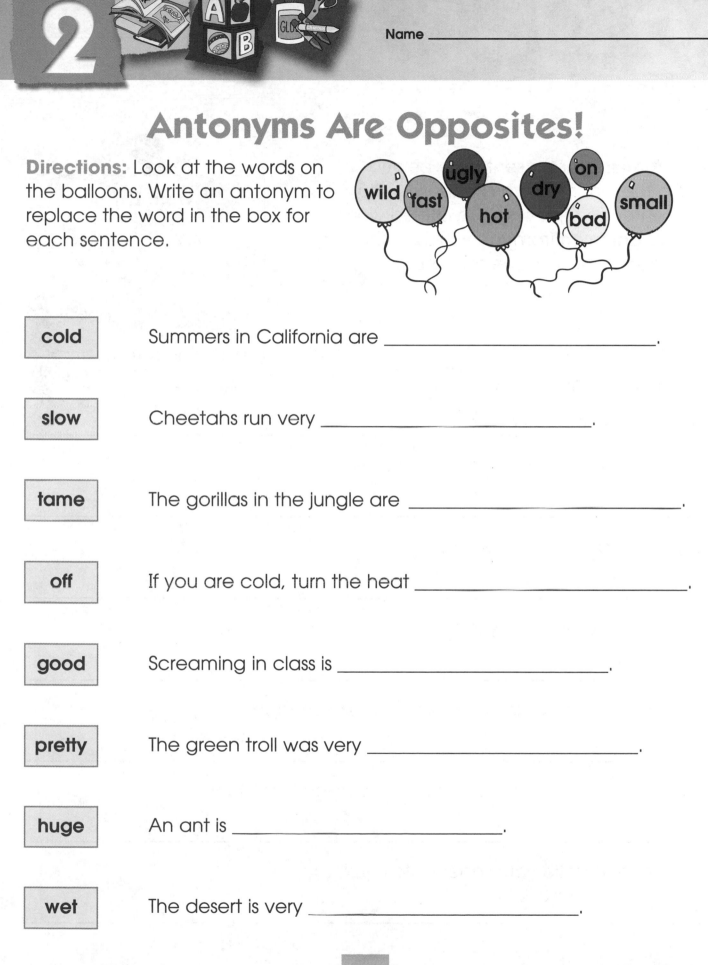

| cold | Summers in California are _____. |

| slow | Cheetahs run very _____. |

| tame | The gorillas in the jungle are _____. |

| off | If you are cold, turn the heat _____. |

| good | Screaming in class is _____. |

| pretty | The green troll was very _____. |

| huge | An ant is _____. |

| wet | The desert is very _____. |

Name _____

# Trading Places

**Directions:** In each sentence below, circle the incorrect word. Then, rewrite the sentence replacing the circled word with its **antonym** from the word list. The first one has been done for you.

### Word List

| | |
|---|---|
| happy | tall |
| full | tie |
| loud | lock |
| dangerous | |

Swimming in the dark was (safe.)

**Swimming in the dark was dangerous.** _____

The gorilla's scream sounded very quiet.

_____

The packed room was empty.

_____

My 6-foot brother is very short.

_____

George, the funny clown, makes me very unhappy.

_____

In an unsafe place, you should always unlock the door.

_____

You need to untie your shoes before you run.

_____

# I Meant to Say!

Molly meant to say the **opposite** of what she said in the sentences below.

**Directions:** Help Molly fix her mistakes by circling the incorrect word in each sentence. Then, choose a word from the word list to replace it. Rewrite the sentence using the new word.

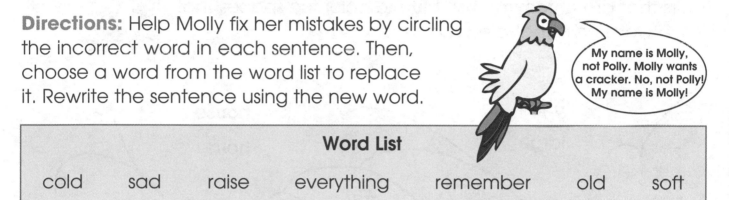

My name is Molly, not Polly. Molly wants a cracker. No, not Polly! My name is Molly!

**Word List**

| cold | sad | raise | everything | remember | old | soft |

It is always hot in the Arctic.

_____

The hard cushion was very comfortable.

_____

We ate nothing at Thanksgiving.

_____

It makes people happy when you frown.

_____

It is important to forget people's birthdays.

_____

Lower your hand if you want to ask a question.

_____

My great-great-grandma is very young.

_____

Name _____

# Antonym or Synonym?

**Directions:** Use **yellow** to color the spaces that have word pairs that are **antonyms**. Use **blue** to color the spaces that have word pairs that are **synonyms**.

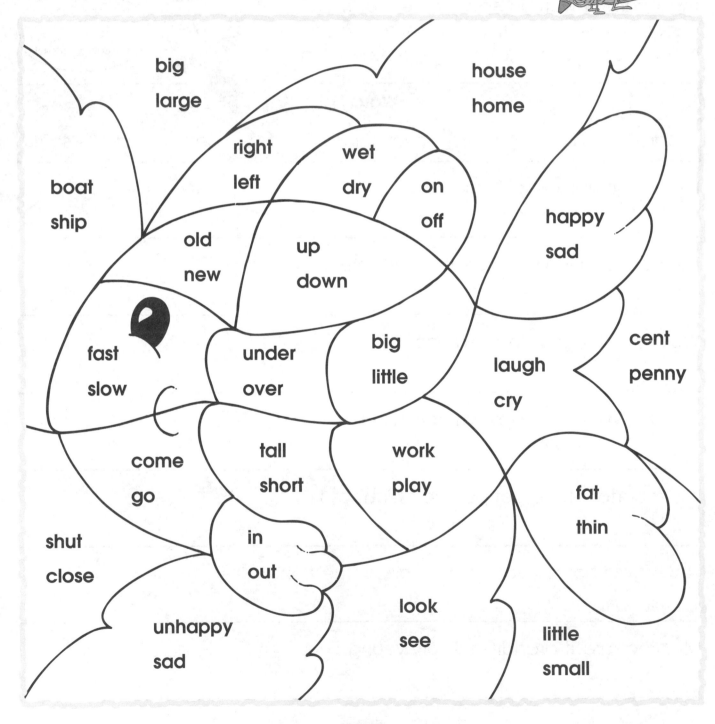

94

Name _____

# Contractions

A **contraction** is a word made up of two words joined together with one or more letters left out. An **apostrophe** is used in place of the missing letters.

**Examples:** I am—**I'm**
do not—**don't**
that is—**that's**

**Directions:** Draw a line to match each contraction to the words from which it was made. The first one is done for you.

| | | | | | |
|---|---|---|---|---|---|
| 1. he's | we are | | 6. they'll | are not |
| 2. we're | cannot | | 7. aren't | they will |
| 3. can't | he is | | 8. I've | you have |
| 4. I'll | she is | | 9. you've | will not |
| 5. she's | I will | | 10. won't | I have |

**Directions:** Write the contraction for each pair of words.

1. you are _____     5. she is _____

2. does not _____     6. we have _____

3. do not _____     7. has not _____

4. would not _____     8. did not _____

Name _____

# Something Is Missing!

| doesn't | it's | she's | |
| don't | aren't | who's | he's |
| didn't | that's | isn't | |

**Directions:** Write the correct contraction for each set of words. Then, circle the letter that was left out when the contraction was made.

1. he is _____

2. are not _____

3. do not _____

4. who is _____

5. is not _____

6. did not _____

7. it is _____

8. she is _____

9. does not _____

10. that is _____

**Directions:** Write the missing contraction on the line.

1. _____ on her way to school.

2. There _____ enough time to finish the story.

3. Do you think _____ too long?

4. We _____ going to the party.

5. Donna _____ like the movie.

6. _____ going to try for a part in the play?

7. Bob said _____ going to run in the big race.

8. They _____ know how to bake a cake.

9. Tom _____ want to go skating on Saturday.

10. Look, _____ where they found the lost watch.

# Highlight Happy!

**Highlighting** is a strategy that will help you with your reading. When you highlight something, you use a light-colored marker to color over a special word or words that you want to remember.

## Highlighting means you...

**Directions:** Follow the directions to highlight words in the sentences below.

1. Highlight three things you might find in the ocean.

   There are many creatures that live in the ocean. If you are lucky, you might see a whale or a dolphin in the ocean. If you are unlucky, you might find a jellyfish or even a shark!

2. Highlight five things you should bring to the beach.

   Spending the day at the beach can be lots of fun. However, you must remember to bring sun block, drinking water, a hat, sandals, a towel, and a snack.

# Tooth Tales!

**Directions:** Read the following information about your teeth.

Did you know that your teeth are made of enamel? Enamel is the hardest material in your entire body. It makes your teeth strong.

There are four different types of teeth in your mouth. Your front four teeth on the top and front four teeth on the bottom are called *incisors*. Ouch! They are sharp teeth used for biting (for biting food that is, not for biting your brother!).

You have two very pointy teeth on the top and two on the bottom called *canines*. They are used for foods that are hard to chew.

In the very back of your mouth, you have twelve wide teeth called *molars*. They are used for grinding food. (These are worth a lot to the Tooth Fairy!)

Finally, you have eight teeth called *bicuspids* for crushing food.

Adults have thirty-two permanent teeth! That's a lot of teeth, so keep smiling!

# Tooth Tales, cont.

**Directions:** Answer the questions from the story about your teeth.

What are your teeth made of?_____
Highlight where you found the answer.


What is the hardest material in your body? _____
Highlight where you found the answer.


How many different types of teeth are in your mouth? _____
Highlight where you found the answer.


What are your two very pointy teeth called? _____
Highlight where you found the answer.


What teeth are used for grinding food? _____
(Hint: The Tooth Fairy likes this type of tooth!)
Highlight where you found the answer.


How many teeth do adults have?_____
Highlight where you found the answer.


What teeth are used for biting? _____
Highlight where you found the answer.


How many molars do people have? _____
Highlight where you found the answer.

Name _____

# The World's Greatest Tree House!

**Directions:** Create the world's greatest tree house by following the directions below to finish the picture. Use crayons to draw or color each part as indicated.

1. Draw a super cool clubhouse door with a special doorknocker.

2. Draw windows (any shape!) and curtains for the windows.

3. Draw a ladder leading up to the tree house.

4. Draw a sign over the door of the tree house.

5. Draw a swing hanging from the tree.

6. Draw two children using the tree house.

## Extra! Extra! Read All About It!

Write a story about this tree house. Does anyone live there? Was it hard to build? Is it used for a secret club or does an entire family live there?

_____

_____

_____

_____

# Clue Caper!

**Directions:** Read the clues below. Write each child's name under the correct picture. Color the hats using the following clues.

_____   _____   _____   _____

- Anna is tall and wearing a green top hat. There is a red baseball cap on top of her top hat!

- Sara is short and wearing a blue polka dotted hat.

- Talia has long hair and is standing between Anna and Sara. Talia is wearing a pretty ribbon in her hair with a flower on it.

- Kessia is standing next to Sara. She is wearing a white baker's hat with a purple veil!

How many hats do you count on the page? _____

Name _____

# Something's Fruity!

**Directions:** Find and circle **twelve** things that are wrong with this picture.

Name _____

# Make the Touchdown!

**Directions:** Read the directions. Draw a line as you move from space to space.

1. Start at the football player running with the football.
2. Go up 2 spaces.
3. Go right 3 spaces. Oops!
4. Now, go down 3 spaces.
5. Hurry and go left 1 space.
6. Turn and go down 2 spaces.
7. Now, quickly turn right and go 3 spaces.
8. You were almost tackled. Go up 3 spaces.
9. Move quickly to the right 1 space.
10. Hurray! You made the touchdown!

**Directions:** Draw a brown football under the goalpost.

# Coach's Call

**Directions:** Follow the directions to draw and color the football player's uniform.

1. Color the pants yellow with a thin, blue stripe down the outside of each leg.

2. Color the top part of Teddy's socks blue, but leave the bottom part white.

3. Color a large yellow number 83 on the chest of the jersey and two yellow stripes on each sleeve. Then, color the rest of the shirt blue.

4. Draw and color black shoes with white stripes. Draw cleats on the bottom of the shoes.

5. Draw a yellow helmet on his head with a blue stripe down the center. Add a face mask.

6. Draw a brown football in Teddy's left hand. Now he's ready to play!

Name _____

# Game Story

**Directions:** Put the basketball story in order. Write the numbers **1–5** on the blanks to show when each event happened.

_____ At the end of the regulation game, the score was tied.

_____ The teams warmed up before the game.

_____ The score at the half was Cougars, 25; Lions, 20.

_____ Kim made the first basket of the game.

_____ When the overtime ended, the Lions had won the game 50–49.

Name _____

# Story Sequence

Look at picture number 4. What do you think happened before Donna went to the beach? What might happen when she is at the beach?

**Directions:** You get to decide how the story will go from beginning to end. Write a number in the empty square in each of the other pictures. Choose any number from 1 through 7 (except 4). Number 1 will be what happened first. Number 7 will be what you think happened last.

106

Name _____

# How Did It Happen?

**Directions:** Read the story. Then, cut out the pictures. Glue them in order below.

Kim took the ball down the field to start the game. Both teams played hard and tried to score. Michael blocked the ball with his knees, but it went out of bounds. Sarah threw the ball in, and Beth kicked the ball into the net. It was the winning goal of the game.

| 1 | 2 | 3 | 4 |
|---|---|---|---|
|   |   |   |   |

Name _____

# Story Sequence

Look at picture number 4. What do you think happened before Danny went to the amusement park? What might happen when he is at the amusement park?

**Directions:** You get to decide how the story will go from beginning to end. Write a number in the empty square in each of the other pictures. Choose any number from 1 through 7 (except 4). Number 1 will be what happened first. Number 7 will be what you think happened last.

Name _____

# Same/Different: Shell Homes

Read the story about shells.

Shells are the homes of some animals. Snails live in shells on the land. Clams live in shells in the water. Clam shells open. Snail shells stay closed. Both shells keep the animals safe.

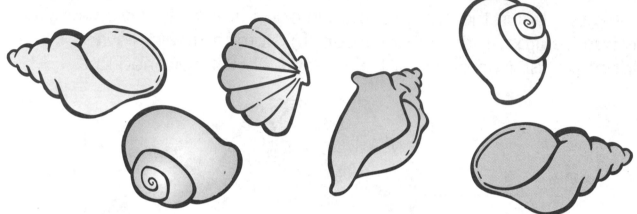

**Directions:** Answer the questions. For numbers 1 and 2, circle the correct answer.

1. Snails live in shells on the

   water.          land.


2. Clam shells are different from snail shells because

   they open.

   they stay closed.


3. Write one way all shells are the same. _____

_____

# Same/Different: Venn Diagram

A **Venn diagram** is a diagram that shows how two things are the same and different.

**Directions:** Choose two outdoor sports. Then, follow the instructions to complete the Venn diagram.

1. Write the first sport name under the first circle. Write some words that describe the sport. Write them in the first circle.

2. Write the second sport name under the second circle. Write some words that describe the sport. Write them in the second circle.

3. Where the 2 circles overlap, write some words that describe both sports.

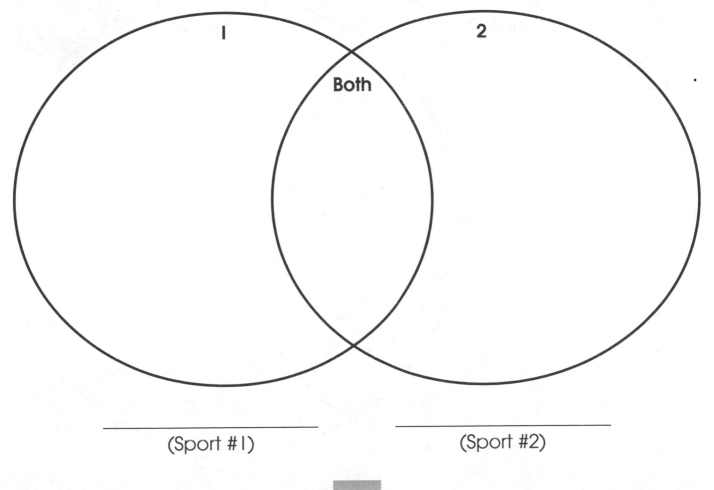

1                    Both                    2

_____          _____
(Sport #1)                              (Sport #2)

Name _____

# Same/Different: Dina and Dina

**Directions:** Read the story. Then, complete the Venn diagram, telling how Dina, the duck, is the same or different than Dina, the girl.

One day in the library, Dina found a story about a duck named Dina!

My name is Dina. I am a duck, and I like to swim. When I am not swimming, I walk on land or fly. I have two feet and two eyes. My feathers keep me warm. Ducks can be different colors. I am gray, brown, and black. I really like being a duck. It is fun.

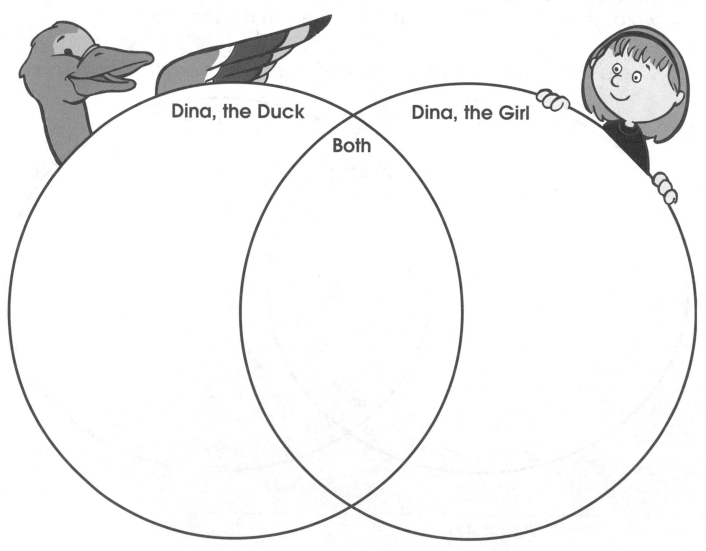

Dina, the Duck          Dina, the Girl

Both

Name _____

# Same/Different: Ann and Lee Have Fun

**Directions:** Read about Ann and Lee. Then, write how they are the same and different in the Venn diagram.

Ann and Lee like to play ball. They like to jump rope. Lee likes to play a card game called "Old Maid." Ann likes to play a card game called "Go Fish."

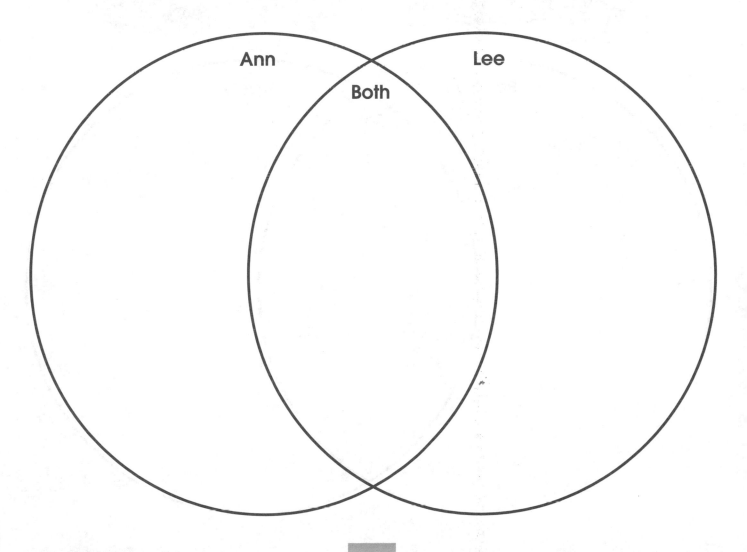

Ann          Both          Lee

# Same/Different: Cats and Tigers

**Directions:** Read about cats and tigers. Then, complete the Venn diagram, telling how they are the same and different.

Tigers are a kind of cat. Pet cats and tigers both have fur. Pet cats are small and tame. Tigers are large and wild.

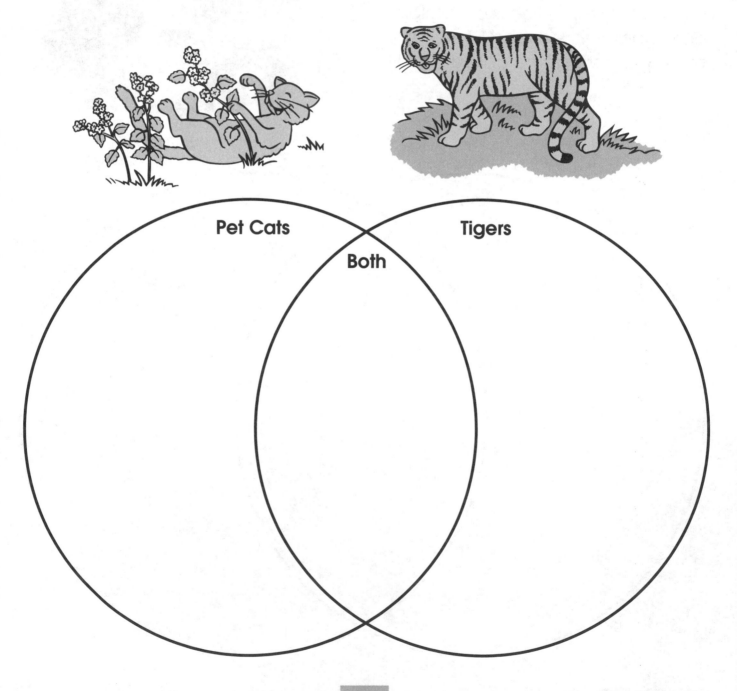

Pet Cats

Tigers

Both

# Same/Different: Marvin and Mugsy

**Directions:** Read about Marvin and Mugsy. Then, complete the Venn diagram, telling how they are the same and different.

Marcy has two dogs, Marvin and Mugsy. Marvin is a black-and-white spotted Dalmatian. Marvin likes to run after balls in the backyard. His favorite food is Canine Crunchy Crunch. Marcy likes to take Marvin for walks, because dogs need exercise. Marvin loves to sleep in his doghouse. Mugsy is a big, furry brown dog, who wiggles when she is happy. Since she is big, she needs lots of exercise. So, Marcy takes her for walks in the park. Her favorite food is Canine Crunchy Crunch. Mugsy likes to sleep on Marcy's bed.

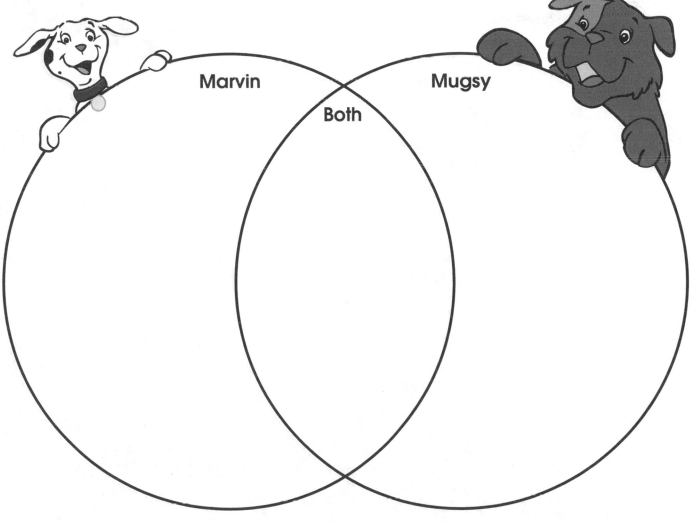

Marvin     Both     Mugsy

Name _____

# Same/Different: Bluebirds and Parrots

**Directions:** Read about bluebirds and parrots. Then, complete the Venn diagram, telling how they are the same and different.

Bluebirds and parrots are both birds. Bluebirds and parrots can fly. They both have beaks. Parrots can live inside a cage. Bluebirds must live outdoors.

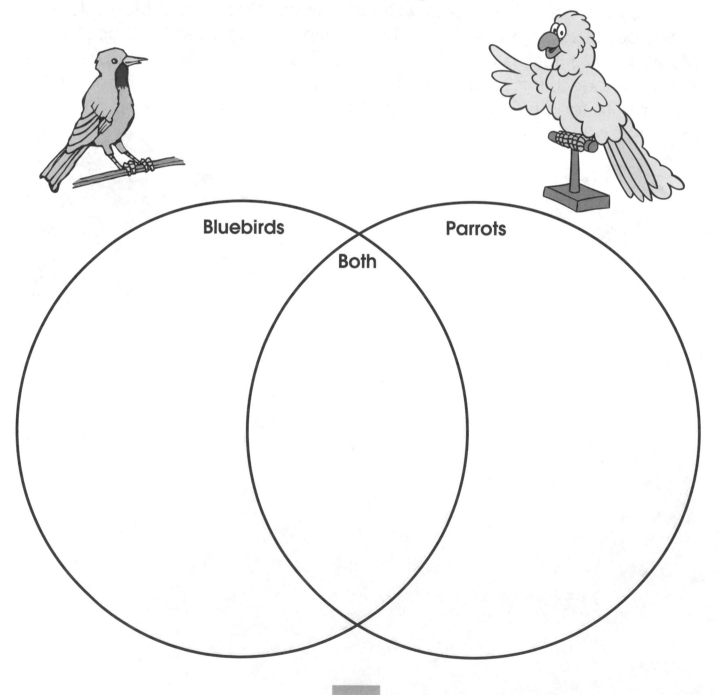

**Bluebirds**          **Parrots**

**Both**

Name _____

# Same/Different: Sleeping Whales

**Directions:** Read about whales. Then, complete the Venn diagram, telling how whales and people are the same and different.

Whales do not sleep like we do. They take many short naps. Like us, whales breathe air. Whales live in very cold water, but they have fat that keeps them warm.

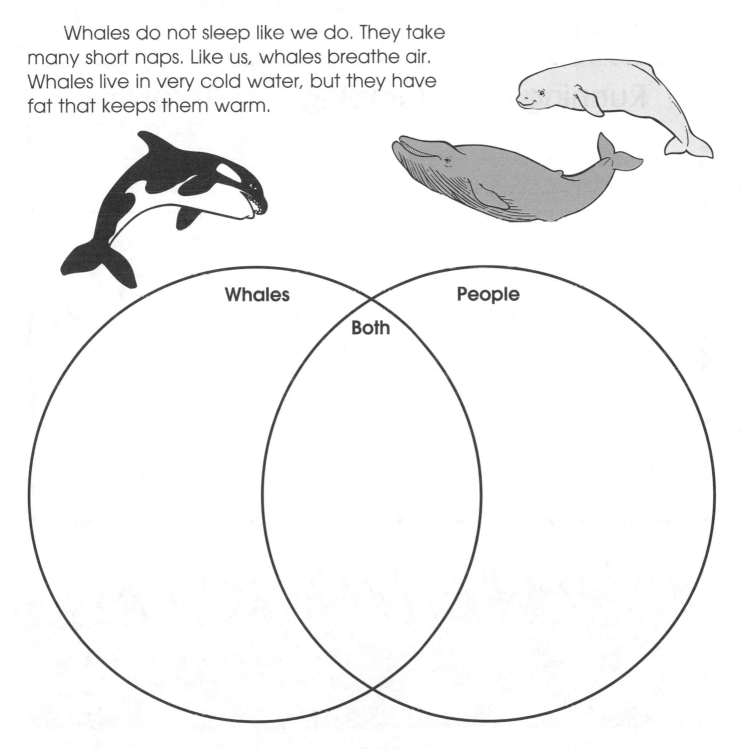

**Whales**      **People**

**Both**

Name _____

# Running! Jumping! Throwing!

To be a strong athlete in track and field events you must be good at running, jumping, and throwing. Many track and field words are listed below.

**Directions:** Write the words under the correct track and field event.

| Running | Jumping | Throwing |
|---------|---------|----------|
| _____ | _____ | _____ |
| _____ | _____ | _____ |
| _____ | _____ | _____ |
| _____ | _____ | _____ |
| _____ | _____ | _____ |
| _____ | _____ | _____ |
| _____ | _____ | _____ |

lap    javelin    high jump    baton    relay    long jump

discus    cross country    broad jump    shot put

track    pole vault    hurdles    triple jump    hammer

Name _____

# Classifying

Sometimes, you want to put things in groups. One way to put things in groups is to sort them by how they are alike. When you put things together that are alike in some way, you classify them.

You can classify the things in your room. In one group, you can put toys and fun things. In the other group, you can put things that you wear.

**Directions:** Look at the words on the bedroom door. Put the toys and playthings in the toy box. Put the things you wear in the dresser drawers.

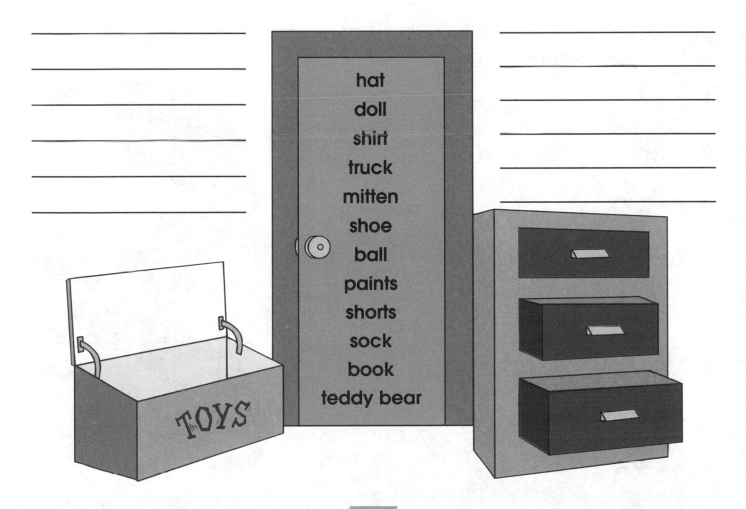

hat
doll
shirt
truck
mitten
shoe
ball
paints
shorts
sock
book
teddy bear

Name _____

# Shrews

A shrew (*shroo*) is a small animal. It looks like a mouse with a sharp, pointed nose. This animal is sometimes mistaken for a mouse. It has tiny eyes and ears. Its body is covered with short, dark hair. A shrew moves very fast. A shrew eats all day. The shrew's long, pointed nose can fit into tiny holes to find the insects and worms it eats.

The shrew lives in fields, woodlands, gardens, and marshes. Shrews are harmless to humans. They are helpful in gardens because they eat grubs and other insects. The smallest shrew weighs as little as a United States penny.

**Directions:** After reading about the shrew, put an **X** on one word that does **not** belong in each group.

1. small          large          tiny

2. bugs           corn           insects

3. move           run            sleep

4. bird           mouse          dish

5. fast           quick          water

6. sharp          pointed        hair

7. nickel         penny          rain

8. garden         fields         sun

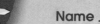

Name _____

# Birds

There are <u>many</u> kinds of birds. The cardinal is a <u>red</u> bird. The cardinal lays <u>three</u> or <u>four</u> eggs. The brown-headed cowbird is <u>black</u> with a <u>brown</u> head. The hummingbird is a very <u>small</u> bird. It lays <u>two</u> eggs. The bald eagle is a <u>large</u> bird. It is brown with a <u>white</u> head. The bald eagle lays from <u>one</u> to <u>four</u> eggs. Bluebirds are <u>blue</u> with <u>orange</u> or light <u>blue</u> breasts. The bluebird lays up to <u>six</u> eggs.

**Directions:** In the story above, the underlined words are called **adjectives**. Put these describing words in the nests where they belong.

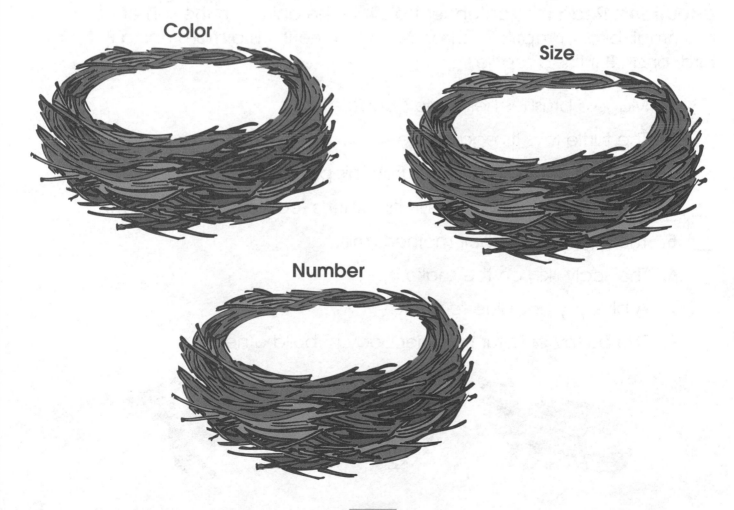

Name _____

# All Animals

There are many kinds of animals. Three kinds of animals are mammals, birds, and reptiles.

Mammals have fur or hair. Baby mammals drink milk from their mothers' bodies. A whale is a mammal.

Birds are the only animals that have feathers. A robin is a bird.

Reptiles have scaly skin. Most reptiles lay eggs on the land. An alligator is a reptile.

**Directions:** Read the sentences below. Is the animal in the sentence a mammal, bird, or reptile? Put an **M** on the line if it is a mammal, a **B** if it is a bird, or an **R** if it is a reptile.

___ **1.** Maggie brushes her horse's coat.

___ **2.** The turtle lays its eggs in the sand.

___ **3.** Adam cleans the feathers from his pet's cage.

___ **4.** The baby penguin hides in its father's feathers to stay warm.

___ **5.** The piglets drink their mother's milk.

___ **6.** The scaly skin on the snake is dry.

___ **7.** A blue jay has blue feathers.

___ **8.** The bunny pulls fur from her body to build a nest.

Name _____

# Baby Animal Names

Many animals are called special names when they are young. A baby deer is called a fawn. A baby cat is called a kitten.

Some young animals have the same name as other kinds of baby animals. A baby elephant is a calf. A baby whale is a calf. A baby giraffe is a calf. A baby cow is a calf.

Some baby animals are called cubs. A baby lion, a baby bear, a baby tiger, and a baby fox are all called cubs.

Some baby animals are called colts. A young horse is a colt. A baby zebra is a colt. A baby donkey is a colt.

**Directions:** Use the story about baby animal names to complete the chart below. Write the kind of animal that belongs with each special baby name.

| calf | cub | colt |
|------|-----|------|
|      |     |      |

# Baby Animal Names, cont.

**Directions:** Look at the pictures of the mother animals and their babies. Write the name of the baby on the line. Use page 123, if needed.

1.

_____

2.

_____

3.

_____

4.

_____

5.

_____

6.

_____

124

Name _____

# Around the Ball Park

**Directions:** Read the sentences in each box. Then, cut out the pictures at the bottom of the page. Glue each picture in the box that matches the sentence.

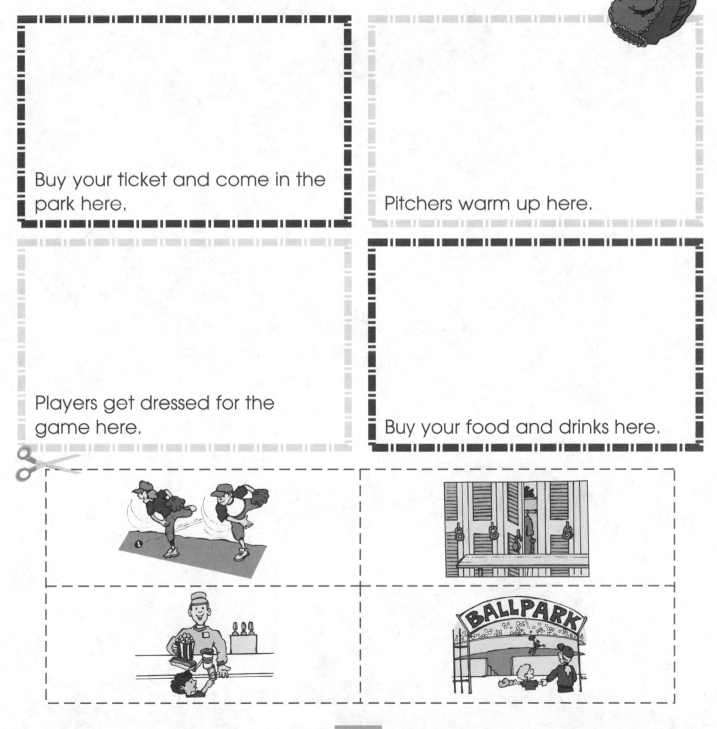

Buy your ticket and come in the park here.

Pitchers warm up here.

Players get dressed for the game here.

Buy your food and drinks here.

# Winter's Sleepers

**Directions:** Read about hibernation. Then, complete page 128.

As days grow shorter and it gets colder, some animals get ready for their winter's sleep. This winter's sleep is called *hibernation*. Scientists do not know all the secrets of hibernating animals. They do know enough to put hibernating animals into two groups. One group is called "true hibernators." The other group is called "light sleepers."

True hibernators go into a very deep sleep. To get ready for this long winter's sleep, true hibernators will eat and eat so they become fat. As these animals sleep, their body temperature drops below normal. If the animal gets too cold, it will shiver to warm itself. The breathing of true hibernators slows so much that they hardly seem to breathe at all.

True hibernators are animals such as woodchucks, some ground squirrels, the

jumping mouse, brown bat, frogs, and snapping turtles.

Light sleepers include skunks, raccoons, the eastern chipmunk, and the grizzly bear.

Some light sleepers will store up food to have during winter while others will eat and become fat. A big difference between light sleepers and true hibernators is that the light sleeper's body temperature drops only a little, and its breathing only slows. These animals are easy to wake and may even get up if the temperature warms. They then go back to sleep when it becomes colder again.

# Winter Sleepers, cont.

**Directions:** Read all of the word groups. Then, place them under the correct hibernation type. Use the story on page 127.

will shiver to warm itself
body temperature drops a little
hardly breathes at all
seems more dead than alive
moves about and then goes back to sleep
breathing only slows
easily awakens
stores up food
body temperature drops far below normal
uses body fat while sleeping

**True Hibernator**

_____

_____

_____

_____

_____

_____

**Light Sleeper**

_____

_____

_____

_____

Name _____

# Use the Clues

**Context clues** can help you figure out words you do not know. Read the words around the new word. Think of a word that makes sense.

Kate swam in a _____?_____.

Did Kate swim in a cake or a lake? The word **swim** is a context clue.

**Directions:** Kate wrote this letter from camp. Read the letter. Use context clues to write the missing words from the word box. What clues did you use?

| lake | six |
| pancakes | forest |

Dear Mom and Dad,

_____

– – – – – – – – – – – –

I woke up at _____ o'clock and got

_____

– – – – – – – – – – – –

dressed. My friends and I ate _____ for

_____

– – – – – – – – – – – –

breakfast. We went hiking in the _____ .

_____

– – – – – – – – – – – –

Then, we went swimming in the _____ .
Camp is fun!

Love,
Kate

# Clues for Clothes

**Directions:** Read the story. Use context clues to figure out the missing words. Write the words from the word box. Then, answer the questions.

| socks | scarf | sweaters | mittens |
|---|---|---|---|

Maria bundles up. She sticks her arms through

_____

_ _ _ _ _ _ _ _ _ _ _

two _____ . She tugs three pairs of

_____                          _____

_ _ _ _ _ _ _ _ _                          _ _ _ _ _ _ _ _ _ _

_____ over her feet. She wraps a _____

                                             _____

                                             _ _ _ _ _ _ _ _ _ _

around her neck. At last, she pulls her _____
onto her hands. Maria goes outside to play. Nobody is warmer
than Maria.

**I.** What clue words helped you figure out sweaters?

_____

_ _ _ _ _ _ _ _ _ _ _ _ _ _ _ _ _ _ _ _

_____

**2.** What clue words helped you figure out mittens?

_____

_ _ _ _ _ _ _ _ _ _ _ _ _ _ _ _ _ _ _ _

_____

Name _____

# Context Clues in Action

**Directions:** Read the story. Use context clues to figure out the meanings of the **boldfaced** words. Draw a line from the word to its meaning. The first one is done for you.

Jack has a plan. He wants to take his parents out to lunch to show that he **appreciates** all the nice things they do for him. His sister Jessica will go, too, so she won't feel left out. Jack is **thrifty**. He saves the **allowance** he earns for doing **chores** around the house. So far, Jack has saved ten dollars. He needs only five dollars more. He is excited about paying the check himself. He will feel like an **adult**.

| appreciates | jobs |
| --- | --- |
| allowance | grown-up |
| chores | is grateful for |
| thrifty | money earned for work |
| adult | careful about spending money |

Name _____

# Cathy Uses Context Clues

When you read, it is important to know about context clues. **Context clues** can help you figure out the meaning of a word, or a missing word, just by looking at the **other words** in the sentence.

**Directions:** Read each sentence below. Circle the context clues, or other words in the sentence that give you hints.

Write the answer that fits in each blank. The first one is done for you.

1. The (joke) was so ____**funny**____ I couldn't stop (laughing.)

   bad            long            nice            funny

   The correct answer is **funny** because of the context clues **joke** and **laughing**. They are hints that go best with the word **funny**. Now you try it.

2. We baked a sweet cinnamon apple pie. It smelled _____.

   sour            delicious            funny            odd

3. You have such a long walk home. Do you need a
   _____ home from school?

   letter            balloon            ride            scooter

4. My brother loves to _____. He has visited over fifty different countries!

   travel            shout            buy            play

Name _____

# Cathy Uses More Context Clues

When you read, it is important to know about context clues. **Context clues** can help you figure out the meaning of a word, or a missing word, just by looking at the **other words** in the sentence.

**Directions:** Read each sentence below. Circle the context clues.

Write the answer that fits in each blank.

1. I am a very good _____. I love to draw, paint, and sculpt. My art teacher says I have a lot of talent.

   teacher          boss          captain          artist

2. Playing the _____ is fun. I like to sit on the bench and press those black and white keys.

   violin          piano          rubberband          desk

3. The telephone rings so _____ in my house that I can never fall asleep.

   softly          beautifully          loudly          ugly

4. Summer is my _____ season because I go to camp and have fun!

   favorite          hungry          bad          study

5. The eagle flew so _____ that it looked like a dot in the sky.

   middle          low          high          deep

Name _____

# Chris's Context Clues

**Context clues** can help you figure out the meaning of a word just by looking at the **other words** in the sentence.

**Directions:** Read each sentence below. Circle the context clues. Choose a word from the word list to replace each word in **bold**. Write it on the line.

| Word List | | |
|:---:|:---:|:---:|
| long | extra | happy |
| weak | hot | limped |

1. I have lost my pen. Do you have a **spare** one I could borrow? _____

2. Your smiling brother seems so **content** with his new birthday toy. _____

3. The old, old man was so **feeble** that he looked like he would break! _____

4. Don't touch that steaming pot on the stove! It is full of **scalding** water! _____

5. The athlete got hurt and **hobbled** off the football field. _____

6. The play was quite **lengthy**. I thought it would never end! _____

Name _____

# Chris's Context Clues, cont.

**Context clues** can help you figure out the meaning of a word just by looking at the **other words** in the sentence.

**Directions:** Read each sentence below. Circle the context clues. Choose a word from the word list to replace each word in **bold**. Write it on the line.

| Word List | | |
|---|---|---|
| fix | ran | neat |
| fly | delicate | |

1. The boy is very **tidy**. He always puts away his toys. _____

2. The athletes were like cheetahs. They **sprinted** to the finish line! _____

3. A hawk can **soar** very high. _____

4. I didn't even want to touch the **fragile** crystal vase. _____

5. If you broke it, you need to **repair** it. _____

# Comprehension: Ladybugs

**Directions:** Read about ladybugs. Then, answer the questions.

Have you ever seen a ladybug? Ladybugs are red. They have black spots. They have six legs. Ladybugs are pretty!

1. What color are ladybugs? _____

2. What color are their spots? _____

3. How many legs do ladybugs have? _____

Name _____

# Making History

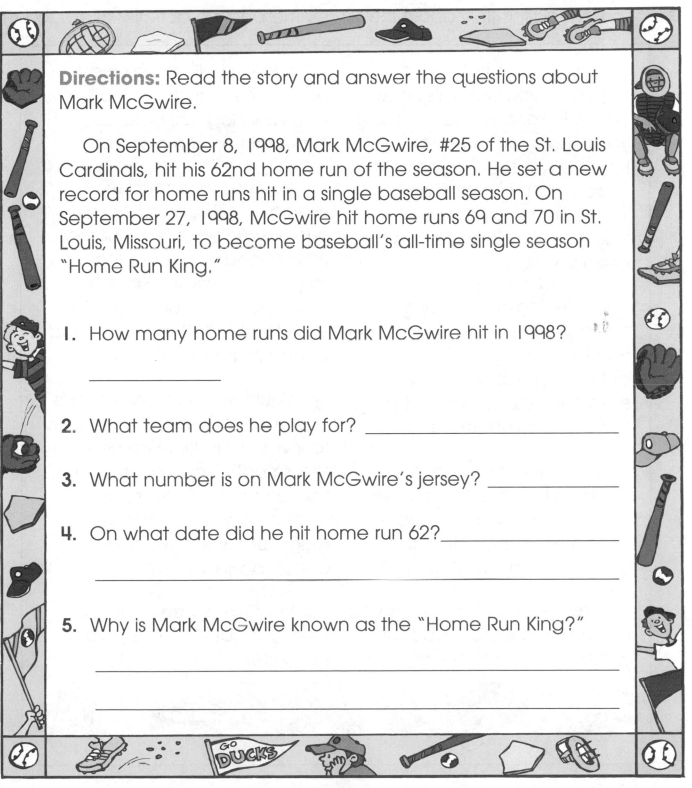

**Directions:** Read the story and answer the questions about Mark McGwire.

On September 8, 1998, Mark McGwire, #25 of the St. Louis Cardinals, hit his 62nd home run of the season. He set a new record for home runs hit in a single baseball season. On September 27, 1998, McGwire hit home runs 69 and 70 in St. Louis, Missouri, to become baseball's all-time single season "Home Run King."

1. How many home runs did Mark McGwire hit in 1998?

    _____

2. What team does he play for? _____

3. What number is on Mark McGwire's jersey? _____

4. On what date did he hit home run 62?_____

    _____

5. Why is Mark McGwire known as the "Home Run King?"

    _____

    _____

# Five Senses

**Directions:** Read this story about the senses. Then, do the activities on page 139.

As you use your eyes to read this, you are using one of your five senses. You are using your sight. Your sense of sight lets you see faces, places, shapes, letters, and words. Your sight helps you see beautiful things and helps keep you safe.

Bells ringing, children singing, and your mother calling you to dinner all use the sense of hearing. Your ears catch sound waves that travel through the air and you hear them.

Your sense of hearing warns you with a *beep-beep* that a truck is backing up. A phone rings and you hear it. Could it be a friend calling?

Your sense of smell lets you know that a pizza is cooking without you even seeing it.

Your nose smells the fresh sheets on your bed and lets you know that your dog has been playing in the rain or with a skunk.

You use your tongue for tasting. Foods can taste salty, sweet, sour, or bitter. Your sense of smell and taste work together so you can enjoy food. Dill pickles or tangy oranges are tasty treats. Cotton candy and popcorn are also tasty treats.

Your largest sense organ is your skin. Your sense of touch is found in your skin. You can feel smooth, soft, rough, sharp, hot, and cold. Velvet is a smooth touch. Sandpaper is rough. Snow is cold, and cotton balls are soft.

Your five senses help to keep you safe and help you enjoy life.

# Five Senses, cont.

**Directions:** Draw a line to match the sense to the body part that works with it.

eyes     taste

ears     smell

nose     sight

tongue    hearing

skin     touch

**Directions:** List three of your favorites under each sense. An example is given.

**Taste** ___pretzel_____

_____

**Smell** ___baking cookies_____

_____

**Sight** ___Mommy_____

_____

**Hearing** ___barking dog_____

_____

**Touch** ___cold snow_____

_____

Name _____

# Comprehension: Playing Store

**Directions:** Read about playing store. Then, answer the questions.

Tyson and his friends like to play store. They use boxes and cans. They line them up. Then, they put them in bags.

1. Circle the main idea:

   Tyson and his friends use boxes, cans, and bags to play store.

   You need bags to play store.

2. Circle your answer:

   Who likes to play store?

   all kids          some kids

3. Do you like to play store?_____

# Comprehension: Playful Cats

**Directions:** Read about cats. Then, follow the instructions.

Cats make good pets. They like to play. They like to jump. They like to run. Do you?

1. Circle your answer:

   Cats make good _____.

   pets.

   friends.

2. Write three things cats like to do:

   _____

   _____

   _____

3. Think of a good name for a cat. Write it on the cat's tag.

Name _____

# Comprehension: Types of Tops

The **main idea** is the most important point or idea in a story.

**Directions:** Read about tops. Then, answer the questions.

Tops come in all sizes. Some tops are made of wood. Some tops are made of tin. All tops do the same thing. They spin! Do you have a top?

1. Circle the main idea:

   There are many kinds of tops.

   Some tops are made of wood.

2. What are some tops made of? _____

3. What do all tops do? _____

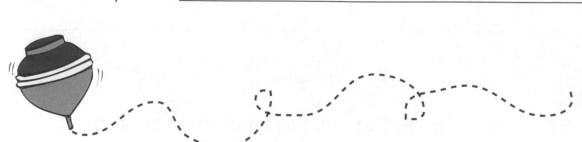

# Comprehension: Singing Whales

**Directions:** Read about singing whales. Then, follow the instructions.

Some whales can sing! We cannot understand the words. But we can hear the tune of the humpback whale. Each season, humpback whales sing a different song.

1. Circle the main idea:

    All whales can sing.

    Some whales can sing.

2. Name the kind of whale that sings.

    _____

3. How many different songs does the humpback whale sing each year?

    1          2          3          4

# Hermit Crabs

The hermit crab lives in a shell in or near the ocean. It does not make its own shell. It moves into a shell left by another sea animal. As the hermit crab grows, it gets too big for its shell. It will hunt for a new shell. It will feel the new shell with its claw. If the shell feels just right, the crab will leave its old shell and move into the bigger one. It might even take a shell away from another hermit crab.

**Directions:** Read about hermit crabs. Use what you learn to finish the sentences.

1. This story is mostly about the _____.

2. The hermit crab lives _____.

3. When it gets too big for its shell, it will _____.

4. The crab will feel the shell with its _____.

5. It might take a shell away from _____.

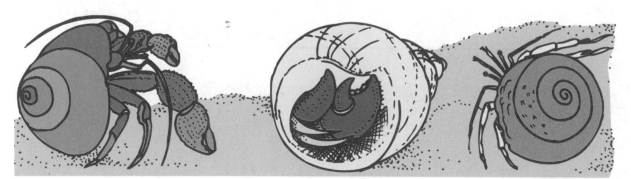

Name _____

# The Statue of Liberty

The Statue of Liberty is a symbol of the United States. It stands for freedom. It is the tallest statue in the United States.

The statue is of a woman wearing a robe. She is holding a torch in her right hand. She is holding a book in her left hand. She is wearing a crown. The Statue of Liberty was a gift from the country of France.

Each year, people come from all over the world to visit the statue. Not only do they look at it, they can also go inside the statue. At one time, visitors could go all the way up into the arm. In 1916, the arm was closed to visitors because it was too dangerous. The Statue of Liberty is located on an island in New York Harbor.

**Directions:** Read the facts above. Then, read each sentence below. If it is true, put a **T** on the line. If it is false, put an **F** on the line.

_____ 1. The Statue of Liberty is a symbol of the United States.

_____ 2. People cannot go inside the statue.

_____ 3. The statue was a gift from Mexico.

_____ 4. People used to be able to climb up into the statue's arm.

_____ 5. It is a very short statue.

_____ 6. The woman statue has a torch in her right hand.

_____ 7. People come from all over to see the statue.

# Venus Flytraps

Many insects eat plants. There is one kind of plant that eats insects. It is the Venus flytrap. The Venus flytrap works like a trap. Each leaf is shaped like a circle. The circle is in two parts. When the leaf closes, the two parts fold together. The leaf has little spikes all the way around it. Inside the leaf, there are little hairs. If an insect touches the little hairs, the two sides of the Venus flytrap leaf will clap together. The spikes will trap the insect inside. The Venus flytrap will then eat the insect.

**Directions:** Read about the Venus flytrap. Then, read each sentence below. If it is true, circle the sentence. If it is **not** true, draw an **X** on the sentence.

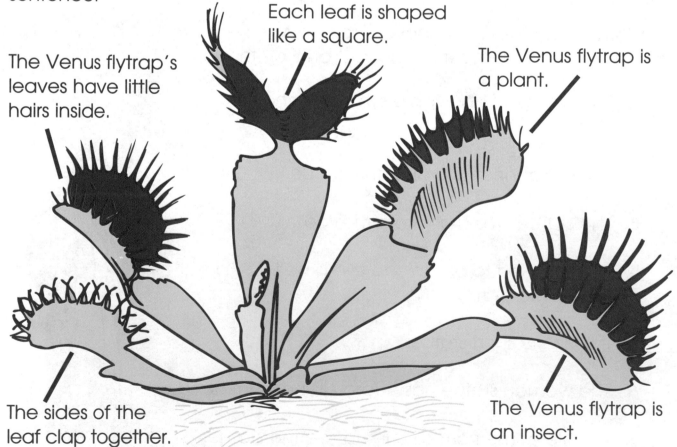

Each leaf is shaped
like a square.

The Venus flytrap's
leaves have little
hairs inside.

The Venus flytrap is
a plant.

The sides of the
leaf clap together.

The Venus flytrap is
an insect.

Name _____

# Sticklebacks

Sticklebacks are small fish. They have small spines along their backs. The spines keep other fish from trying to swallow them.

Stickleback fish are odd because the male builds the nest for the eggs. He makes the nest out of water plants and sticks. He makes it in the shape of a barrel and glues it together. He uses a thread-like material from his body to glue the nest together.

When the nest is ready, the mother fish comes. She lays her eggs and goes away. The father stays by the nest and guards the eggs. After the eggs hatch, he stays with the baby fish for a few days. If other sea animals try to eat the baby sticklebacks, he will fight them. He keeps the baby fish safe until they can care for themselves.

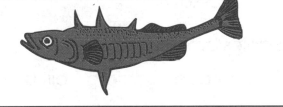

**Directions:** Read about the stickleback fish. Use the story to help pick the correct answers to fill in the blanks. Circle the correct answer.

1. The story is mostly about ____.

   spines       enemy sea animals       stickleback fish

2. The stickleback is unusual because ____.

   the female lays eggs       the male builds a nest       the eggs are in the nest

3. The nest is made of ____.

   mud and grass       water plants and sticks       string and glue

4. If an animal tries to eat the baby fish, the stickleback father will ____.

   fight it off       swim away       jump out of the water

# Eagles

Eagles are large birds. They eat small animals such as mice and rabbits. Eagles make their nests in high places such as the tops of trees. Their nests are made of sticks, weeds, and dirt. Eagles can live in the same nest for many years.

The mother eagle lays one or two eggs each year. When she sits on the eggs, the father eagle brings her food. Baby eagles are called *eaglets*.

**Directions:** Read about eagles. Then, circle the correct ending to each sentence below.

1. Eagles are

   large dogs.     large birds.

2. Eagles eat

   small animals.

   plants and trees.

3. Eagles

   build a nest each year.

   live in the same nest for many years.

4. The mother eagle lays

   one or two eggs.

   three or four eggs.

5. Baby eagles are called

   igloos.          eaglets.

# Seals

Seals live in the oceans and on land. They eat different kinds of sea animals, such as fish, shrimp, squid, and krill. They are very good swimmers. They use their flippers to help them move in the water and on the land. They talk to each other by making barking sounds.

**Directions:** Read the facts above. Then, answer each question using complete sentences.

1. What do seals eat? _____

_____

2. For what do seals use their flippers? _____

_____

3. Where do seals live? _____

_____

4. How do seals talk? _____

_____

Name _____

# Main Idea

The **main idea** tells about the **whole picture**.

**Directions:** Which sentence tells the main idea of the picture? Fill in the circle next to the correct answer.

○ The dog is happy.

○ The dog is hot.

○ The garden was in bloom.

○ The garden was messy.

○ I have a new sister.

○ I want to be a babysitter.

○ I met my new teacher.

○ This is the last day of school.

○ The juggler needed practice.

○ The juggler likes scrambled eggs.

# Main Idea

The **main idea** tells about the **whole picture**.

**Directions:** Which sentence tells the main idea of the picture? Fill in the circle next to the correct answer.

○ She saw a shooting star.

○ She likes to climb hills.

○ She likes to stay up late.

○ Skateboarding can be done anywhere.

○ Skateboarding is easy.

○ Skateboarders should wear helmets.

○ Grandpa is a great storyteller.

○ Grandpa is boring.

○ Grandpa is funny.

○ Mom made me a birthday cake.

○ We ate ice cream.

○ I opened presents.

Name _____

# What's the Main Idea?

The **main idea** tells about the **whole story**.

**Directions:** Read the story below.

Visiting the city zoo with my class was a lot of fun. Everyone in my class got to pet the llamas. Next, we were given a bag of peanuts to feed the elephants. Finally, we were allowed to take pictures in front of the monkeys' cage. Then, my teacher made a joke. She said she had never seen so much monkeying around!

Read each sentence below and decide whether it tells the main idea. Write **yes** or **no**.

Finally, we were allowed to take pictures
in front of the monkeys' cage.                           _____

Then, my teacher made a joke.                            _____

Next, we were given a bag of
peanuts to feed the elephants.                           _____

Visiting the city zoo with my class
was a lot of fun.                                        _____

Write the one sentence that tells the main idea:

_____

_____

Name _____

# Main Idea

The **main idea** tells about the **whole story**.

**Directions:** Read the story carefully. Then, write a sentence that tells the main idea.

My brother, Scott, loves to fly planes. He flies planes every chance he gets. His favorite type of plane is a Cessna 182. He also likes to go scuba diving. He likes to go scuba diving in the Gulf of Mexico best. Sometimes, he goes flying in the morning and scuba diving in the afternoon. Scott is very adventurous!

_____

_____

_____

My dad is a very talented musician. He taught himself how to play the piano and now he is an excellent piano player. When people hear him play, they can't believe he has never taken any lessons! People say he has "natural talent," and it's true!

_____

_____

_____

# The Marvelous Miss Madison!

Miss Madison loves to cook with chocolate chips. She puts chocolate chips in everything she makes! She doesn't make just pancakes, she makes chocolate chip pancakes! When she makes peanut butter sandwiches, she adds chocolate chips. When she heats up hot chocolate (you guessed it!), she adds chocolate chips! Miss Madison could not imagine cooking without chocolate chips!

**Directions:** What is the main idea of this story? Fill in the circle next to the correct answer.

○   Miss Madison likes to eat.

○   Miss Madison loves to cook with chocolate chips.

○   Miss Madison makes pancakes with chocolate chips.

What is one thing Miss Madison makes with chocolate chips?

○   sandwiches

○   hamburgers

○   muffins

Name _____

# Marco Polo!

Marco Polo is a fun summertime game. The game Marco Polo was named after a famous Italian explorer.

This game of tag is played in a swimming pool. One person chooses to be Marco. This person swims around the pool trying to tag someone else—except that she or he must keep his or her eyes closed! To find someone to tag, Marco calls out, "Marco!" Everybody else in the pool answers, "Polo!" Soon, Marco tags someone, and the game is over.

**Directions:** What is the main idea of this story? Fill in the circle next to the correct answer.

○ Marco Polo was a famous explorer.

○ Marco Polo is from Italy.

○ Marco Polo is a fun summertime game.

What is one important rule of the game Marco Polo?

_____

_____

_____

# What's the Big Idea?

The **main idea** is the most important idea in a story. The main idea tells what happens.

**Directions:** Look at the pictures. Read the sentences. Circle **yes** if the sentence tells the main idea of the picture. Circle **no** if it does not. The first one is done for you.

yes    (no)

The hat is too small.

yes    no

The bear is afraid of the mouse.

yes    no

The bear washed three shirts.

yes    no

The circus is fun.

yes    no

The bear has two mittens.

yes    no

The bear walks to school.

Name _____

# Find the Main Idea

**Directions:** Look at the pictures. Read the sentences. In the circle, write the letter of the sentence that tells the main idea.

**A.** The eggs are ready to hatch.

**B.** It is a very windy day.

**C.** The old house looks scary.

**D.** The popcorn popper is too full.

**E.** The girl thinks the music is too loud.

**F.** It is too warm for a snowman.

Name _____

# What's the Idea?

**Directions:** Look at the pictures. Read the sentences in the speech balloons. Fill in the circle beside the sentence that tells the main idea.

My tummy hurts.

○ The mouse wants more to eat.

○ The mouse ate too much cheese.

My hat is blowing away.

○ It is a very windy day.

○ He doesn't want a hat.

I am seven years old today.

○ The cake is very big.

○ Today is her birthday.

I can't find my home.

○ The cat is lost.

○ The cat has a new home.

# Read All About It

**Directions:** Read each part of the paper. Fill in the circle beside the sentence that tells the main idea.

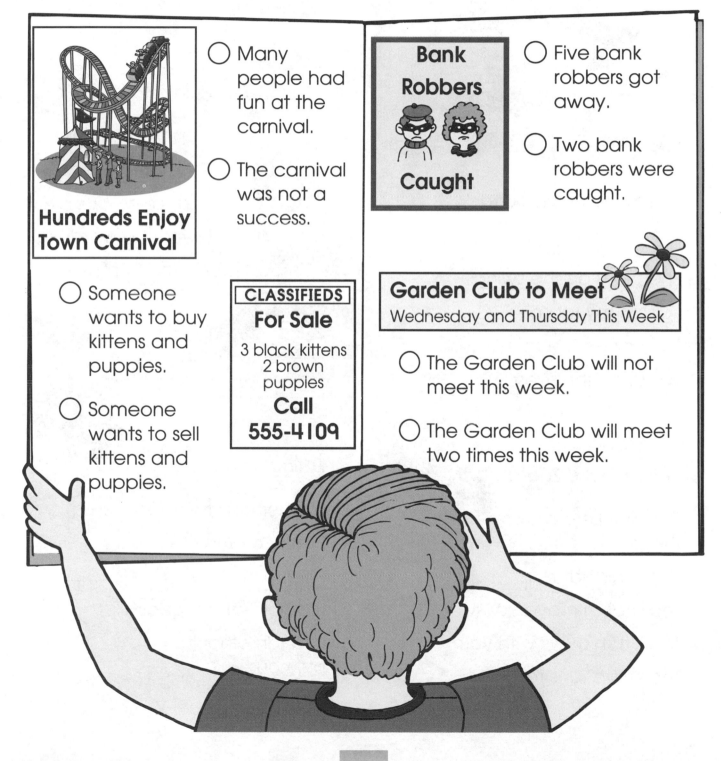

**Hundreds Enjoy Town Carnival**

○ Many people had fun at the carnival.

○ The carnival was not a success.

○ Someone wants to buy kittens and puppies.

○ Someone wants to sell kittens and puppies.

CLASSIFIEDS
**For Sale**
3 black kittens
2 brown puppies
**Call 555-4109**

**Bank Robbers Caught**

○ Five bank robbers got away.

○ Two bank robbers were caught.

**Garden Club to Meet**
Wednesday and Thursday This Week

○ The Garden Club will not meet this week.

○ The Garden Club will meet two times this week.

# What Doesn't Belong?

**Directions:** Read the sentences under each title. Cross out the sentence that does **not** tell about the main idea.

## Fun at the Playground

He runs to the slide.

She plays on the swings.

I clean my room.

They climb the monkey bars.

We sit on the seesaw.

## Doing My Homework

I open my book.

I take a bath.

I read the book.

I write the words.

I add the numbers.

## Going to the Zoo

The monkeys climb the trees.

The seals eat fish.

The snakes move slowly.

The kitten plays with yarn.

The zebra runs fast.

## Eating Dinner

Mother cuts the meat.

Father chews the corn.

Sister drinks the milk.

Brother eats his peas.

Grandmother has a big house.

Name _____

# Main Ideas About Meals

**Directions:** Read each story to find the main idea. Fill in the circle beside the phrase that tells the main idea.

## Open Wide!

An anteater slowly walked up to a log. Many ants were inside the log. The anteater put on a bib. Then, she laid a plate and a big spoon down on the ground. She began to eat and eat. When she was finished, she had eaten 30,000 ants!

○ many ants
○ a log on the ground
○ a hungry anteater

## Bite Down!

It's a good thing that Rollo Rabbit likes to chew. He nibbles on carrots, lettuce, and cabbage all day long. Every time he chews, he wears down his teeth. If Rollo did not chew so much, his front teeth could grow to be ten feet long!

○ good vegetables
○ wearing down teeth
○ a fluffy rabbit

Name _____

# Ouch!

**Directions:** Read the story below. Then, complete the activity at the bottom of the page.

    Marsha and I went for a bike ride on Sunday morning. The streets weren't crowded so we rode down Main Street. A delivery truck in front of us had just gone over a huge bump. Suddenly, a box labeled NAILS flew off the truck and into the air…

Tell what happens next:

_____

_____

_____

_____

_____

_____

_____

Name _____

# What Will Happen Next?

**Directions:** Write what happens next:

_____

_____

Name _____

# What's Next?

**Directions:** Draw a picture of what will happen next in the boxes below:

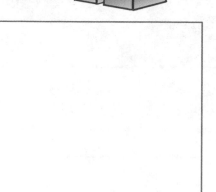

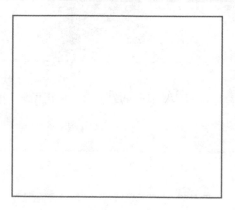

Name _____

# What Happens Next?

**Directions:** Read each paragraph. Predict what will happen next by placing an **X** in front of the best answer.

**1.** Robin went hiking with her friend. It was very hot outside. In the distance, they saw a blue glimmering lake.

____ They turned around and went home.

____ They yelled for help.

____ They waded into the cool water.

**2.** Jack and Tina are brother and sister. They love to watch basketball games. They also like to practice basketball in their driveway. Their grandma wants to get them the best birthday present ever. What should she get them?

____ Four pairs of shoes.

____ Season tickets to see the Los Angeles Lakers.

____ A new video game.

# What Will They Do?

**Directions:** Read each sentence. Fill in the circle beside the best prediction. Then, circle the picture that matches your answer.

The boy is putting on his skates.

○ He will go swimming.

○ He will go skating.

The girl fills her glass with milk.

○ She will drink the milk.

○ She will drink water.

The woman wrote a letter to her friend.

○ She will call her friend on the phone.

○ She will put the letter in the mailbox.

The kids gave Sally a birthday gift.

○ She will open the gift.

○ She will throw the gift away.

# Pup Predictions

**Directions:** Read the story.

When Donald tells Dudley to sit, Dudley rolls over. If Donald asks him to come, Dudley runs away. To surprise Dad, Donald tries to teach Dudley to fetch the newspaper. Dudley rips it up! Donald will take Dudley to dog obedience school.

**Directions:** Make predictions. Draw three things Dudley will probably learn in obedience school.

# How Will It End?

**Directions:** Read each story. Fill in the circle beside the sentence that tells what will happen next.

It is a snowy winter night. The lights flicker once, twice, and then they go out. It is cold and dark. Dad finds the flashlight and matches. He brings logs in from outside. What will Dad do?

○ Dad will make a fire.

○ Dad will cook dinner.

○ Dad will clean the fireplace.

Maggie has a garden. She likes fresh, homegrown vegetables. She says they make salads taste better. Maggie is going to make a salad for a picnic. What will Maggie do?

○ Maggie will buy the salad at the store.

○ Maggie will buy the vegetables at the store.

○ Maggie will use vegetables from her garden.

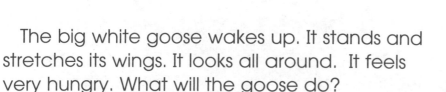

The big white goose wakes up. It stands and stretches its wings. It looks all around. It feels very hungry. What will the goose do?

○ The goose will go swimming.

○ The goose will look for food.

○ The goose will go back to sleep.

# Five Polliwogs

**A Cut-and-Fold Book**

**Directions:** The pages of your Cut-and-Fold Book are on the back of this sheet. First, follow the directions below to make the book. Next, color the pictures. Then, read the story to a family member or friend. Stop reading after page three. Ask your listener to predict what will happen next. Then, finish reading the story.

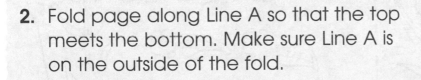

1. Tear the page out of the book.

2. Fold page along Line A so that the top meets the bottom. Make sure Line A is on the outside of the fold.

3. Fold along Line B to make the book.

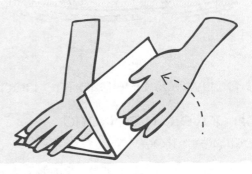

3

The fourth one said, "My legs are getting strong."

The fifth one said, "It will not be very long."

Line B

Line A

---

2

The second one said, "I have a funny tail."

The third one said, "And a tail can help me sail."

---

# Five Polliwogs

Five polliwogs swam near the shore.

The first one said, "I have never been this way before."

1

---

Five polliwogs deep in the bog.

Each gave a croak and became a frog.

4

Name _____

# Boa Constrictors

Boa constrictors are very big. They may grow up to 14 feet (4.3 meters) long. A boa kills its prey by squeezing it. Then, the prey is swallowed.

Boas do not eat cows or other large animals. They do eat animals that are larger than their own heads. The bones in their jaws stretch so they can swallow small animals such as rodents and birds.

Boa constrictors hunt while hanging from trees. They watch for their prey. Then, they attack. After eating, they may sleep for a week. Boas do not need to eat often. They can live without food for many months.

Boas are not poisonous. They defend themselves by striking and biting with their sharp teeth.

Boa constrictors give birth to live baby snakes. They do not lay eggs. They may have up to fifty baby snakes at one time.

**Directions:** Use facts from the story to help predict what will happen. Fill in the circle next to the correct answer.

1. A boa is hanging from a tree. Suddenly, a bird hops under it. The boa will ____.

   ○ strike and bite it
   ○ squeeze it, then swallow it
   ○ poison it, then eat it
   ○ sleep for one week

2. The boa is hungry and hunting for food. Which type of prey will the snake most likely eat?

   ○ cow      ○ panther      ○ horse      ○ mouse

3. A boa constrictor is slithering through the grass. Out of the grass comes a hunter walking toward it. The boa will probably ____.

   ○ strike the hunter
   ○ slither up a tree to sleep
   ○ squeeze and kill the hunter
   ○ poison the hunter

Name _____

# Fact or Opinion?

In sports, there are many facts and opinions. A **fact** is something that is true. An **opinion** is a belief someone has about something.

**Directions:** Read the sports sentences below. Next to each sentence, write **F** if it is a fact and **O** if it is an opinion.

1. _____ In bowling, a poodle is a ball that rolls down the gutter.

2. _____ I think poodles are cute.

3. _____ Julio is my favorite football player.

4. _____ A football player is a person who plays in a football game.

5. _____ A catcher's mask protects the catcher's face.

6. _____ My catcher's mask is too tight.

7. _____ I had a great putt!

8. _____ A putt is when a golfer hits the ball into the hole on a green.

9. _____ A referee is a person who enforces the rules in a game.

10. _____ Josh thought the referee did a good job.

11. _____ This silly javelin is really hard to throw!

12. _____ A metal spear that is thrown for a distance is called a javelin.

13. _____ Jake said, "The defense tried its best to block the ball."

Name _____

# Fact and Opinion: Games!

A **fact** is something that can be proven. An **opinion** is a feeling or belief about something and cannot be proven.

**Directions:** Read these sentences about different games. Then, write **F** next to each fact and **O** next to each opinion.

_____ **1.** Tennis is cool!

_____ **2.** There are red and black markers in a Checkers game.

_____ **3.** In football, a touchdown is worth six points.

_____ **4.** Being a goalie in soccer is easy.

_____ **5.** A yo-yo moves on a string.

_____ **6.** June's sister looks like the queen on the card.

_____ **7.** The six kids need three more players for a baseball team.

_____ **8.** Table tennis is more fun than court tennis.

_____ **9.** Hide-and-Seek is a game that can be played outdoors or indoors.

_____ **10.** Play money is used in many board games.

Name _____

# Fact and Opinion: Recycling

**Directions:** Read about recycling. Then, follow the instructions.

What do you throw away every day? What could you do with these things? You could change an old greeting card into a new card. You could make a puppet with an old paper bag. Old buttons make great refrigerator magnets. You can plant seeds in plastic cups. Cardboard tubes make perfect rockets. So, use your imagination!

I.  Write **F** next to each fact and **O** next to each opinion.

_____ Cardboard tubes are ugly.

_____ Buttons can be made into refrigerator magnets.

_____ An old greeting card can be changed into a new card.

_____ Paper-bag puppets are cute.

_____ Seeds can be planted in plastic cups.

_____ Rockets can be made from cardboard tubes.

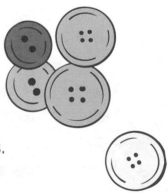

2.  What could you do with a cardboard tube? _____

_____

Name _____

# Fact and Opinion: An Owl Story

**Directions:** Read the story. Then, follow the instructions.

My name is Owen Owl, and I am a bird. I go to Nocturnal School. Our teacher is Mr. Screech Owl. In his class I learned that owls are birds and can sleep all day and hunt at night. Some of us live in nests in trees. In North America, it is against the law to harm owls. I like being an owl!

Write **F** next to each fact and **O** next to each opinion.

_____ **1.** No one can harm owls in North America.

_____ **2.** It would be great if owls could talk.

_____ **3.** Owls sleep all day.

_____ **4.** Some owls sleep in nests.

_____ **5.** Mr. Screech Owl is a good teacher.

_____ **6.** Owls are birds.

_____ **7.** Owen Owl would be a good friend.

_____ **8.** Owls hunt at night.

_____ **9.** Nocturnal School is a good school for smart owls.

_____ **10.** This story is for the birds.

Name _____

# Fact and Opinion: A Bounty of Birds

**Directions:** Read the story. Then, follow the instructions.

Tashi's family likes to go to the zoo. Her favorite animals are all the different kinds of birds. Tashi likes birds because they can fly, they have colorful feathers, and they make funny noises.

Write **F** next to each fact and **O** next to each opinion.

_____ 1. Birds have two feet.

_____ 2. All birds lay eggs.

_____ 3. Parrots are too noisy.

_____ 4. All birds have feathers and wings.

_____ 5. It would be great to be a bird and fly south for the winter.

_____ 6. Birds have hard beaks or bills instead of teeth.

_____ 7. Pigeons are fun to watch.

_____ 8. Some birds cannot fly.

_____ 9. Parakeets make good pets.

_____ 10. A penguin is a bird.

Name _____

# Fact and Opinion: Henrietta the Humpback

**Directions:** Read the story. Then, follow the instructions.

My name is Henrietta, and I am a humpback whale. I live in cold seas in the summer and warm seas in the winter. My long flippers are used to move forward and backward. I like to eat fish. Sometimes, I show off by leaping out of the water.  Would you like to be a humpback whale?

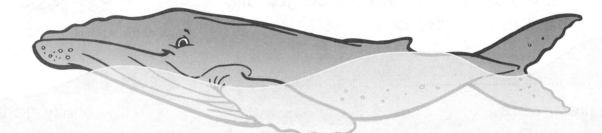

Write **F** next to each fact and **O** next to each opinion.

_____ **1.** Being a humpback whale is fun.

_____ **2.** Humpback whales live in cold seas during the summer.

_____ **3.** Whales are fun to watch.

_____ **4.** Humpback whales use their flippers to move forward and backward.

_____ **5.** Henrietta is a great name for a whale.

_____ **6.** Leaping out of water would be hard.

_____ **7.** Humpback whales like to eat fish.

_____ **8.** Humpback whales show off by leaping out of the water.

# Strings Attached!

**Directions:** Draw a line to connect each string of words on the left with a string of words on the right to make a complete sentence. Make sure that each sentence you form makes sense.

**Hint:** There are several ways to connect the groups of words. Try out different combinations to find the ones you like best.

**MATCHING**

A
B
C
D

**All of the Above**

The tired mom

the stinky garbage.

We picked apples

had a shaky voice.

I threw out

smelled bad.

The nervous man

and made a pie!

I love to eat

rocked her baby.

The wet cat

vanilla ice cream.

# Best Guess!

**Directions:** Read each sentence below. Using the information in the first sentence, decide which answer best completes each question. Fill in the circle next to your answer choice.

"Is it cold in here?" asked my grandma as she shivered.

What do you think your grandma would like you to do?

○ Open a window.

○ Turn on the heat.

○ Give her a hug.

James' stomach growled really loudly in class today!

What would help James?

○ medicine

○ a new toy

○ food

# Who Will Help Me?

**Directions:** Write the best choice from the word list to answer each question.

| Word List | | | |
|---|---|---|---|
| captain | dentist | fireman | doctor |
| plumber | police | teacher | baker |

I think I have a cavity in my tooth.
Who can help me?

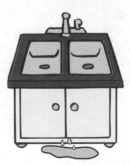

_____

My mom needs to order a wedding cake
for my uncle. Who can help her?

_____

I hurt my ankle during gym class.
Who can help me?

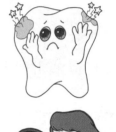

_____

My pipes are leaking.
Who can help me?

_____

Name _____

# What Could I Be?

**Directions:** Write the answer to each riddle. Use a word from the word list.

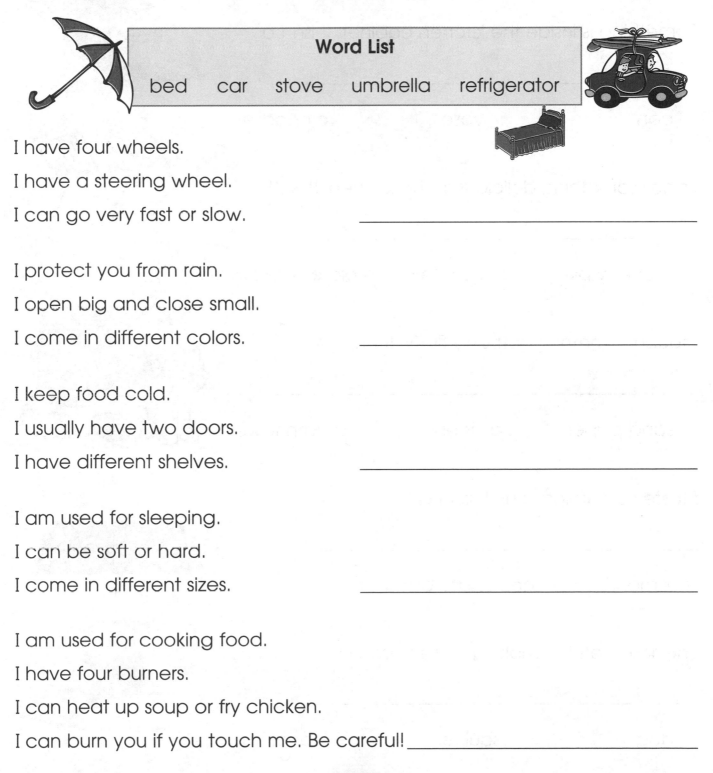

| Word List |
| --- |
| bed    car    stove    umbrella    refrigerator |

I have four wheels.

I have a steering wheel.

I can go very fast or slow. _____

I protect you from rain.

I open big and close small.

I come in different colors. _____

I keep food cold.

I usually have two doors.

I have different shelves. _____

I am used for sleeping.

I can be soft or hard.

I come in different sizes. _____

I am used for cooking food.

I have four burners.

I can heat up soup or fry chicken.

I can burn you if you touch me. Be careful! _____

Name _____

# It Isn't!

**Directions:** Finish the sentences about the stories.

Something is inside the kitchen cabinet. It isn't a

_____ .

    can               vase            crocodile

I smell something delicious in the kitchen. It isn't

_____ .

    a cherry pie      dirty socks      a plate of brownies

I touch something soft and fluffy. It isn't

_____ .

    sand paper      a kitten      a bath towel

I taste something sour. It isn't a

_____ .

    lemon      chocolate bar

I hear something making noise. It isn't a

_____ .

    dog           squirrel           book

Name _____

# Making Inferences

Not every story tells you all the facts. Sometimes, you need to put together details to understand what is happening in a story. When you put details together, you **make inferences**.

**Directions:** Read each story. Fill in the circle beside the inference you can make from the details you have.

Everyone on the Pine School baseball team wears a blue shirt on Mondays. It is Monday and Brenda is wearing a blue shirt.

○ Brenda always wears blue clothes.

○ Brenda cannot find her red shirt.

○ Brenda is on the baseball team.

My cat has brown and white stripes. It meows when it wants to be fed. My cat is meowing now.

○ The cat wants to go outside.

○ The cat is hungry.

○ The cat doesn't like brown and white stripes.

Every afternoon the children run outside when they hear a bell ring. At 2:00, Mr. Chocovan drives by in his ice-cream truck. The children hear a bell ringing. They run outside.

○ It is time for ice cream.

○ It is time for the children to go home.

○ It is time for a fire drill.

# Figure It Out

**Directions:** Read the story.

It is a rainy day. Mom tells Tosh to stay inside until the weather clears up. Tosh lies on his bed and pouts. He sings one song over and over. Now and then, he checks to see if the rain has stopped.

**Directions:** Use details in the story to make inferences. Fill in the circle beside the phrase that completes each sentence.

Tosh probably wants to
- ◯ go outside and play.
- ◯ lie in bed all day.

Tosh probably feels
- ◯ happy.
- ◯ bored and grumpy.

The song Tosh probably sings is
- ◯ "Rain, Rain, Go Away."
- ◯ "Jingle Bells."

# Inferences About Characters

**Directions:** Read this story. Look for clues about Tom. Then, follow the directions below the story.

"You can't get me!" Goldie teased Tom when she saw him looking at her.

"I never said that I wanted to get you, anyway," answered Tom, knowing that Goldie was right. He walked away, waving his fluffy tail proudly.

Although Goldie had once been afraid of Tom, she now liked to tease him.

"It's fun to tease Tom. When he is upset, all his fur stands straight up," she thought.

Soon Goldie heard noises. Someone else was home. "It is almost time for dinner," thought Goldie. "I'm really glad to be a goldfish. I'm safe and sound and very well fed."

What does Tom look like? Draw a picture of Tom.

Circle the picture that tells how Goldie feels.

Name _____

# Mind-Reading Tricks

Samantha thought of a good joke. She bragged that she could read Maria's mind. She put her hand on Maria's head, closed her eyes, and said, "You had red punch with your lunch!"

"Wow! You're right!" replied Maria, not realizing that she had a little red ring around her lips.

"That was easy. But I bet you can't tell me what I just ate," said Thomas.

"That's a bunch of baloney," answered Samantha.

"How did you know?" gasped Thomas.

"It's my little secret," said Samantha, with a sigh of relief.

"Here comes your mom," said Maria. "Can you read her mind, too?"

Samantha looked down at her watch. She should have been home half an hour ago. As she ran to meet her mother, she yelled back, "Yes, I know exactly what she's thinking!"

**Directions:** Make inferences about Samantha's mind-reading tricks. Fill in the circle beside the correct inference.

**1.** Was Samantha sure that Thomas had eaten bologna for lunch?

○ No, she was just lucky.

○ Yes, she saw him eat his bologna sandwich.

**2.** What was Samantha's mother probably thinking?

○ Samantha was a great mind reader.

○ Samantha was late.

Name _____

# What Is It?

When you don't get the whole picture, you may need to **draw conclusions** for yourself. To draw a conclusion, think about what you see or read. Think about what you already know. Then, make a good guess.

**Directions:** Look at each picture. Use what you know and what you see to draw a conclusion. Draw a line to the sentence that tells about each picture.

It must be a clown.

It must be a cowhand.

It must be a baby.

It must be a ballet dancer.

It must be a football player.

Name _____

# Who Said It?

**Directions:** Use what you see, what you read, and what you know to draw conclusions. Draw a line from the animal to what it might say.

"I save lots of bones and bury them in the yard."

"I live in the ocean and have sharp teeth."

"I love to walk in the snow and slide on the ice."

"I hop on lily pads in a pond with my webbed feet."

"I slither on the ground because I have no arms or legs."

Name _____

# What Happened?

**Directions:** Look at the pictures. Fill in the circle beside the sentence that tells what happened in the missing picture. Draw a picture that shows what happened.

## What happened?

○ The boy dropped the string.

○ The boy took his kite home.

## What happened?

○ The angry baby played in its bed.

○ The hungry baby drank the milk.

Name _____

# My Conclusion Is . . .

**Directions:** Read the sentences. Look at the pictures. Circle the picture that completes the last sentence.

1. Emily is on a class trip. She sees cows eating grass and horses in the barn. Hens are sitting on their eggs. She must be visiting a . . .

2. Timmy wore his best suit. He sat in a tall chair. He combed his hair. A man said, "Say cheese!" The man is a . . .

3. Mark spilled milk on the floor. He had to clean up the mess. He went to the closet and got a . . .

Name _____

# I Conclude!

**Directions:** Read each story. Fill in the circle beside the answer that completes the last sentence.

The little house is in the backyard. Inside is a bowl of water. Next to the bowl is a big bone. This house belongs to . . .

○ some birds.        ○ a family of elves.        ○ a puppy.

The yellow cat is fluffy. The black cat is thin. The tan and white cat acts friendly. The little gray cat is shy. Cats are all . . .

○ different.        ○ angry.        ○ silly.

Lois keeps her pet in an aquarium. Her pet can hop. It eats flies and is green. Her pet is . . .

○ a bunny.        ○ a frog.        ○ very tall.

We played a game. We ran away from Sofia. When she tapped Raymond, he was It. We were playing . . .

○ soccer.        ○ basketball.        ○ tag.

# Clues to Conclusions

**Directions:** Read each story. Fill in the circle beside the correct conclusion.

Joe tried to read the book. He pulled it closer to his face and squinted. What is wrong?

- ◯ The book isn't very interesting.
- ◯ Joe needs glasses.
- ◯ The book is closed.

"My shoes are too tight," said Eddie, "and my pants are too short!" What has happened?

- ◯ Eddie has put on his older brother's clothes.
- ◯ Eddie has become shorter.
- ◯ Eddie has grown.

Patsy went to the beach. She stayed outside for hours. When she came home, she looked in the mirror. Her face was very red. Why did she look different?

- ◯ Patsy had gotten a bad sunburn.
- ◯ Patsy got red paint all over herself.
- ◯ Patsy was very cold.

Name _____

# Cause and Effect

**Cause:** An action or act that makes something happen.

**Effect:** Something that happens because of an action or cause.

Look at the following example of cause and effect.

 We forgot to put the lid on the trash can.

 The raccoons ate the trash.

**Directions:** Now, draw a line connecting each cause on the left side of the page to its effect on the right side of the page.

Name _____

# How Did It Happen?

**Directions:** Read the stories below. Then, write the missing cause or effect.

Audrey left her bike outside in the rain for weeks. When she finally put it back inside the garage, it had rusted.

**Cause:** Audrey left her bike outside in the rain.

What was the **effect**? _____

I dropped a heavy box on my foot by accident. Yoweeeee! That hurt! My mom took me to the doctor.

**Cause:** _____

**Effect:** _____

Noah Webster loved words so much that he decided to write a dictionary!

**Cause:** _____

**Effect:** _____

# Do You Know Why?

**Directions:** Write the cause from the answer box for each sentence.

---

**Answer Box**

The bathtub overflowed.

I studied all the spelling words.

Gill tried to grab the cat.

I didn't water my plants.

A tornado hit our town.

---

1. _____

The cat ran away.

2. _____

The floor got wet.

3. _____

There was a lot of damage.

4. _____

My plants died.

5. _____

I won the school spelling bee!

Name _____

# Weather Effects!

**Directions:** Write two effects from the answer box to answer each question.

---

**Answer Box**

The kids got wet walking to school.

Everyone came outside to see it.

The roads were closed because of the snow.

People lost electricity for a day.

The street drains overflowed.

People took pictures and artists sat on the grass to draw it.

---

What happened when it rained everyday for a month?

_____

_____

What happened when a blizzard hit the town?

_____

_____

What happened when there was a beautiful rainbow outside?

_____

_____

# Tricky Cause and Effect

Things that happen can make other things happen. The event that happens is the **effect**. Why the event happens is the **cause**.

**Example:** Marcie tripped on the step and fell down.
    **Cause:** Marcie tripped on the step.
    **Effect:** Marcie fell down.

**Directions:** Read the story.

Marcie knows a magic trick. She can make a ring seem to go up and down by itself on a pencil. Marcie has to get ready ahead of time. She ties a piece of skinny thread under the pencil's eraser. Then, she ties the thread to a button on her blouse. In front of her audience, Marcie puts a ring on the pencil. When Marcie leans forward, the thread goes loose, so the ring goes down. Then, Marcie leans back. The thread tightens and makes the ring go up the pencil.

**Directions:** Write the cause to complete each sentence.

I. The audience cannot see the thread because

_____

- - - - - - - - - - - - - - - - - - - - - - - -

_____

2. - - - - - - - - - - - - - - - - - - - - - - -

_____

makes the ring go down.

Name _____

# Why Did It Happen?

**Directions:** Read the effects. Fill in the circle beside the sentence that tells what caused the effect.

The soccer coach is cheering.

○ Her team lost the game.

○ Her team won the game.

Patty found only one cookie in the cookie jar.

○ Someone ate all the other cookies.

○ It was a brand new cookie jar.

Fred has a new pair of glasses.

○ Fred was having trouble seeing the chalkboard.

○ There was a sale on glasses.

Lynn turned the fan to high.

○ It was a very cold day.

○ It was a very hot day.

Jason took his umbrella to school.

○ The sky was cloudy.

○ The sun was shining.

Name _____

# Chain of Effects

**Directions:** Read the story.

At night, Tran set his alarm clock for seven o'clock. When it rang the next morning, he was so tired he turned the alarm off. Then, he went back to sleep. Tran finally woke up at eight o'clock. Tran had missed the school bus. He had to walk to school. It was a long walk. Tran was very late!

**Directions:** Draw a line to match a cause to an effect.

| | |
|---|---|
| Because he was tired, | Tran missed the school bus. |
| Because Tran turned off the alarm, | he had to walk to school. |
| Because he woke up at eight o'clock, | Tran turned off the alarm. |
| Because Tran missed the bus, | Tran was late for school. |
| Because he had a long walk, | he overslept. |

# A Cause-and-Effect Fable

**Directions:** Read the story.

Four animals caught a talking fish. "If you let me go, I will grant each of you one wish," announced the fish.

"Make my trunk smaller!" demanded the vain elephant. "I wish to be the most beautiful elephant that ever lived."

"Make my legs longer!" commanded the alligator. "I want to be taller than all my alligator friends."

"Make my neck shorter!" ordered the giraffe. "I am tired of always staring at the tops of trees."

"Dear Fish, please make me be satisfied with who-o-o-o-o I am," whispered the wise old owl.

Poof! Kazaam! Their wishes were granted. However, soon after, only one of these animals was happy. Can you guess who-o-o-o-o?

**Directions:** Draw a line to match a cause to an effect.

| | |
|---|---|
| Because of its short trunk, | the giraffe could no longer eat leaves from treetops. |
| Because of its long legs, | the elephant could no longer spray water on its back. |
| Because of its short neck, | the owl was happy about his wish. |
| Because he could still do all the things he needed, | the alligator could no longer hide in shallow water. |

Name _____

# Fiction or Nonfiction?

Some stories are made up and some are true. **Fiction** stories are made up, and **nonfiction** stories are true.

**Directions:** Read the passages below. Then, write if they are **fiction** or **nonfiction**.

Following a balanced diet is important for good health. Your body needs many kinds of vitamins and minerals found in different types of food. For example, oranges provide vitamin C, and bananas are a good source of the mineral potassium.

_____

We call my dog the alphabet dog. Why? Because my dog can sing the alphabet! That's right! My dog, Smarty Pants, is a dog genius! Smarty Pants can sing the entire alphabet! "S.P.," as we sometimes call her, is also starting her own dog academy to teach other dogs how to sing the alphabet. You should sign up your dog for classes with Smarty Pants today!

_____

Name _____

# Fiction/Nonfiction: Heavy Hitters

**Fiction** is a make-believe story. **Nonfiction** is a true story.

**Directions:** Read the stories about two famous baseball players. Then, write **fiction** or **nonfiction** in the baseball bats.

In 1998, Mark McGwire played for the St. Louis Cardinals. He liked to hit home runs. On September 27, 1998, he hit home run number 70, to set a new record for the most home runs hit in one season. The old record was set in 1961 by Roger Maris, who later played for the St. Louis Cardinals (1967 to 1968), when he hit 61 home runs.

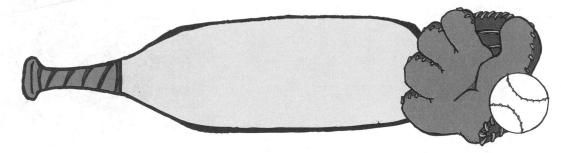

The Mighty Casey played baseball for the Mudville Nine and was the greatest of all baseball players. He could hit the cover off the ball with the power of a hurricane. But, when the Mudville Nine was behind 4 to 2 in the championship game, Mighty Casey struck out with the bases loaded. There was no joy in Mudville that day, because the Mudville Nine had lost the game.

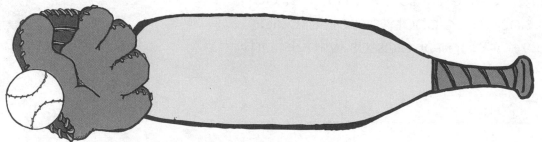

# Nonfiction: Tornado Tips

**Directions:** Read about tornadoes. Then, follow the instructions.

A tornado begins over land with strong winds and thunderstorms. The spinning air becomes a funnel. It can cause damage. If you are inside, go to the lowest floor of the building. A basement is a safe place. A bathroom or closet in the middle of a building can be a safe place, too. If you are outside, lie in a ditch. Remember, tornadoes are dangerous.

Write five facts about tornadoes.

1. _____

_____

2. _____

_____

3. _____

_____

4. _____

_____

5. _____

_____

# Fiction: Hercules

The **setting** is where a story takes place. The **characters** are the people in a story or play.

**Directions:** Read about Hercules. Then, answer the questions.

Hercules was born in the warm Atlantic Ocean. He was a very small and weak baby. He wanted to be the strongest hurricane in the world. But he had one problem. He couldn't blow 75-mile-per-hour winds. Hercules blew and blew in the ocean, until one day, his sister, Hola, told him it would be more fun to be a breeze than a hurricane. Hercules agreed. It was a breeze to be a breeze!

1.  What is the setting of the story? _____

2.  Who are the characters? _____

3.  What is the problem? _____

4.  How does Hercules solve his problem? _____

_____

# Fiction/Nonfiction: The Fourth of July

**Directions:** Read each story. Then, write whether it is fiction or nonfiction.

One sunny day in July, a dog named Stan ran away from home. He went up one street and down the other looking for fun, but all the yards were empty. Where was everybody? Stan kept walking until he heard the sound of band music and happy people. Stan walked faster until he got

to Central Street. There he saw men, women, children, and dogs getting ready to walk in a parade. It was the Fourth of July!

Fiction or nonfiction? _____

Americans celebrate the Fourth of July every year, because it is the birthday of the United States of America. On July 4, 1776, the United States got its independence from Great Britain. Today, Americans celebrate this holiday with parades, picnics, and fireworks as they proudly wave the red, white, and blue American flag.

Fiction or nonfiction? _____

# Fiction and Nonfiction: Which Is It?

**Directions:** Read about fiction and nonfiction books. Then, follow the instructions.

There are many kinds of books. Some books have make-believe stories about princesses and dragons. Some books contain poetry and rhymes, like Mother Goose. These are fiction.

Some books contain facts about space and plants. And still other books have stories about famous people in history like Abraham Lincoln. These are nonfiction.

Write **F** for **fiction** and **NF** for **nonfiction**.

_____ 1. nursery rhyme

_____ 2. fairy tale

_____ 3. true life story of a famous athlete

_____ 4. Aesop's fables

_____ 5. dictionary entry about foxes

_____ 6. weather report

_____ 7. story about a talking tree

_____ 8. story about how a tadpole becomes a frog

_____ 9. story about animal habitats

_____ 10. riddles and jokes

# What Is a Character?

A **character** is the person, animal, or object that a story is about. You cannot have a story without a character.

Characters are usually people, but sometimes they can be animals, aliens (!), or even objects that come to life. You can have many characters in a story.

**Directions:** Read the story below, and then answer the questions about character on the next page.

**Adventurous Alenna!**

Alenna was seven years old and lived on a tropical island. She had long, blond hair and sea-green eyes. Alenna was very adventurous and was always exploring new things. She started an Adventure Club at her school and led her friends on long bike rides. She also was the youngest person in her family to learn to water-ski!

When her dad asked, "Who wants to go snorkeling to see some fish?"

Alenna answered, "I want to go snorkeling!" Alenna was very adventurous.

**The End**

Name _____

# Character, cont.

First, authors must decide who their main character is going to be. Next, they decide what their main character looks like. Then, they reveal the character's personality by:

**what the character does**

**what the character says**

**Directions:** Answer the questions about the story you just read.

Who is the main character in "Adventurous Alenna!"?

_____

What does Alenna look like? Describe her appearance on the line below:

_____

Give two examples of what Alenna **does** that shows that she is adventurous:

1. _____

2. _____

Give an example of what Alenna **says** that reveals she is adventurous.

_____

_____

Name _____

# Character Interview—Lights! Camera! Action!

An **interview** takes place between two people, usually a reporter and another person. The interviewer asks questions for the person to answer.

**Directions:** Pretend that you are a reporter. Choose a character from a book you read. If you could ask the character anything you wanted to, what would you ask?

Make a **list of questions** you would like to ask your character:

1. _____

2. _____

3. _____

4. _____

Now, pretend your character has come to life and could **answer your questions**. Write what you think he, she, or it would say:

1. _____

2. _____

3. _____

4. _____

Name _____

# Setting—Place

Every story has a **setting**. The setting is the **place** where the story happens. Think of a place that you know well. It could be your room, your kitchen, your backyard, your classroom, or an imaginary place.

**Directions:** Brainstorm some words and ideas about that place. Think about what you see, hear, smell, taste, or feel in that place.

Brainstorm your ideas for a setting below:

_____

_____

_____

_____

see    hear    smell

taste    touch

_____

_____

_____

_____

_____

Where are we?_____

Name _____

# Setting—Place

**Directions:** Read the story below and answer the questions about the setting.

## The Amazing Amazon

The Amazon jungle is a huge rain forest in South America. It is full of gigantic green trees, thick jungle vines, and many species of dangerous animals. It is very humid in the jungle.

What is the temperature like in the Amazon jungle?

_____

Where is the Amazon jungle located?

_____

Would it be easy to travel in the Amazon jungle? Why or why not?

_____

_____

_____

Does it rain a lot in the Amazon jungle?

_____

Name _____

# Setting—Time

The **setting** is the **place** where the story happens. The setting is also the **time** in which the story happens. A reader needs to know **when** the story is happening. Does it take place at night? On a sunny day? In the future? During the winter?

**Time** can be:

time of day

a holiday

a season of the year

a time in the future

a time in history

**Directions:** Read the following story. Then, answer the questions below.

### Knock, Knock!

One windy fall night there was a knock at the door. "Who is it?" I asked.

"It's your dog, Max. Please let me in," Max said.

"Oh, good. I was getting worried about you!" I said. Then, I let Max inside.

I thought to myself how glad I was that scientists had invented voice boxes for dogs. How did people in the olden days ever know when to let their dogs inside if their dogs couldn't talk? The Doggie Voice Box is such a wonderful invention. I'm so happy that I live in the year 2090!

What time of day is it? _____

What season is it? _____

What year does this story take place? _____

# Make a Map!

In a story or book you read, the character or characters may have taken a journey or simply walked around their town. Where did the main events in the story take place?

"I can't wait to tell you about my story!"

**Directions:** Create a detailed map showing the place where the characters lived. You may wish to ask an adult for help.

1.  Draw the outline of your map on a sheet of paper.

2.  Be sure to write the title and the author of the book at the top of the map.

3.  Think about what places you want to include on your map and draw them.

4.  Label the important places, adding a short sentence about what happened there.

5.  Add color and details.

6.  Share your map with friends, and tell them about the story you read.

Name _____

# Travel Brochure

A travel brochure gives information about interesting places to visit. Travel brochures usually include beautiful color pictures and descriptive sentences that make people want to visit that place. They also give useful facts about a place.

**Directions:** Plan a travel brochure for the **setting** of a book you have read.

First, brainstorm and write down some ideas about the setting in your book. What would you want to talk about in your travel brochure: What it looked like? local plants and animals? an unusual restaurant? interesting places to visit there?

Take a sheet of paper and fold it into three sections. You can write on both the front and back sides.

Color your brochure with crayons or markers.

Share your brochure with friends, and tell them about the setting of the book you read.

# Postcard

Have you ever received or written a postcard? Usually, people send postcards when they are on vacation. A postcard usually shows a **picture** of the place someone is visiting and provides room for a **short message** about the trip.

**Directions:** Create a postcard about a book you have just read.

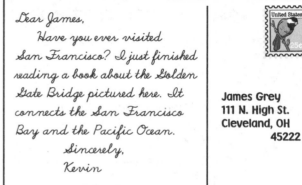

Dear James,
    Have you ever visited San Francisco? I just finished reading a book about the Golden Gate Bridge pictured here. It connects the San Francisco Bay and the Pacific Ocean.
        Sincerely,
        Kevin

Golden Gate Bridge • San Francisco, California

James Grey
111 N. High St.
Cleveland, OH
        45222

1. Brainstorm a list of parts of the book that you liked best.

2. On scrap paper, sketch a picture that illustrates your favorite part.

3. Copy your picture onto the blank side of a large index card.

4. Write a message on the lined side of the index card. Tell about the book you read, your favorite part, and the picture that goes with it.

5. Address the card to someone you know or to a character from the book.

6. Show your postcard to your friends and tell them about your book.

# Extra! Extra! Read All About It!

Newspaper reporters have very important jobs. They have to catch a reader's attention and, at the same time, **tell the facts**.

Newspaper reporters write their stories by answering **who**, **what**, **where**, **when**, **why**, and **how**.

**Directions:** Think about a book you just read and answer the questions below.

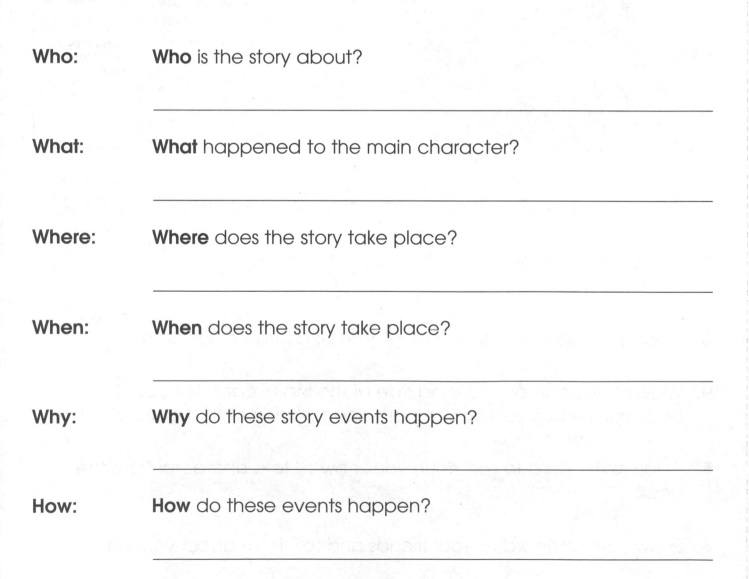

**Who:**      **Who** is the story about?

_____

**What:**      **What** happened to the main character?

_____

**Where:**      **Where** does the story take place?

_____

**When:**      **When** does the story take place?

_____

**Why:**      **Why** do these story events happen?

_____

**How:**      **How** do these events happen?

_____

# Extra! Extra! Read All About It!

**Directions:** Use your answers on page 216 to write a newspaper article about the book you read.

# BIG CITY TIMES

Title

_____

(Write a catchy title for your article.)

_____

_____

_____

_____

_____

_____

_____

_____

Name _____

# Common Nouns

A **common noun** names a person, place, or thing.

**Example:** The **boy** had several **chores** to do.

**Directions:** Fill in the circle below each common noun.

1. First, the boy had to feed his puppy.
   ◯        ◯          ◯          ◯

2. He got fresh water for his pet.
          ◯      ◯       ◯ ◯

3. Next, the boy poured some dry food into a bowl.
          ◯            ◯        ◯         ◯

4. He set the dish on the floor in the kitchen.
   ◯      ◯          ◯           ◯

5. Then, he called his dog to come to dinner.
       ◯          ◯              ◯

6. The boy and his dad worked in the garden.
       ◯         ◯     ◯          ◯

7. The father turned the dirt with a shovel.
       ◯       ◯       ◯        ◯

8. The boy carefully dropped seeds into little holes.
       ◯      ◯              ◯         ◯

9. Soon, tiny plants would sprout from the soil.
          ◯       ◯      ◯          ◯

10. Sunshine and showers would help the radishes grow.
    ◯          ◯                  ◯      ◯

Name _____

# Proper Nouns

A **proper noun** names a specific or certain person, place, or thing. A proper noun always begins with a capital letter.

**Example: Becky** flew to **St. Louis** in a **Boeing 747**.

**Directions:** Put a ✔ in front of each proper noun.

| | |
|---|---|
| _____ I. uncle | _____ 9. New York Science Center |
| _____ 2. Aunt Retta | _____ 10. Ms. Small |
| _____ 3. Forest Park | _____ II. Doctor Chang |
| _____ 4. Gateway Arch | _____ 12. Union Station |
| _____ 5. Missouri | _____ 13. Henry Shaw |
| _____ 6. school | _____ 14. museum |
| _____ 7. Miss Hunter | _____ 15. librarian |
| _____ 8. Northwest Plaza | _____ 16. shopping mall |

**Directions:** Underline the proper nouns.

I. Becky went to visit Uncle Harry.

2. He took her to see the Cardinals play baseball.

3. The game was at Busch Stadium.

4. The St. Louis Cardinals played the Chicago Cubs.

5. Mark McGwire hit a home run.

Name _____

# Singular Nouns

A **singular noun** names one person, place, or thing.

**Example:** My **mother** unlocked the old **trunk** in the **attic**.

**Directions:** If the noun is singular, draw a line from it to the trunk. If the noun is **not** singular, draw an **X** on the word.

| | | | |
|---|---|---|---|
| teddy bear | hammer | picture | sweater |
| bonnet | letters | seashells | fiddle |
| kite | ring | feather | books |
| postcard | crayon | doll | dishes |
| blocks | hats | bicycle | blanket |

Name _____

# Plural Nouns

A **plural noun** names more than one person, place, or thing.

**Example:** Some **dinosaurs** ate **plants** in **swamps**.

**Directions:** Underline each plural noun.

1. Large animals lived millions of years ago.

2. Dinosaurs roamed many parts of the Earth.

3. Scientists look for fossils.

4. The bones can tell a scientist many things.

5. These bones help tell what the creatures were like.

6. Some had curved claws and whip-like tails.

7. Others had beaks and plates of armor.

8. Some dinosaurs lived on the plains, and others lived in forests.

9. You can see the skeletons of dinosaurs at some museums.

10. We often read about these animals in books.

# Action Verbs

A **verb** is a word that can show action.

**Example:**    I **jump**.    He **kicks**.    He **walked**.

**Directions:** Underline the verb in each sentence. Write it on the line.

1. Our school plays games on Field Day.    _____

2. Juan runs 50 yards.    _____

3. Carmen hops in a sack race.    _____

4. Paula tosses a ball through a hoop.    _____

5. One girl carries a jellybean on a spoon.    _____

6. Lola bounces the ball.    _____

7. Some boys chase after balloons.    _____

8. Mark chooses me for his team.    _____

9. The children cheer for the winners.    _____

10. Everyone enjoys Field Day.    _____

# Ready for Action!

**Directions:** Draw a line to match each action word to the picture that shows it.

kick

catch

slide

run

jump

# Irregular Verbs

Verbs that do not add **ed** to show what happened in the past are called **irregular verbs**.

**Example: Present      Past**
    run, runs   ran
    fall, falls   fell

Jim **ran** past our house yesterday.
He **fell** over a wagon on the sidewalk.

**Directions:** Fill in the verbs that tell what happened in the past in the chart. The first one is done for you.

| Present | Past |
| --- | --- |
| hear, hears | heard |
| draw, draws | |
| do, does | |
| give, gives | |
| sell, sells | |
| come, comes | |
| fly, flies | |
| build, builds | |
| know, knows | |
| bring, brings | |

# Linking Verbs

A **linking verb** does not show action. Instead, it links the subject with a word in the predicate. **Am, is, are, was,** and **were** are **linking verbs.**

**Example:** Many people **are** collectors.
(**Are** connects **people** and **collectors.**)
The collection **was** large.
(**Was** connects **collection** and **large.**)

**Directions:** Underline the linking verb in each sentence.

1. I am happy.

2. Toy collecting is a nice hobby.

3. Mom and Dad are helpful.

4. The rabbit is beautiful.

5. Itsy and Bitsy are stuffed mice.

6. Monday was special.

7. I was excited.

8. The class was impressed.

9. The elephants were gray.

10. My friends were a good audience.

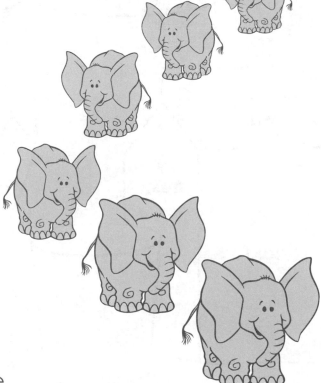

# Adjectives

An **adjective** is a word that describes a noun.
It tells **how many**, **what kind**, or **which one**.

**Example:** Yolanda has a **tasty** lunch.

**Directions:** Color each space that has an adjective. Do not color the other spaces.

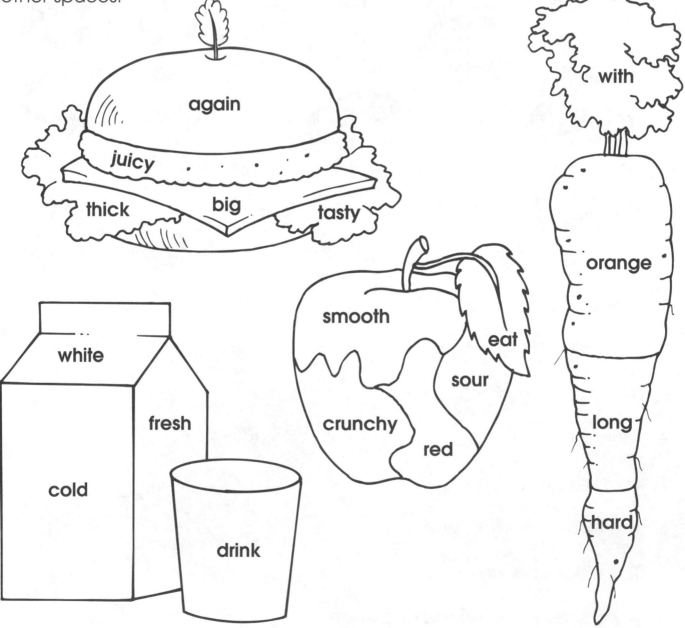

# Add the Adjectives

**Directions:** Write a describing word on each line. Draw a picture to match each sentence.

**high** mountain

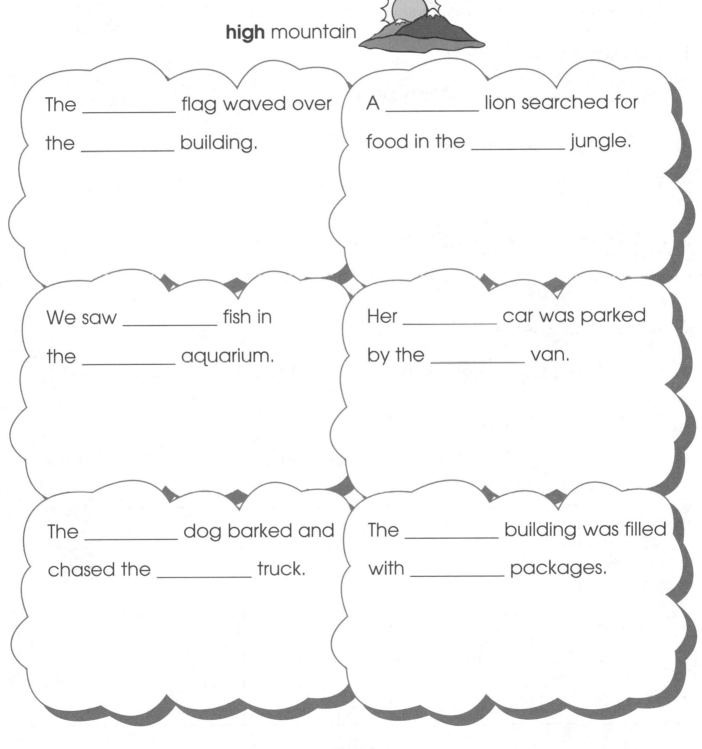

The _____ flag waved over the _____ building.

A _____ lion searched for food in the _____ jungle.

We saw _____ fish in the _____ aquarium.

Her _____ car was parked by the _____ van.

The _____ dog barked and chased the _____ truck.

The _____ building was filled with _____ packages.

Name _____

# Better Sentences

**Directions:** Describing words like adjectives can make a better sentence. Write a word on each line to make the sentences more interesting. Draw pictures of your sentences.

1. The skater won a medal.

   The _____ skater won a _____ medal.

2. The jewels were in the safe.

   The _____ jewels were in the _____ safe.

3. The airplane flew through the storm.

   The _____ airplane flew through the _____ storm.

4. A fireman rushed into the house.

   A _____ fireman rushed into the _____ house.

5. The detective hid behind the tree.

   The _____ detective hid behind the _____ tree.

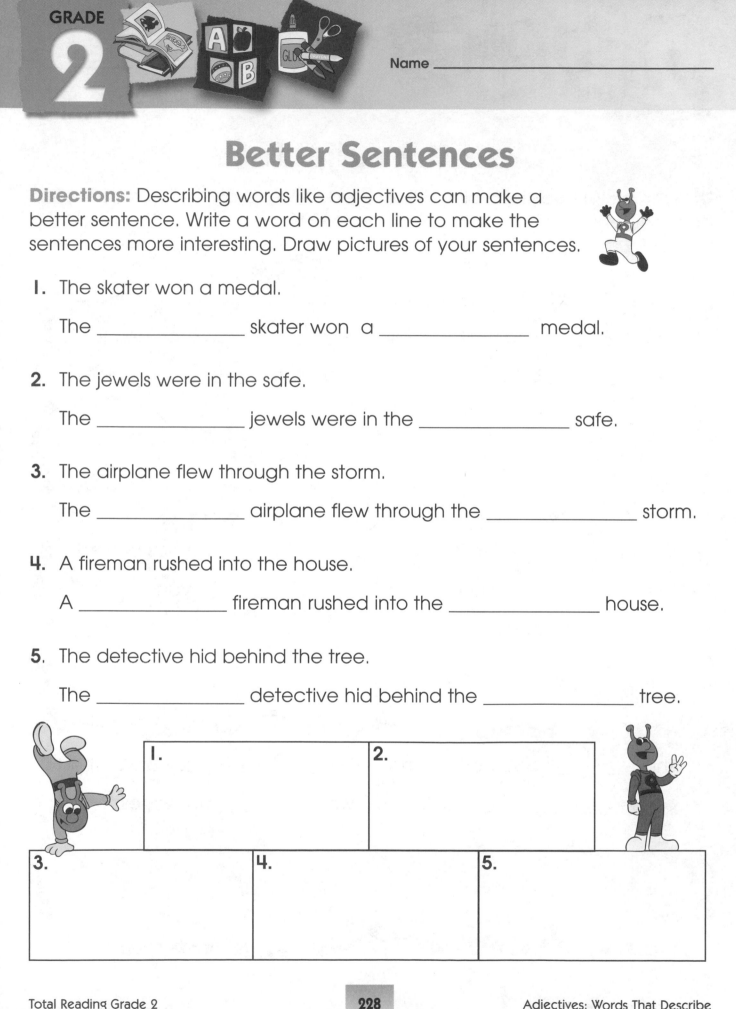

| 1. | 2. |
|---|---|
| 3. | 4. | 5. |

# Describing People

**Directions:** Choose two words from the box that describe each character. Then, complete each sentence to tell why you chose those words.

| understanding | spoiled | responsible | lazy | helpful | upset | happy |
|---|---|---|---|---|---|---|
| busy | caring | kind | mean | confused | unhappy | patient | nice |

The girl is _____ and _____

because she _____

_____

_____

_____

Mother is _____ and _____

because she _____

_____

_____

_____

Father is _____ and _____

because he _____

_____

_____

_____

Name _____

# Using Exact Adjectives

Use an **adjective** that best describes the noun or pronoun. Be specific.

**Example:** David had a nice birthday.
David had a **fun** birthday.

**Directions:** Rewrite each sentence, replacing **nice** or **good** with a better adjective from the box or one of your own.

| sturdy | new | great | chocolate | delicious | special |

1. David bought a nice pair of in-line skates.

   _____

2. He received a nice helmet.

   _____

3. He got nice knee pads.

   _____

4. Father baked a good cake.

   _____

5. David made a good wish.

   _____

6. Mom served good ice cream.

   _____

# Subjects of Sentences

The **subject** of a sentence tells **who** or **what** does something.

**Example: Some people** eat foods that may seem strange to you.

**Directions:** Underline the subject of each sentence.

1. Some people like crocodile steak.

2. The meat tastes like fish.

3. Australians eat kangaroo meat.

4. Kangaroo meat tastes like beef.

5. People in the Southwest eat rattlesnake meat.

6. Snails make a delicious treat for some people.

7. Some Africans think roasted termites are tasty.

8. Bird's-nest soup is a famous Chinese dish.

9. People in Florida serve alligator meat.

10. Almost everyone treats themselves with ice cream.

Name _____

# Predicates of Sentences

The **predicate** of a sentence tells what the subject is or does. It is the verb part of the sentence.

**Examples:** Sally Ride **flew in a space shuttle**.

She **was an astronaut**.

**Directions:** Underline the predicate in each sentence.

1. She was the first American woman astronaut in space.

2. Sally worked hard for many years to become an astronaut.

3. She studied math and science in college.

4. Ms. Ride passed many tests.

5. She learned things quickly.

6. Sally trained to become a jet pilot.

7. This astronaut practiced using a robot arm.

8. Ms. Ride used the robot arm on two space missions.

9. She conducted experiments with it.

10. The robot arm is called a remote manipulator.

# Wheelies

Build sentences using a subject part and a predicate part.

You will need: disk patterns below (may be enlarged), tagboard, rubber cement, scissors, a fastener, writing paper, pencils

**Directions:** With an adult, cut out the two disks below. Cut out two more from tagboard. Using rubber cement, glue the tagboard disks to the disks with the words. Let them dry and laminate them. Place the smaller disk on top and secure it in the center with the brad.

Then, turn the top disk to match a subject part (large circle) and a predicate part (smaller circle). Then, write the two parts to form a sentence. Keep the circles in the same position and write the other sentences formed.

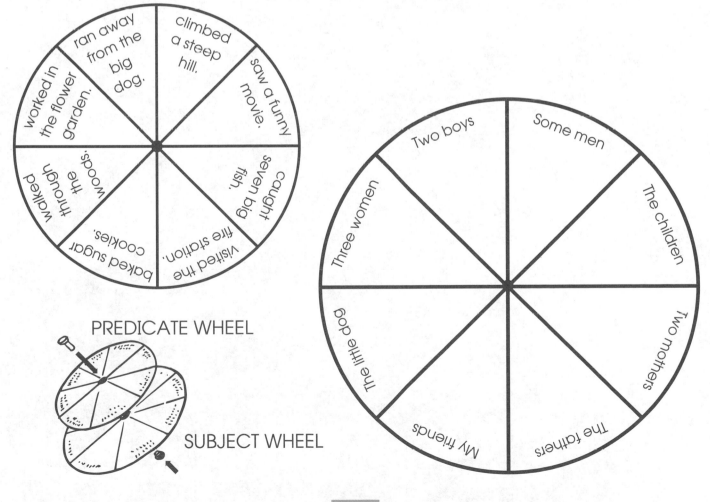

PREDICATE WHEEL

SUBJECT WHEEL

# Compound Subjects

A **compound subject** has two or more subjects joined by the word **and**.

**Example: Owls** are predators. **Wolves** are predators.

**Owls and wolves** are predators. (compound subject)

**Directions:** If the sentence has a compound subject, write **CS**. If it does not, write **No**.

_____ 1. A predator is an animal that eats other animals.

_____ 2. Prey is eaten by predators.

_____ 3. Robins and bluejays are predators.

_____ 4. Some predators eat only meat.

_____ 5. Crocodiles and hawks eat meat only.

_____ 6. Raccoons and foxes eat both meat and plants.

**Directions:** Combine the subjects of the two sentences to make a compound subject. Write the new sentence on the line.

1. Snakes are predators. Spiders are predators.

_____

2. Frogs prey on insects. Chameleons prey on insects.

_____

Name _____

# Compound Predicates

A **compound predicate** has two or more predicates joined by the word **and**.

**Example:** Abe Lincoln was born in Kentucky. Abe Lincoln lived in a log cabin there.
Abe Lincoln **was born in Kentucky and lived in a log cabin there**.

Kentucky

**Directions:** If the sentence has a compound predicate, write **CP**. If it does not, write **No**.

_____ I. Abe Lincoln cut trees and chopped wood.

_____ 2. Abe and his sister walked to a spring for water.

_____ 3. Abe's family packed up and left Kentucky.

_____ 4. They crossed the Ohio River to Indiana.

_____ 5. Abe's father built a new home.

_____ 6. Abe's mother became sick and died.

_____ 7. Mr. Lincoln married again.

_____ 8. Abe's new mother loved Abe and his sister and cared for them.

Name _____

# Complete Sentences

A **sentence** is a group of words that tells a whole idea. It has a subject and a predicate.

**Examples:** Some animals have stripes.
(sentence)
Help to protect.
(not a sentence)

**Directions:** Write **S** in front of each sentence. Write **No** if it is **not** a sentence.

_____ 1. There are different kinds of chipmunks.

_____ 2. They all have.

_____ 3. They all have stripes to help protect them.

_____ 4. The stripes make them hard to see in the forest.

_____ 5. Zebras have stripes, too.

_____ 6. Some caterpillars also.

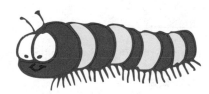

_____ 7. Other animals have spots.

_____ 8. Some dogs have spots.

_____ 9. Beautiful, little fawns.

_____ 10. Their spots help to hide them in the woods.

Name _____

# Summer Camp

A **statement** is a telling sentence. It begins with a capital letter and ends with a period.

**Directions:** Write each statement correctly on the lines.

1. everyone goes to breakfast at 6:30 each morning

_____

2. only three people can ride in one canoe

_____

3. each person must help clean the cabins

_____

4. older campers should help younger campers

_____

5. all lights are out by 9:00 each night

_____

6. everyone should write home at least once a week

_____

Name _____

# Questions

A **question** is an asking sentence. It begins with a capital letter and ends with a question mark.

**Directions:** Write each question correctly on the line.

1. is our class going to the science museum

_____

2. will we get to spend the whole day there

_____

3. will a guide take us through the museum

_____

4. do you think we will see dinosaur bones

_____

5. is it true that the museum has a mummy

_____

6. can we take lots of pictures at the museum

_____

7. will you spend the whole day at the museum

_____

# More Questions

**Directions:** Write five questions about the picture.

_____

_____

_____

_____

_____

# Kinds of Sentences

A **statement** ends with a period. **.**   A **question** ends with a question mark. **?**

**Directions:** Write the correct mark in each box.

1. Would you like to help me make an aquarium ☐

2. We can use my brother's big fish tank ☐

3. Will you put this colored sand in the bottom ☐

4. I have three shells to put on the sand ☐

5. Can we use your little toy boat, too ☐

6. Let's go buy some fish for our aquarium ☐

7. Will twelve fish be enough ☐

8. Look, they seem to like their new home ☐

9. How often do we give them fish food ☐

10. Let's tell our friends about our new aquarium ☐

Name _____

# Writing Sentences

Every sentence begins with a capital letter.

Come to the Fourth of July Picnic.
Town Park—All Day

**Directions:** Write three statements about the picture.

_____

_____

_____

**Directions:** Write three questions about the picture.

_____

_____

_____

Name _____

# Four Kinds of Sentences

A **statement** tells something. A **question** asks something. An **exclamation** shows surprise or strong feeling. A **command** tells someone to do something.

**Example:** The shuttle is ready for takeoff. (statement)
Are all systems go? (question)
What a sight! (exclamation)
Take a picture of this. (command)

**Directions:** Use the code to color the spaces.

**Code**
statement—**yellow**
question—**red**
exclamation—**blue**
command—**gray**

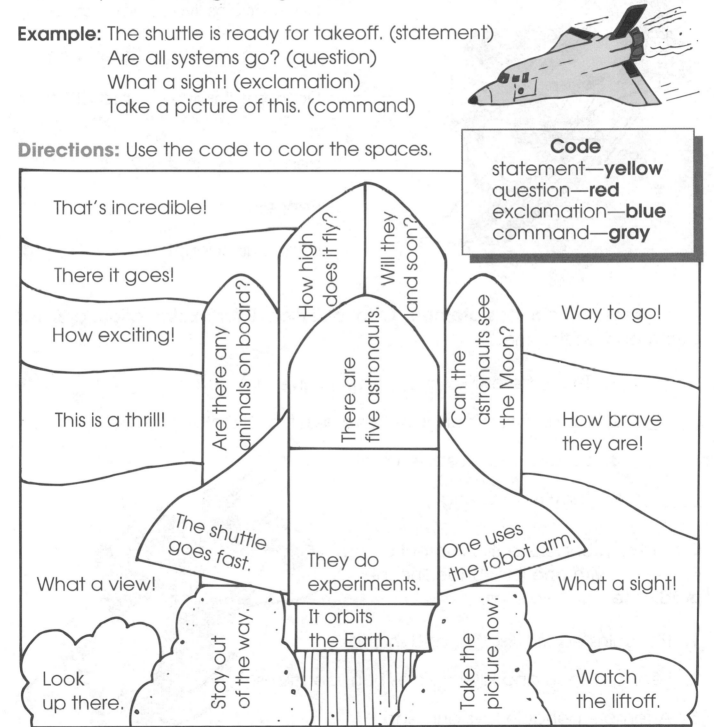

That's incredible!

There it goes!

How exciting!

This is a thrill!

How high does it fly?

Will they land soon?

Are there any animals on board?

There are five astronauts.

Can the astronauts see the Moon?

Way to go!

How brave they are!

The shuttle goes fast.

They do experiments.

One uses the robot arm.

What a view!

Stay out of the way.

It orbits the Earth.

Take the picture now.

What a sight!

Look up there.

Watch the liftoff.

# Review of Sentences

**Directions:** Underline the sentence that is written correctly in each group.

1. Do Penguins live in antarctica?

   do penguins live in Antarctica.

   Do penguins live in Antarctica?

2. penguins cannot fly?

   Penguins cannot fly.

   penguins cannot fly.

**Directions:** Write **S** for **statement**, **Q** for **question**, **E** for **exclamation,** or **C** for **command** on the line.

_____ 1. Two different kinds of penguins live in Antarctica.

_____ 2. Do emperor penguins have black and white bodies?

_____ 3. Look at their webbed feet.

_____ 4. They're amazing!

**Directions:** Underline the **subject** of the sentence with **one** line. Underline the **predicate** with **two** lines.

1. Penguins eat fish, squid, and shrimp.

2. Leopard seals and killer whales hunt penguins.

3. A female penguin lays one egg.

Name _____

# My Bag's Ready!

The first letter of a word is used to put words in alphabetical (ABC) order.

**Directions:** Write the golf words below in ABC order. If two or more words begin with the same letter, go to the next letter to put them in ABC order.

club     tee     bag     ball     scorecard     cart     towel

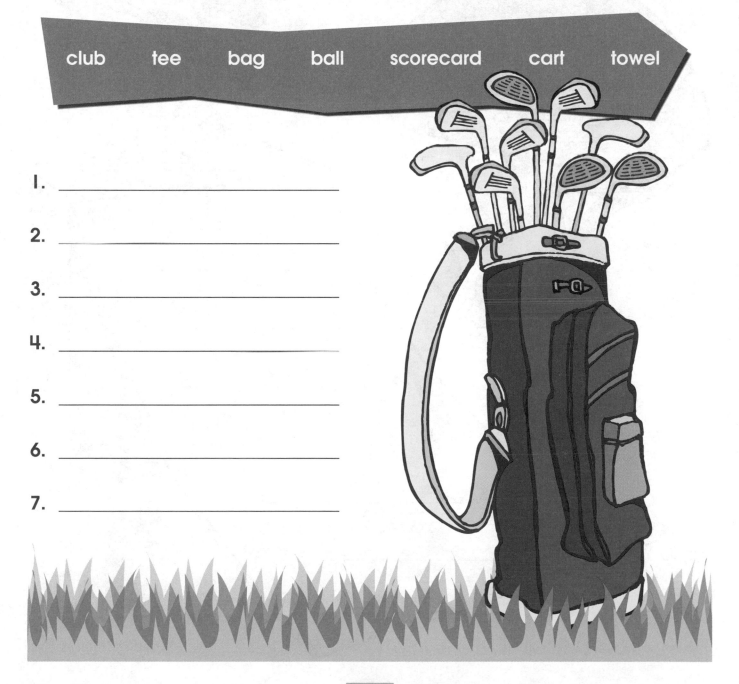

1. _____

2. _____

3. _____

4. _____

5. _____

6. _____

7. _____

Name _____

# Drop In!

**Drop in** means to start at the top of a ramp.

**Directions:** Write the words in ABC order. "Drop in" from the top of the ramp.

kick-turn

balance        freestyle

stunt        helmet        ramp

1. _____

2. _____

3. _____

4. _____

5. _____

6. _____

Name _____

# Slam Dunk!

**Directions:** Put the words in the box in ABC order.

| coach | points | team | hoop |
| player | game | score | dunk |

1. _____

2. _____

3. _____

4. _____

5. _____

6. _____

7. _____

8. _____

Name _____

# Learning Dictionary Skills

A dictionary is a book that gives the meaning of words. It also tells how words sound. Words in a dictionary are in ABC order. That makes them easier to find. A picture dictionary lists a word, a picture of the word, and its meaning.

**Directions:** Look at this page from a picture dictionary. Then, answer the questions.

**baby**

A very young child.

**band**

A group of people who play music.

**bank**

A place where money is kept.

**bark**

The sound a dog makes.

**berry**

A small, juicy fruit.

**board**

A flat piece of wood.

1. What is a small, juicy fruit? _____

2. What is a group of people who play music?_____

3. What is the name for a very young child? _____

4. What is a flat piece of wood called?_____

Name _____

# Learning Dictionary Skills

**Directions:** Look at this page from a picture dictionary. Then, answer the questions.

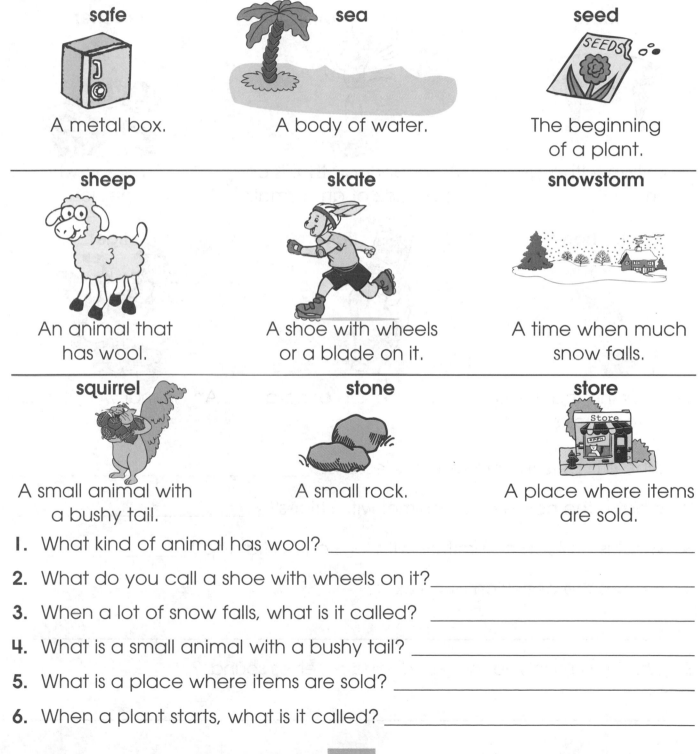

**safe**
A metal box.

**sea**
A body of water.

**seed**
The beginning of a plant.

**sheep**
An animal that has wool.

**skate**
A shoe with wheels or a blade on it.

**snowstorm**
A time when much snow falls.

**squirrel**
A small animal with a bushy tail.

**stone**
A small rock.

**store**
A place where items are sold.

1. What kind of animal has wool? _____

2. What do you call a shoe with wheels on it? _____

3. When a lot of snow falls, what is it called? _____

4. What is a small animal with a bushy tail? _____

5. What is a place where items are sold? _____

6. When a plant starts, what is it called? _____

Name _____

# Learning Dictionary Skills

**Directions:** Look at this page from a picture dictionary. Then, answer the questions.

**table**

Furniture with legs and a flat top.

**tail**

A slender part that is on the back of an animal.

**teacher**

A person who teaches lessons.

**telephone**

A machine that sends and receives sounds.

**ticket**

A paper slip or card.

**tiger**

An animal with stripes.

1. Who is a person who teaches lessons? _____

2. What is the name of an animal with stripes? _____

3. What is a piece of furniture with legs and a flat top? _____

4. What is the definition of a ticket?

_____

5. What is a machine that sends and receives sounds?

_____

Name _____

# Learning Dictionary Skills

The **guide words** at the top of a page in a dictionary tell you what the first and last words on the page will be. Only words that come in ABC order between those two words will be on that page. Guide words help you find the page you need to look up a word.

**Directions:** Write each word from the box in ABC order between each pair of guide words.

| faint | fence | farmer | feet | family |
|-------|-------|--------|------|--------|
| far | feed | fan | farm | face |

face                                                                                    fence

_____          _____

_____          _____

_____          _____

_____          _____

Name _____

# Guide Words

**Directions:** Circle the words that would be found on these dictionary pages. Remember to use the guide words to help you. The first one has been done for you.

| **save** | | **seal** |
|---|---|---|
| (seafood) | sass | sea |
| seafarer | scene | season |
| scuba | seam | salt |
| savage | scurry | say |

| **thirsty** | | **today** |
|---|---|---|
| thirst | toddle | tiff |
| toad | time | togs |
| tissue | third | thumb |
| thirty | thread | toboggan |

| **what** | | **whet** |
|---|---|---|
| where | whey | wheezy |
| whiff | wham | wheel |
| wheat | wart | wharf |
| west | whatever | when |

GRADE 2

# Test Practice Table of Contents

# About the Tests

## What Are Standardized Achievement Tests?

Achievement tests measure what children know in particular subject areas such as reading, language arts, and mathematics. They do not measure your child's intelligence or ability to learn.

When tests are standardized, or *normed*, children's test results are compared with those of a specific group who have taken the test, usually at the same age or grade.

Standardized achievement tests measure what children around the country are learning. The test makers survey popular textbook series, as well as state curriculum frameworks and other professional sources, to determine what content is covered widely.

Because of variations in state frameworks and textbook series, as well as grade ranges on some test levels, the tests may cover some material that children have not yet learned. This is especially true if the test is offered early in the school year. However, test scores are compared to those of other children who take the test at the same time of year, so your child will not be at a disadvantage if his or her class has not covered specific material yet.

## Different School Districts, Different Tests

There are many flexible options for districts when offering standardized tests. Many school districts choose not to give the full test battery, but select certain content and scoring options. For example, many schools may test only in the areas of reading and mathematics. Similarly, a state or district may use one test for certain grades and another test for other grades. These decisions are often based on

the amount of time and money a district wishes to spend on test administration. Some states choose to develop their own statewide assessment tests.

On pages 255–257 you will find information about these five widely used standardized achievement tests:

- California Achievement Test (CAT)
- Terra Nova/CTBS
- Iowa Test of Basic Skills (ITBS)
- Stanford Achievement Test (SAT9)
- Metropolitan Achievement Test (MAT)

However, this book contains strategies and practice questions for use with a variety of tests. Even if your state does not give one of the five tests listed above, your child will benefit from doing the practice questions in this book. If you're unsure about which test your child takes, contact your local school district to find out which tests are given.

## Types of Test Questions

Traditionally, standardized achievement tests have used only multiple-choice questions. Today, many tests may include constructed response (short answer) and extended response (essay) questions as well.

In addition, many tests include questions that tap students' higher-order thinking skills. Instead of simple recall questions, such as identifying a date in history, questions may require students to make comparisons and contrasts or analyze results, among other skills.

## What the Tests Measure

These tests do not measure your child's level of intelligence, but they do show how well your child knows material that he or she has learned and that is

also covered on the tests. It's important to remember that some tests cover content that is not taught in your child's school or grade. In other instances, depending on when in the year the test is given, your child may not yet have covered the material.

If the test reports you receive show that your child needs improvement in one or more skill areas, you may want to seek help from your child's teacher and find out how you can work with your child to improve his or her skills.

# California Achievement Test (CAT/5)

## What Is the California Achievement Test?

The *California Achievement Test* is a standardized achievement test battery that is widely used with elementary through high school students.

## Parts of the Test

The *CAT* includes tests in the following content areas:

**Reading**
- Word Analysis
- Vocabulary
- Comprehension

**Spelling**

**Language Arts**
- Language Mechanics
- Language Usage

**Mathematics**

**Science**

**Social Studies**

Your child may take some or all of these subtests if your district uses the *California Achievement Test*.

# Terra Nova/CTBS (Comprehensive Tests of Basic Skills)

## What Is the Terra Nova/CTBS?

The *Terra Nova/Comprehensive Tests of Basic Skills* is a standardized achievement test battery used in elementary through high school grades.

While many of the test questions on the Terra Nova are in the traditional multiple choice form, your child may take parts of the Terra Nova that include some open-ended questions (constructed-response items).

## Parts of the Test

Your child may take some or all of the following subtests if your district uses the *Terra Nova/CTBS*:

**Reading/Language Arts**
**Mathematics**
**Science**
**Social Studies**

Supplementary tests include:
- Word Analysis
- Vocabulary
- Language Mechanics
- Spelling
- Mathematics Computation

Critical thinking skills may also be tested.

# About the Tests

## Iowa Test of Basic Skills (ITBS)

### What Is the ITBS?

The *Iowa Test of Basic Skills* is a standardized achievement test battery used in elementary through high school grades.

### Parts of the Test

Your child may take some or all of these subtests if your district uses the *ITBS*, also known as the *Iowa*:

**Reading**
- Vocabulary
- Reading Comprehension

**Language Arts**
- Spelling
- Capitalization
- Punctuation
- Usage and Expression

**Math**
- Concepts/Estimate
- Problems/Data Interpretation

**Social Studies**

**Science**

**Sources of Information**

## Stanford Achievement Test (SAT9)

### What Is the Stanford Achievement Test?

The *Stanford Achievement Test, Ninth Edition (SAT9)* is a standardized achievement test battery used in elementary through high school grades.

Note that the *Stanford Achievement Test (SAT9)* is a different test from the *SAT* used by high school students for college admissions.

While many of the test questions on the *SAT9* are in traditional multiple choice form, your child may take parts of *the SAT9* that include some open-ended questions (constructed-response items).

### Parts of the Test

Your child may take some or all of these subtests if your district uses the *Stanford Achievement Test*:

**Reading**
- Vocabulary
- Reading Comprehension

**Mathematics**
- Problem Solving
- Procedures

**Language Arts**

**Spelling**

**Study Skills**

**Listening**
Critical thinking skills may also be tested.

# Metropolitan Achievement Test (MAT7 and MAT8)

## What Is the Metropolitan Achievement Test?

The *Metropolitan Achievement Test* is a standardized achievement test battery used in elementary through high school grades.

## Parts of the Test

Your child may take some or all of these subtests if your district uses the *Metropolitan Achievement Test*:

**Reading**
- Vocabulary
- Reading Comprehension

**Math**
- Concepts and Problem Solving
- Computation

**Language Arts**
- Pre-writing
- Composing
- Editing

**Science**

**Social Studies**

**Research Skills**

**Thinking Skills**

**Spelling**

# Statewide Assessments

Today, the majority of states give statewide assessments. In some cases, these tests are known as *high-stakes assessments*. This means that students must score at a certain level in order to be promoted. Some states use minimum competency or proficiency tests. Often, these tests measure more basic skills than other types of statewide assessments.

Statewide assessments are generally linked to state curriculum frameworks. Frameworks provide a blueprint, or outline, to ensure that teachers are covering the same curriculum topics as other teachers in the same grade level in the state. In some states, standardized achievement tests (such as the five described in this book) are used in connection with statewide assessments.

## When Statewide Assessments Are Given

Statewide assessments may not be given at every grade level. Generally, they are offered at one or more grades in elementary school, middle school, and high school. Many states test at grades 4, 8, and 10.

## State-by-State Information

You can find information about statewide assessments and curriculum frameworks at your state Department of Education Web site. To find the address for your individual state, go to www.ed.gov, click on Topics A–Z, and then click on State Departments of Education. You will find a list of all the state departments of education, mailing addresses, and Web sites.

# How to Help Your Child Prepare for Standardized Testing

## Preparing All Year Round

Perhaps the most valuable way you can help your child prepare for standardized achievement tests is by providing enriching experiences. Keep in mind also that test results for younger children are not as reliable as for older students. If a child is hungry, tired, or upset, this may result in a poor test score. Here are some tips on how you can help your child do his or her best on standardized tests.

**Read aloud with your child.** Reading aloud helps develop vocabulary and fosters a positive attitude toward reading. Reading together is one of the most effective ways you can help your child succeed in school.

**Share experiences.** Baking cookies together, planting a garden, or making a map of your neighborhood are examples of activities that help build skills that are measured on the tests, such as sequencing and following directions.

**Become informed about your state's testing procedures.** Ask about or watch for announcements of meetings that explain about standardized tests and statewide assessments in your school district. Talk to your child's teacher about your child's individual performance on these state tests during a parent-teacher conference.

**Help your child know what to expect.** Read and discuss with your child the test-taking tips in this book. Your child can prepare by working through a couple of strategies a day so that no practice session takes too long.

**Help your child with his or her regular school assignments.** Set up a quiet study area for homework. Supply this area with pencils, paper, markers, a calculator, a ruler, a dictionary, scissors, glue, and so on. Check your child's homework and offer to help if he or she gets stuck. But remember, it's your child's homework, not yours. If you help too much, your child will not benefit from the activity.

**Keep in regular contact with your child's teacher.** Attend parent-teacher conferences, school functions, PTA or PTO meetings, and school board meetings. This will help you get to know the educators in your district and the families of your child's classmates.

**Learn to use computers as an educational resource.** If you do not have a computer and Internet access at home, try your local library.

**Remember**—simply getting your child comfortable with testing procedures and helping him or her know what to expect can improve test scores!

## Getting Ready for the Big Day

There are lots of things you can do on or immediately before test day to improve your child's chances of testing success. What's more, these strategies will help your child prepare him- or herself for school tests, too, and promote general study skills that can last a lifetime.

**Provide a good breakfast on test day.** Instead of sugar cereal, which provides immediate but not long-term energy, have your child eat a breakfast with protein or complex carbohydrates, such as an egg, whole grain cereal or toast, or a banana-yogurt shake.

**Promote a good night's sleep.** A good night's sleep before the test is essential. Try not to overstress the importance of the test. This may cause your child to lose sleep because of anxiety. Doing some exercise after school and having a quiet evening routine will help your child sleep well the night before the test.

**Assure your child that he or she is not expected to know all of the answers on the test.** Explain that other children in higher grades may take the same test, and that the test may measure things your child has not yet learned in school. Help your child understand that you expect him or her to put forth a good effort—and that this is enough. Your child should not try to cram for these tests. Also avoid threats or bribes; these put undue pressure on children and may interfere with their best performance.

**Keep the mood light and offer encouragement.** To provide a break on test days, do something fun and special after school—take a walk around the neighborhood, play a game, read a favorite book, or prepare a special snack together. These activities keep your child's mood light—even if the testing sessions have been difficult—and show how much you appreciate your child's effort.

# Taking Standardized Tests

## What You Need to Know About Taking Tests

You can get better at taking tests. Here are some tips.

## Do your schoolwork. Study in school. Do your homework all the time. These things will help you in school and on any tests you take. Learn new things a little at a time. Then, you will remember them better when you see them on a test.

## Feel your best. One way you can do your best on tests and in school is to make sure your body is ready. Get a good night's sleep. Eat a healthy breakfast.

One more thing: Wear comfortable clothes. You can also wear your lucky shirt or your favorite color on test day. It can't hurt. It may even make you feel better about the test.

## Be ready for the test. Do practice questions. Learn about the different kinds of questions. Books like this one will help you.

## Follow the test directions. Listen carefully to the directions your teacher gives. Read all instructions carefully. Watch out for words such as *not*, *none*, *never*, *all*, and *always*. These words can change the meaning of the directions. You may want to circle words like these. This will help you keep them in mind as you answer the questions.

## Look carefully at each page before you start. Do reading tests in a special order. First, read the directions. Read the questions next. This way you will know what to look for as you read. Then, read the story. Last, read the story again quickly. Skim it to find the best answer.

## On math tests, look at the labels on graphs and charts. Think about what the graph or chart shows. You will often need to draw conclusions about the information to answer some questions.

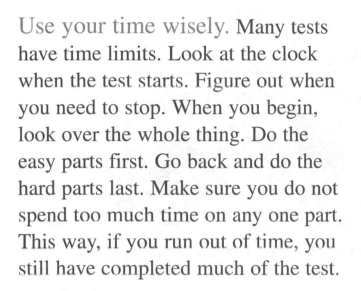
**Use your time wisely.** Many tests have time limits. Look at the clock when the test starts. Figure out when you need to stop. When you begin, look over the whole thing. Do the easy parts first. Go back and do the hard parts last. Make sure you do not spend too much time on any one part. This way, if you run out of time, you still have completed much of the test.

**Fill in the answer circles the right way.** Fill in the whole circle. Make your pencil mark dark, but not so dark that it goes through the paper! Be sure you pick just one answer for each question. If you pick two answers, both will be marked as wrong.

**Use context clues to figure out hard questions.** You may come across a word or an idea you don't understand. First, try to say it in your own words. Then, use context clues—

the words in the sentences nearby— to help you figure out its meaning.

**Sometimes it's good to guess.** Here's what to do. Each question may have four or five answer choices. You may know that two answers are wrong, but you are not sure about the rest. Then, make your best guess. If you are not sure about any of the answers, skip it. Do not guess. Tests like these take away extra points for wrong answers. So it is better to leave them blank.

**Check your work.** You may finish the test before the time is up. Then, you can go back and check your answers. Make sure you answered each question you could. Also, make sure that you filled in only one answer circle for each question. Erase any extra marks on the page.

**Finally—stay calm!** Take time to relax before the test. One good way to relax is to get some exercise. Stretch, shake out your fingers, and wiggle your toes. Take a few slow, deep breaths. Then, picture yourself doing a great job!

Name _____

# READING: WORD ANALYSIS

● **Lesson 1: Word Sounds**

**Directions:** Choose the best answer to each question.

**Example**

A. **Which word has the same beginning sound as sheep?**

- (A) chin
- (B) shake
- (C) seven
- (D) sleep

**Clue** Read all the answer choices before choosing the one you think is correct.

● **Practice**

1. **Which word has the same beginning sound as blue?**
   - (A) blast
   - (B) boy
   - (C) brush
   - (D) few

2. **Which word has the same vowel sound as join?**
   - (F) tool
   - (G) joke
   - (H) spoil
   - (J) cold

3. **Which word has the same ending sound as from?**
   - (A) float
   - (B) barn
   - (C) come
   - (D) fry

4. **Which word has the same vowel sound as found?**
   - (F) down
   - (G) flood
   - (H) road
   - (J) could

5. **Which word has the same ending sound as spend?**
   - (A) seen
   - (B) pound
   - (C) pain
   - (D) spot

6. **Which word has the same beginning sound as another?**
   - (F) about
   - (G) arm
   - (H) clue
   - (J) ace

STOP

Name _____

## READING: WORD ANALYSIS

● **Lesson 2: Rhyming Words**

**Directions:** Choose the best answer to each question.

**Example**

A. Which picture rhymes with the word fun?

Ⓐ          Ⓑ          Ⓒ

**Clue** If you are not sure which answer is correct, take your best guess.

● **Practice**

1. Which picture rhymes with the word seal?

Ⓐ          Ⓑ          Ⓒ

2. Which picture rhymes with the word bag?

Ⓕ          Ⓖ          Ⓗ

3. Which picture rhymes with the word five?

Ⓐ          Ⓑ          Ⓒ

4. Which picture rhymes with the word honey?

Ⓕ          Ⓖ          Ⓗ

STOP

Name _____

# READING: WORD ANALYSIS

● **Lesson 3: Word Sounds**

**Directions:** Choose the word that has the same sound as the underlined part of the word.

**Examples**

**A.  This one has been done for you.**
**u̲mbrella**

- (A) use
- (B) cube
- (C) skunk
- (D) four

**B.  Practice this one with your teacher.**
**gro̲wl**

- (F) food
- (G) couch
- (H) home
- (J) grow

**Clue**  Match the sound of the underlined letter or letters. Look at each answer choice and say each answer choice quietly to yourself.

● **Practice**

**1.  c̲ame**
- (A) rain
- (B) hand
- (C) black
- (D) swam

**2.  he̲r**
- (F) fire
- (G) real
- (H) here
- (J) turn

**3.  e̲asy**
- (A) child
- (B) keep
- (C) ten
- (D) head

**4.  go̲od**
- (F) sound
- (G) but
- (H) could
- (J) hold

**5.  thi̲s**
- (A) their
- (B) still
- (C) kind
- (D) mine

**6.  c̲oat**
- (F) know
- (G) out
- (H) people
- (J) school

STOP

Name _____

## READING: WORD ANALYSIS

● **Lesson 4: Word Study**

Directions: Choose the word that completes each sentence.

**Example**

A. The girls were _____ at the joke.

   (A) book

   (B) cap

   (C) top

**Clue** When deciding which answer is best, try each answer choice in the blank.

● **Practice**

1. She _____ cake and candy to the party.

   (A) taken

   (B) bring

   (C) brought

   (D) buy

2. The boys love to _____ pictures.

   (F) painting

   (G) painted

   (H) paint

   (J) paints

3. Jack's room was the _____ in the house.

   (A) clean

   (B) cleaner

   (C) cleans

   (D) cleanest

4. She saw the _____ star in the sky.

   (F) brightest

   (G) brighted

   (H) brightly

   (J) brights

5. My _____ loves to read.

   (A) teach

   (B) learn

   (C) taught

   (D) teacher

6. The baby _____ through the storm.

   (F) slept

   (G) sleeping

   (H) sleeped

   (J) sleepiest

**STOP**

Name _____

# READING: WORD ANALYSIS

● **Lesson 5: Contractions and Compound Words**

**Directions:** Choose the best answer to each question.

## Examples

**A.** Which word is a compound word, a word that is made up of two smaller words?

- (A) footprint
- (B) remember
- (C) narrow
- (D) explain

**B.** Look at the word. Find the answer that tells what the contraction means.
**aren't**

- (F) are not
- (G) are late
- (H) are most
- (J) are then

**Clue** If a question is too difficult, skip it and come back to it later.

● **Practice**

**1.** Which word is a compound word?

- (A) repeat
- (B) follow
- (C) shopping
- (D) outside

**2.** Which word is a compound word?

- (F) introduce
- (G) overpass
- (H) describe
- (J) unnecessary

**3.** Which word is a compound word?

- (A) being
- (B) enough
- (C) family
- (D) everyone

**4. don't**

- (F) did it
- (G) drive in
- (H) do think
- (J) do not

**5. they're**

- (A) they rest
- (B) they are
- (C) they run
- (D) they care

**6. she'll**

- (F) she falls
- (G) she all
- (H) she will
- (J) she likes

STOP

Name _____

# READING: WORD ANALYSIS

● **Lesson 6: Root Words and Suffixes**

**Directions:** Choose the best answer to each question.

### Examples

**A.** Which word is the root or base word for the word **mostly**?

- (A) cost
- (B) tly
- (C) ly
- (D) most

**B.** Which word is the ending or suffix for the word **helpless**?

- (F) elp
- (G) help
- (H) less
- (J) ess

**Clue** Stay with your first answer. Change it only if you are sure it is wrong and another answer is better.

● **Practice**

**1.** Which word is the root word for **kindness**?

- (A) in
- (B) ness
- (C) kind
- (D) ind

**2.** Which word is the root word for **trying**?

- (F) try
- (G) ing
- (H) rying
- (J) tri

**3.** Which word is the root word for **faster**?

- (A) fas
- (B) fast
- (C) aster
- (D) ter

**4.** Which word is the suffix for **rested**?

- (F) ted
- (G) rest
- (H) ed
- (J) sted

**5.** Which word is the suffix for **softly**?

- (A) ftly
- (B) soft
- (C) sof
- (D) ly

**6.** Which word is the suffix for **treatment**?

- (F) treat
- (G) eat
- (H) ment
- (J) nt

STOP

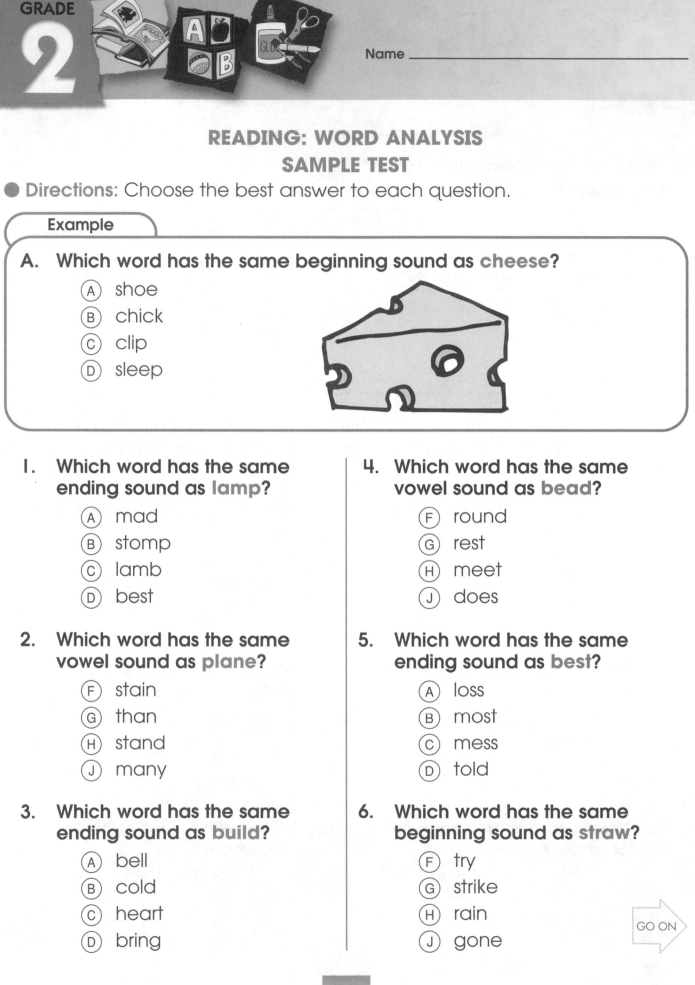

Name _____

# READING: WORD ANALYSIS
## SAMPLE TEST

● **Directions:** Choose the best answer to each question.

**Example**

A. Which word has the same beginning sound as cheese?

  (A) shoe
  (B) chick
  (C) clip
  (D) sleep

1. Which word has the same ending sound as lamp?

  (A) mad
  (B) stomp
  (C) lamb
  (D) best

2. Which word has the same vowel sound as plane?

  (F) stain
  (G) than
  (H) stand
  (J) many

3. Which word has the same ending sound as build?

  (A) bell
  (B) cold
  (C) heart
  (D) bring

4. Which word has the same vowel sound as bead?

  (F) round
  (G) rest
  (H) meet
  (J) does

5. Which word has the same ending sound as best?

  (A) loss
  (B) most
  (C) mess
  (D) told

6. Which word has the same beginning sound as straw?

  (F) try
  (G) strike
  (H) rain
  (J) gone

GO ON

Name _____

# READING: WORD ANALYSIS
## SAMPLE TEST

● **Directions:** Choose the best answer to each question.

**Example**

B.   Which picture rhymes with the word **more**?

Ⓕ          Ⓖ          Ⓗ

7.   Which picture rhymes with the word **far**?

Ⓐ          Ⓑ          Ⓒ

8.   Which picture rhymes with the word **rain**?

Ⓕ          Ⓖ          Ⓗ

9.   Which picture rhymes with the word **dragon**?

Ⓐ          Ⓑ          Ⓒ

10.  Which picture rhymes with the word **soon**?

Ⓕ          Ⓖ          Ⓗ

GO ON

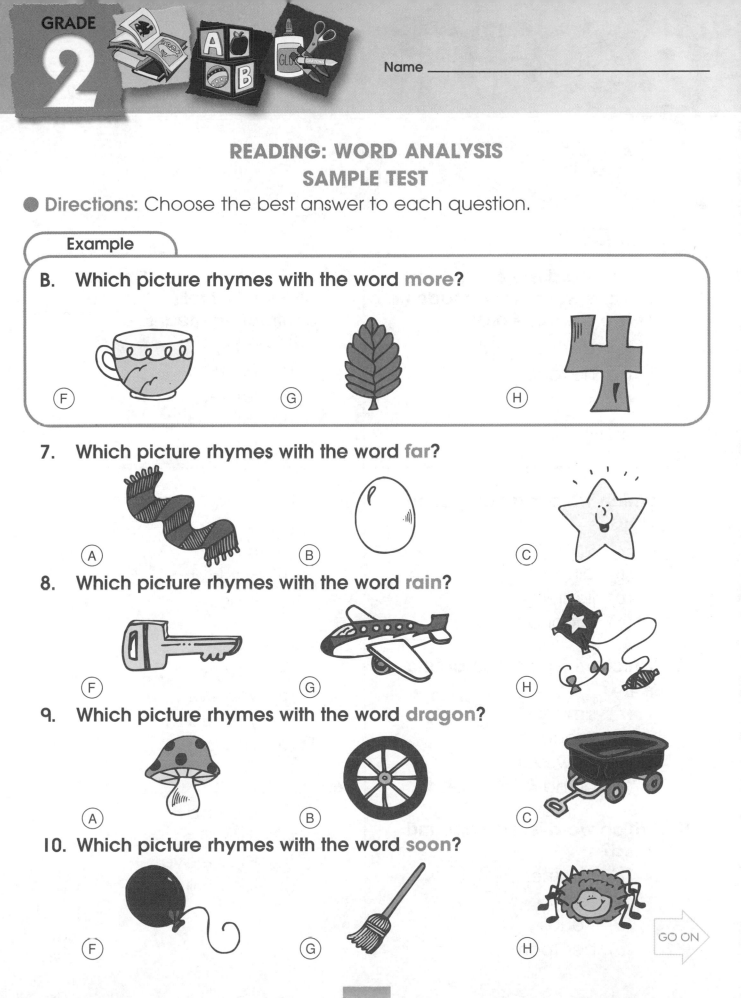

Name _____

# READING: WORD ANALYSIS
## SAMPLE TEST

● **Directions:** Choose the best answer to each question.

**Example**

**C. Which word is a compound word, a word that is made up of two smaller words?**

- (A) started
- (B) haircut
- (C) stand
- (D) tried

**D. Look at the word. Find the answer that tells what the contraction means.**
**let's**

- (F) let sister
- (G) let see
- (H) let us
- (J) let go

**11. Which word is a compound word?**

- (A) someday
- (B) dinner
- (C) jumping
- (D) second

**12. Which word is a compound word?**

- (F) simple
- (G) probably
- (H) however
- (J) going

**13. Which word is a compound word?**

- (A) summer
- (B) turned
- (C) trouble
- (D) bedroom

**14. isn't**

- (F) is now
- (G) is not
- (H) is thinking
- (J) is nose

**15. you're**

- (A) you read
- (B) you eat
- (C) you are
- (D) you is

**16. they'll**

- (F) they ball
- (G) they like
- (H) they leave
- (J) they will

GO ON

Name _____

# READING: WORD ANALYSIS
## SAMPLE TEST

● **Directions:** Choose the best answer to each question.

**Example**

**E.** Which word is the root or base word for the word **dreaming**?

- (A) ing
- (B) eam
- (C) aming
- (D) dream

**F.** Which word is the ending or suffix for the word **brighter**?

- (F) ight
- (G) er
- (H) bright
- (J) ghter

**17.** Which word is the root word for **calling**?

- (A) ing
- (B) call
- (C) all
- (D) alling

**18.** Which word is the root word for **sadness**?

- (F) sad
- (G) ness
- (H) adness
- (J) bad

**19.** Which word is the root word for **asked**?

- (A) mask
- (B) ed
- (C) ked
- (D) ask

**20.** Which word is the suffix for **darkly**?

- (F) ly
- (G) dark
- (H) arkly
- (J) door

**21.** Which word is the suffix for **helpful**?

- (A) help
- (B) ful
- (C) elpful
- (D) pful

**22.** Which word is the suffix for **picked**?

- (F) pick
- (G) sick
- (H) icked
- (J) ed

**STOP**

Name _____

## READING: VOCABULARY

● **Lesson 7: Picture Vocabulary**

**Directions:** Choose the word that matches the picture.

**Examples**

A. **This one has been done for you.**

- (A) bottle
- (B) pour
- (C) glass
- (D) spill

B. **Practice this one with your teacher.**

- (F) sleep
- (G) baby
- (H) blanket
- (J) awake

**Clue** Look at the picture carefully and then read the choices.

● **Practice**

1.
- (A) clean
- (B) sing
- (C) blow
- (D) eat

2.
- (F) crying
- (G) happy
- (H) smiling
- (J) talking

3.
- (A) baby
- (B) stand
- (C) come
- (D) crib

4.
- (F) out
- (G) whisper
- (H) shout
- (J) laugh

**STOP**

Name _____

# READING: VOCABULARY

● **Lesson 8: Word Meaning**

**Directions:** Look at the underlined words in each sentence. Which word means the same thing?

**Example**

A.  Which word is <u>part of your hand</u>?

   (A)  toe
   (B)  tooth
   (C)  ring
   (D)  finger

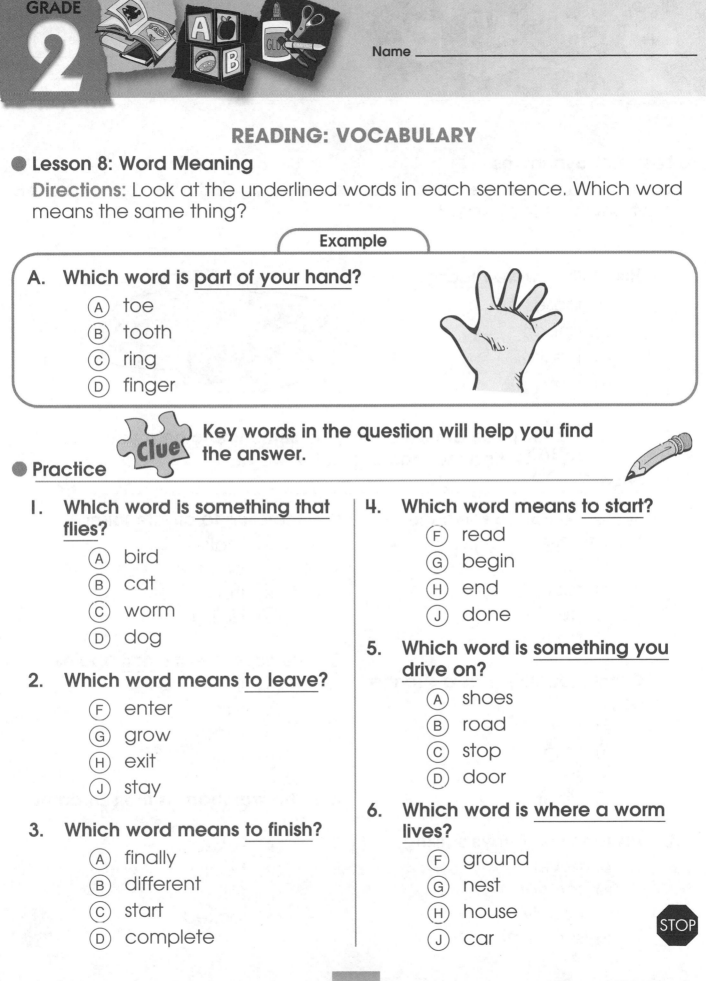

**Clue** Key words in the question will help you find the answer.

● **Practice**

1.  Which word is <u>something that flies</u>?

   (A)  bird
   (B)  cat
   (C)  worm
   (D)  dog

2.  Which word means <u>to leave</u>?

   (F)  enter
   (G)  grow
   (H)  exit
   (J)  stay

3.  Which word means <u>to finish</u>?

   (A)  finally
   (B)  different
   (C)  start
   (D)  complete

4.  Which word means <u>to start</u>?

   (F)  read
   (G)  begin
   (H)  end
   (J)  done

5.  Which word is <u>something you drive on</u>?

   (A)  shoes
   (B)  road
   (C)  stop
   (D)  door

6.  Which word is <u>where a worm lives</u>?

   (F)  ground
   (G)  nest
   (H)  house
   (J)  car

**STOP**

Name _____

## READING: VOCABULARY

● **Lesson 9: Synonyms**

**Directions:** Look at the underlined word in each sentence. Which word is a synonym for that word?

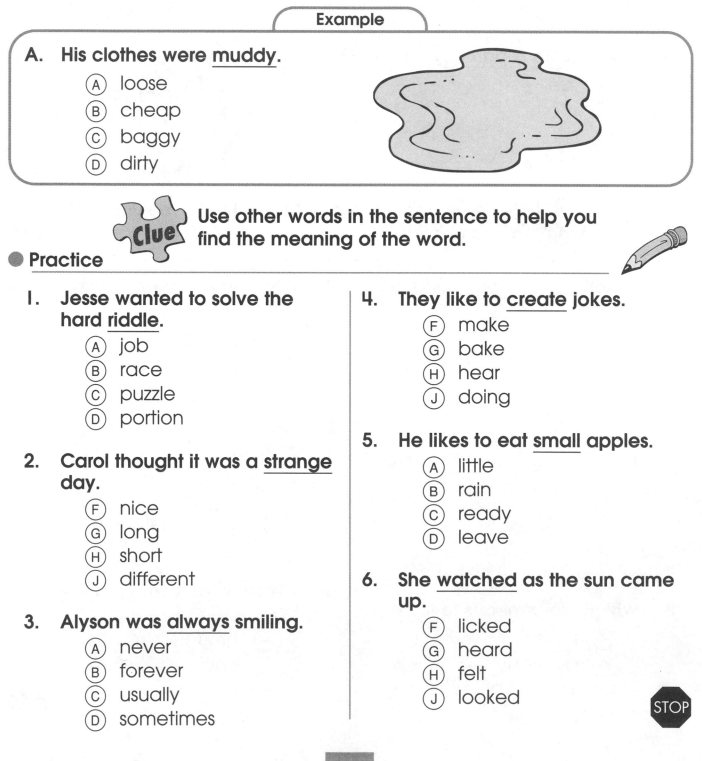

**Example**

A.   His clothes were <u>muddy</u>.

- Ⓐ loose
- Ⓑ cheap
- Ⓒ baggy
- Ⓓ dirty

**Clue**  Use other words in the sentence to help you find the meaning of the word.

● **Practice**

1.   Jesse wanted to solve the hard <u>riddle</u>.

- Ⓐ job
- Ⓑ race
- Ⓒ puzzle
- Ⓓ portion

2.   Carol thought it was a <u>strange</u> day.

- Ⓕ nice
- Ⓖ long
- Ⓗ short
- Ⓙ different

3.   Alyson was <u>always</u> smiling.

- Ⓐ never
- Ⓑ forever
- Ⓒ usually
- Ⓓ sometimes

4.   They like to <u>create</u> jokes.

- Ⓕ make
- Ⓖ bake
- Ⓗ hear
- Ⓙ doing

5.   He likes to eat <u>small</u> apples.

- Ⓐ little
- Ⓑ rain
- Ⓒ ready
- Ⓓ leave

6.   She <u>watched</u> as the sun came up.

- Ⓕ licked
- Ⓖ heard
- Ⓗ felt
- Ⓙ looked

STOP

Name _____

## READING: VOCABULARY

● **Lesson 10: Antonyms**

**Directions:** Look at the underlined word in each sentence. Choose the word that is the antonym of the underlined word.

**Example**

A. His room was <u>large</u>.

- Ⓐ pretty
- Ⓑ big
- Ⓒ small
- Ⓓ noisy

**Clue** Look for the answer that means the opposite of the underlined word. Skip difficult questions and come back to them later.

● **Practice**

1. Her brother was <u>young</u>.
   - Ⓐ busy
   - Ⓑ new
   - Ⓒ tired
   - Ⓓ old

2. The family took a trip to the <u>city</u>.
   - Ⓕ zoo
   - Ⓖ park
   - Ⓗ country
   - Ⓙ building

3. The bedroom was always <u>messy</u>.
   - Ⓐ lost
   - Ⓑ neat
   - Ⓒ sand
   - Ⓓ dirty

4. She was the <u>best</u> at spelling.
   - Ⓕ worst
   - Ⓖ simple
   - Ⓗ good
   - Ⓙ rest

5. They had <u>real</u> money to go shopping.
   - Ⓐ need
   - Ⓑ less
   - Ⓒ fake
   - Ⓓ his

6. My <u>sister</u> likes ice cream.
   - Ⓕ mother
   - Ⓖ father
   - Ⓗ brother
   - Ⓙ uncle

STOP

Name _____

# READING: VOCABULARY

● **Lesson 11: Words in Context**

**Directions:** Choose the word that best fits in the blank.

### Examples

The ___(A)___ was easy to enter. All you had to do was go to the park. To win, you had to ___(B)___ how many jelly beans were in the jar.

**A.**
- Ⓐ door
- Ⓑ contest
- Ⓒ tunnel

**B.**
- Ⓕ guess
- Ⓖ read
- Ⓗ count

**Clue** When deciding which answer is best, try each answer choice in the blank.

● **Practice**

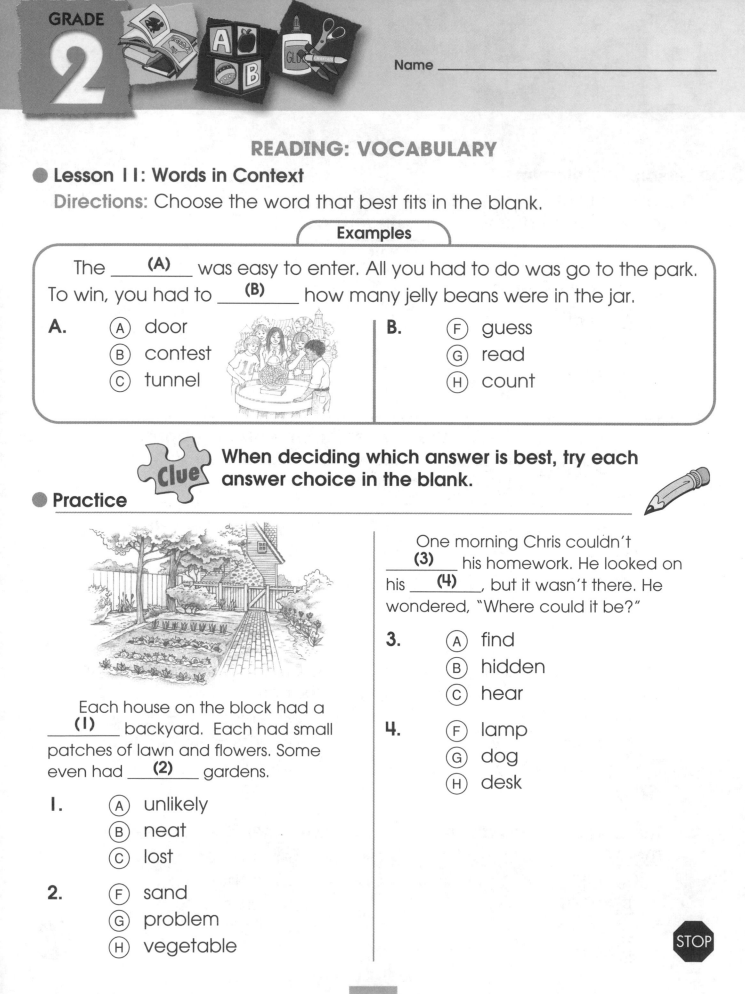

Each house on the block had a ___(1)___ backyard. Each had small patches of lawn and flowers. Some even had ___(2)___ gardens.

1.
- Ⓐ unlikely
- Ⓑ neat
- Ⓒ lost

2.
- Ⓕ sand
- Ⓖ problem
- Ⓗ vegetable

One morning Chris couldn't ___(3)___ his homework. He looked on his ___(4)___, but it wasn't there. He wondered, "Where could it be?"

3.
- Ⓐ find
- Ⓑ hidden
- Ⓒ hear

4.
- Ⓕ lamp
- Ⓖ dog
- Ⓗ desk

STOP

Name _____

# READING: VOCABULARY

● **Lesson 12: Multiple Meaning Words**

**Directions:** Some words have more than one meaning. Choose the word that will make sense in both blanks.

**Examples**

A.  I _____for the door.
   She bumped her _____ when she fell.
   (A) went
   (B) leg
   (C) self
   (D) head

**Clue** Remember, the correct answer must make sense in both blanks.

● **Practice**

1.  _____ the light over here.
   The _____ on this pencil broke.
   (A) point
   (B) eraser
   (C) shine
   (D) top

2.  The boat began to _____. Dad washed the dishes in the _____.
   (F) wait
   (G) tub
   (H) sink
   (J) pan

3.  Hit the _____ with the hammer.
   The _____ on my little finger is broken.
   (A) tack
   (B) nail
   (C) skin
   (D) wood

4.  Did you _____ your visitor well?
   My dog loves to get a _____ from me.
   (F) feed
   (G) snack
   (H) enjoy
   (J) treat

5.  The brown _____ was sleeping in the cave.
   She could not _____ to hear any more scary stories.
   (A) hear
   (B) fox
   (C) bear
   (D) take

**STOP**

Name _____

# READING: VOCABULARY
## SAMPLE TEST

● **Directions:** Choose the action word that best matches the picture.

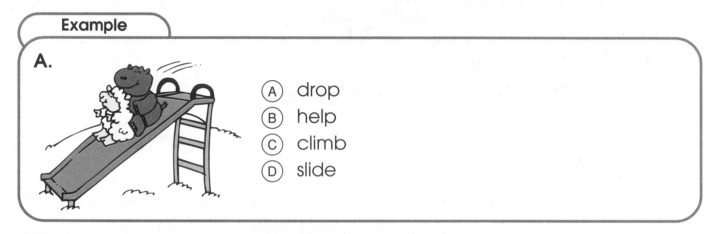

**Example**

**A.**

- (A) drop
- (B) help
- (C) climb
- (D) slide

**Look at the picture carefully and then read the choices.**

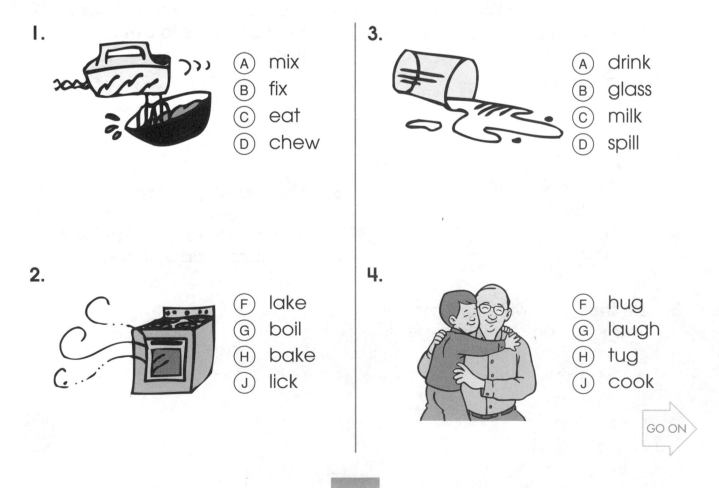

**1.**

- (A) mix
- (B) fix
- (C) eat
- (D) chew

**3.**

- (A) drink
- (B) glass
- (C) milk
- (D) spill

**2.**

- (F) lake
- (G) boil
- (H) bake
- (J) lick

**4.**

- (F) hug
- (G) laugh
- (H) tug
- (J) cook

GO ON

Name _____

## READING: VOCABULARY
## SAMPLE TEST

● **Directions:** Choose the best answer.

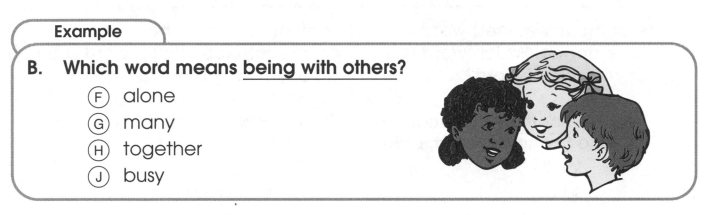

**Example**

**B.** **Which word means <u>being with others</u>?**
- Ⓕ alone
- Ⓖ many
- Ⓗ together
- Ⓙ busy

**Key words in the question will help you find the answer.**

5. **Which word is <u>to lift up</u>?**
- Ⓐ find
- Ⓑ raise
- Ⓒ release
- Ⓓ haul

6. **Which word means <u>to be quick</u>?**
- Ⓕ slow
- Ⓖ fast
- Ⓗ walk
- Ⓙ run

7. **Which word means <u>to drop down</u>?**
- Ⓐ fall
- Ⓑ lift
- Ⓒ wish
- Ⓓ see

8. **Which word is <u>part of a tree</u>?**
- Ⓕ shade
- Ⓖ cool
- Ⓗ leaf
- Ⓙ moist

9. **Which word is <u>something cold</u>?**
- Ⓐ short
- Ⓑ small
- Ⓒ fire
- Ⓓ ice

10. **Which word is <u>part of a flower</u>?**
- Ⓕ petal
- Ⓖ dirt
- Ⓗ bee
- Ⓙ pot

GO ON

Name _____

# READING: VOCABULARY
## SAMPLE TEST

**Examples**

Look at the underlined word in each sentence. Which word is a synonym for that word?

C. She was **certain** she would be able to fix the broken clock.
- Ⓐ loose
- Ⓑ sure
- Ⓒ baggy
- Ⓓ dirty

Look at the underlined word in each sentence. Which word is an antonym for that word?

D. He was very **nervous** to talk in front of the class.
- Ⓕ calm
- Ⓖ annoyed
- Ⓗ frightened
- Ⓙ excited

11. Flossie **actually** knew a lot about social studies.
- Ⓐ rarely
- Ⓑ really
- Ⓒ seldom
- Ⓓ never

12. Jack found a giant rock to add to his **rock** garden.
- Ⓕ sand
- Ⓖ stone
- Ⓗ marble
- Ⓙ apple

13. She knew where the **hidden** key was kept.
- Ⓐ open
- Ⓑ known
- Ⓒ friendly
- Ⓓ secret

14. The plane was going to fly very **high**.
- Ⓕ low
- Ⓖ land
- Ⓗ middle
- Ⓙ people

15. Alan's doctor said he was **healthy**.
- Ⓐ wound
- Ⓑ heal
- Ⓒ sick
- Ⓓ find

16. She was always **early** to school.
- Ⓕ help
- Ⓖ late
- Ⓗ same
- Ⓙ funny

GO ON

Name _____

# READING: VOCABULARY
## SAMPLE TEST

● **Directions:** Choose the word that best fits in the blanks.

> **Examples**
>
> Beth watched the rain ____(E)____ down the window. Rain meant no picnic in the park with Grandma. Beth likes going to the park because it has ____(F)____ birds and a swing set.
>
> **E.**
>   (A) jump
>   (B) walk
>   (C) slide
>
> **F.**
>   (F) laughing
>   (G) singing
>   (H) crying

## When deciding which answer is best, try each answer choice in the blank.

Matt and Alan ____(17)____ with their kites to the top of the high hill. They laid down in the ____(18)____ grass and watched the clouds.

**17.**
  (A) raced
  (B) picked
  (C) took

**18.**
  (F) stop
  (G) winter
  (H) soft

Alicia and her brother Randy hurried out the ____(19)____ in their heavy snowsuits. They played in the snow. They made a big snowman in the ____(20)____.

**19.**
  (A) door
  (B) window
  (C) space

**20.**
  (F) backyard
  (G) sand
  (H) garage

Name _____

# READING: COMPREHENSION

● **Lesson 13: Picture Comprehension**

**Directions:** Look at the picture. Then, choose the word that best fits in the blank.

**Example**

A.  The train is _____ in a few minutes.
   - (A) whistled
   - (B) arriving
   - (C) hours
   - (D) floating

**Clue** Look back at the picture when you choose an answer to fit in the blank.

● **Practice**

1.  The line for the movie _____ around the corner.
   - (A) went
   - (B) ran
   - (C) skipped
   - (D) sang

2.  This was a film that everyone wanted to _____.
   - (F) like
   - (G) hear
   - (H) see
   - (J) drink

3.  Jenna caught small fish on her new fishing _____.
   - (A) bait
   - (B) camp
   - (C) box
   - (D) rod

4.  Her _____ helped her take it off the hook.
   - (F) mom
   - (G) dad
   - (H) baby
   - (J) brother

STOP

Name _____

# READING: COMPREHENSION

● **Lesson 14: Critical Reading**

**Directions:** Read each sentence. Choose the sentence that describes something that could **not** happen.

**Example**

**A.** ⒜ The wind was blowing hard and it was snowing.

ⓑ Because of the storm, school was closed.

ⓒ Pedro and Juanita dressed in warm clothing to play outside.

ⓓ Their dog, Barney, dressed himself in a hat and gloves too.

**Clue** — **Read the sentences carefully. Think about what could and could not happen.**

● **Practice**

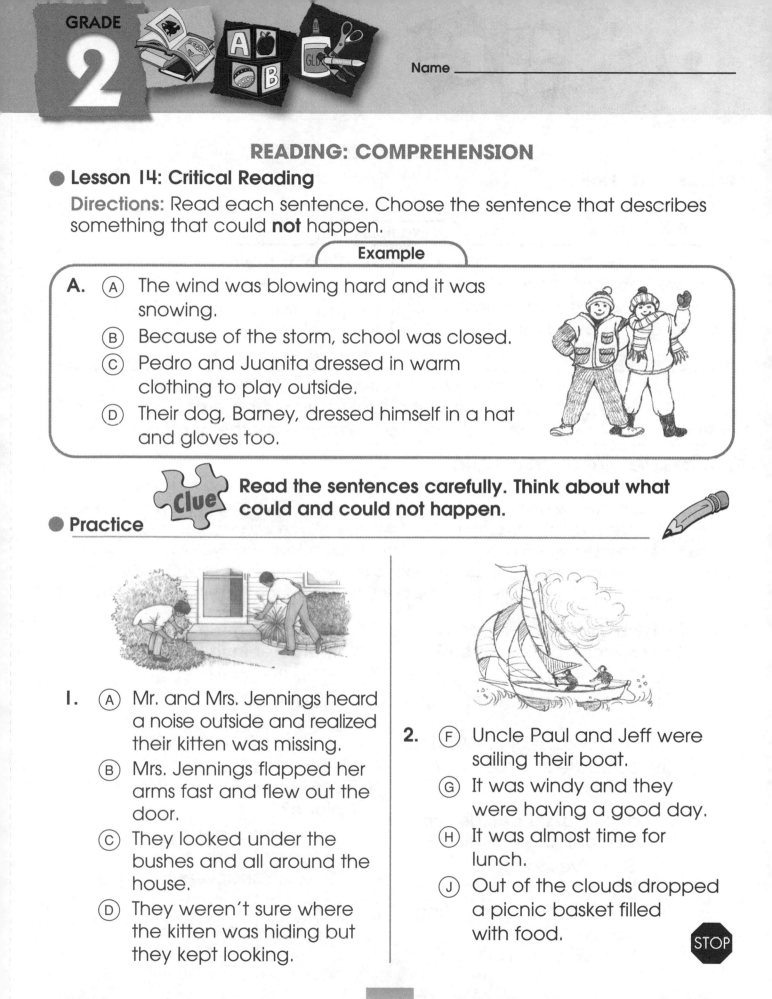

**1.** ⒜ Mr. and Mrs. Jennings heard a noise outside and realized their kitten was missing.

ⓑ Mrs. Jennings flapped her arms fast and flew out the door.

ⓒ They looked under the bushes and all around the house.

ⓓ They weren't sure where the kitten was hiding but they kept looking.

**2.** Ⓕ Uncle Paul and Jeff were sailing their boat.

ⓖ It was windy and they were having a good day.

ⓗ It was almost time for lunch.

ⓙ Out of the clouds dropped a picnic basket filled with food.

STOP

# READING: COMPREHENSION

● **Lesson 15: Fiction**

**Directions:** Read or listen to the story below and answer the questions that follow.

**Examples**

| | |
|---|---|
| Camels are strong, sturdy animals that live in the desert. Camels are able to live in the desert because their bodies are designed for it. | **A. What is the main idea?**<br>Ⓐ camels are strong animals<br>Ⓑ living in the desert<br>Ⓒ bodies<br>Ⓓ animals in the desert |

**Read or listen to the paragraph below. It tells about a girl who thinks it would be great if no one could see her. Then, answer the questions.**

● **Practice**

## If Cassie Were Invisible

Cassie kicked at the dirty clothes on her floor. She was upset. Her dad told her to clean her room. Cassie wished she was invisible. Then she wouldn't have to clean anything! If she were invisible, she would go to school and not do any work. She would stay up late. She would never have to take baths. Best of all, her brother couldn't pick on her. But, wait! If she were invisible, she wouldn't get any apple pie. And no one would ask her to play. Cassie would never get to hug her grandparents. Maybe being invisible wouldn't be so much fun after all.

1. **In the beginning, why does Cassie want to be invisible?**
   Ⓐ Because she wants to play.
   Ⓑ Because she loves apple pie.
   Ⓒ Because she didn't like dad.
   Ⓓ Because she didn't want to clean her room.

2. **Why does Cassie decide she doesn't want to be invisible?**
   Ⓕ She loves to clean.
   Ⓖ Her mom misses her.
   Ⓗ She wouldn't get to hug her grandparents.
   Ⓙ She wants to be smart.

3. **Who is the main character in the story?**
   Ⓐ the dad
   Ⓑ Cassie
   Ⓒ the grandparents
   Ⓓ the teacher

4. **Where does the story take place?**
   Ⓕ at school
   Ⓖ at Cassie's grandparents
   Ⓗ at the park
   Ⓙ at Cassie's house

GO ON

## READING: COMPREHENSION

● **Lesson 15: Fiction (cont.)**

**Directions:** Read or listen to the story below. It tells about Sam being the oldest child in his family. Then, answer the questions.

## *The Oldest*

Sometimes, Sam likes being the oldest. He can stay up one hour later. He can go places by himself. He also gets a bigger allowance for helping around the house. When his friend Brennan asks him to spend the night, Sam's mom says yes. He even gets to stay at his friend's house to eat dinner sometimes. Sam thinks it's great that he can read, ride a bike, and spell better than his brother. Sam's sister loves when he reads stories to her. Sam likes it too. When his mom needs help cooking, she asks Sam because he is the oldest.

Sometimes, Sam doesn't like being the oldest. He has to babysit his sister. She likes to go where he does. He also has to act more like a grown-up. Sam always has more jobs to do around the house. He has to help wash the dishes and take out the trash. His brother and sister get help when they have to clean their rooms. Sam doesn't get help. Sam doesn't like to be the oldest when his brother and sister want him to play with them all the time.

5. **What can Sam do better than his brother?**
   - (A) play soccer
   - (B) eat candy
   - (C) ride a bike
   - (D) watch movies

6. **What does Sam think about having to act more like a grown-up?**
   - (F) He likes it.
   - (G) He thinks his brother should act more grown-up.
   - (H) It is one reason why he doesn't like to be the oldest.
   - (J) He wants his parents to treat his brother like they treat him.

7. **Who is the main character in the story?**
   - (A) Brennan
   - (B) the sister
   - (C) the brother
   - (D) Sam

8. **What is the main idea of the story?**
   - (F) washing dishes
   - (G) eating dinner
   - (H) playing outside
   - (J) being the oldest

## READING: COMPREHENSION

● **Lesson 16: Nonfiction**

**Directions:** Read or listen to the paragraph below that tells how to make a peanut butter and jelly sandwich. Then, answer the questions.

# How to Make a Peanut Butter and Jelly Sandwich

You will need peanut butter, jelly, and two pieces of bread. First, spread peanut butter on one piece of bread. Next, spread jelly on the other piece. Then, put the two pieces of bread together. Next, cut the sandwich in half. Last, eat your sandwich and enjoy!

1. **What is the paragraph explaining?**
   - (A) how to make peanut butter
   - (B) how to cut sandwiches
   - (C) how to make peanut butter and jelly sandwiches
   - (D) how to put bread together

2. **Which of these is an opinion?**
   - (F) Peanut butter and jelly sandwiches have jelly in them.
   - (G) The paragraph says to cut the sandwich.
   - (H) You can use two pieces of bread.
   - (J) Peanut butter and jelly sandwiches are great.

3. **What does the paragraph say to do after you spread peanut butter on one piece of bread?**
   - (A) cut the sandwich
   - (B) spread jelly on the other piece of bread
   - (C) put the two pieces together
   - (D) eat your sandwich and enjoy eating it

4. **What don't you need to make a peanut butter and jelly sandwich?**
   - (F) bread
   - (G) peanut butter
   - (H) milk
   - (J) jelly

GO ON

## READING: COMPREHENSION

● **Lesson 16: Nonfiction (cont.)**

**Directions:** Read or listen to the paragraph below that tells about dolphins and sharks. Then, answer the questions.

# Dolphins and Sharks

Dolphins and sharks both live in the ocean, but they are very different. Dolphins are mammals. Sharks are fish. Both animals swim underwater. Sharks breathe through gills, and dolphins have lungs. Dolphins breathe through a blowhole on their heads. Dolphins have smooth, slippery skin, but sharks have scales. Dolphins give birth to live young. Sharks lay eggs. When the eggs hatch, young sharks come out. Sharks and dolphins live in water, but they have many differences.

5. **Which animal has smooth, slippery skin?**
   - (A) dolphins
   - (B) sharks
   - (C) eggs
   - (D) fish

6. **Why did the author write about dolphins and sharks?**
   - (F) to feel the smooth skin of the dolphins
   - (G) to learn how to swim
   - (H) to tell others about dolphins and sharks
   - (J) to breathe through the gills

7. **What do you know about dolphins and sharks?**
   - (A) They are mostly alike.
   - (B) They both have blowholes.
   - (C) There are many different things about them.
   - (D) They live in rivers and streams.

8. **What do sharks need to breathe?**
   - (F) lungs
   - (G) blowholes
   - (H) noses
   - (J) gills

Name _____

## READING: COMPREHENSION
## SAMPLE TEST

● **Directions:** Read or listen to the story below. Then, answer the questions. The story is about two boys who are best friends.

**Example**

### Best Friends

In second grade, Chad and Ryan were best friends. Both boys loved all kinds of sports. In the spring, they played baseball.

**A. What is a fact about Chad and Ryan?**

- Ⓐ They were best friends.
- Ⓑ They did not like sports.
- Ⓒ Playing outside is not allowed.
- Ⓓ They always wore socks when taking a bath.

During the summer, Chad and Ryan enjoyed swimming and street hockey. Chad swam on a swim team. Ryan went to meets so he could cheer for Chad. In the fall, the boys played pee-wee football. They won most of their games and made several new friends. During the winter months, both boys played basketball. Ryan also played on a weekend ice-hockey team. Chad went to the games so he could yell for Ryan and his team. The two boys decided to call themselves "Best Sports Pals" and stay friends forever.

**1. What does the phrase "cheer for Chad" mean?**

- Ⓐ to play football
- Ⓑ to yell for Chad to do a good job
- Ⓒ to scream for Chad to make a mistake
- Ⓓ to listen carefully to your parents

**2. What sport do the boys play in the fall?**

- Ⓕ football
- Ⓖ basketball
- Ⓗ hockey
- Ⓙ baseball

**3. What is another title for the story?**

- Ⓐ Hockey Is Fun
- Ⓑ Play Football!
- Ⓒ Friends That Always Win
- Ⓓ Best Sports Pals

**4. What do you think Chad would do if Ryan decided to play soccer and baseball in the spring?**

- Ⓕ Chad would never go see Ryan play a game.
- Ⓖ Chad would cry.
- Ⓗ Chad would quit playing.
- Ⓙ Chad would make sure to go to see Ryan play soccer.

GO ON

Name _____

# READING: COMPREHENSION
## SAMPLE TEST

● **Directions:** Read or listen to the story below. Then, answer the questions. The story is about a new boy named Raj who is deaf and comes to Patsy's school. Raj was born in India, and he knows sign language, English, and Hindi, his family's language in India. The story tells about Patsy's first experience with Raj.

## *A New Friend*

"Can I sit here?" asked Raj in an unusual voice. He signed while he talked, and it was a little difficult to understand him.

"Sure," answered Patsy. She was very nervous, and her words barely came out. "What am I supposed to do?" she asked herself. "I've never met a deaf person before."

All that morning, Patsy kept looking over at Raj. He seemed to be able to understand what was going on in class. "How does he do that?" she wondered to herself. That afternoon, Mrs. Martin took some time to let Raj and the other students get to know each other better. Patsy was surprised to find that her friend Kyle actually knew sign language. Soon, Patsy found she could understand most of what Raj was saying.

That afternoon, Raj and Patsy walked home together. Patsy learned some signs and told Raj about her family. By the time they reached Raj's house, she was able to sign "good-bye."

5. **What do you think about Raj from reading the story?**
   - (A) He is embarrassed.
   - (B) He is pleasant.
   - (C) He is unfriendly.
   - (D) He is very tall.

6. **What do you think Patsy will do in a few weeks?**
   - (F) She will forget sign language.
   - (G) She won't walk home with Raj.
   - (H) She will look for other friends.
   - (J) She will have learned more sign language.

7. **What would you conclude from reading this story?**
   - (A) Raj makes new friends easily.
   - (B) Raj has a hard time learning languages.
   - (C) Raj was more frightened than Patsy.
   - (D) Raj was not a nice person.

8. **Which of the following is a fact?**
   - (F) Patsy isn't a nice girl.
   - (G) Patsy will never learn sign language.
   - (H) Raj knows sign language.
   - (J) Raj and Patsy will become best friends.

GO ON

Name _____

## READING: COMPREHENSION
## SAMPLE TEST

● **Directions:** Read or listen to the paragraphs about how people talk in the country of India. Then answer the questions. India is a country near China. Much like the U.S.A. is next to Canada, India is next to China. Have you ever heard of the country of India?

# *India*

In the U.S.A. most people speak English. In India, there are over 1,000 different languages. This has caused many problems. Many of the people speak the words in different ways. Hindi was made the main language to speak to solve the problem. However, it is still hard for people to talk to each other.

There are many ways to let others know what you think without words. Some actions mean different things in India. For example, to show an older person that you respect him, bow down and touch his feet. If you want to be rude, sit with the bottoms of your shoes showing. To show you are clean, never wear your shoes in the house or in the kitchen. If you don't want to be polite, point at your feet.

**9.  What can you do to be rude in India?**

   (A) Never wear your shoes in the house.
   (B) Learn how to read.
   (C) Sit with the bottoms of your shoes showing.
   (D) Go to the store.

**10.  What is the main idea of the paragraphs?**

   (F) It is fun to live in India.
   (G) Learning to read is important.
   (H) Never point at your feet or show the bottom of your shoes.
   (J) There are many ways to let others know what you think in India.

**11.  What do you think people feel about talking to each other in India?**

   (A) It is easy to talk to others.
   (B) It is mostly easy to talk to others.
   (C) It is hard to talk to others.
   (D) It is just like in the U.S.A.

**12.  What can you do to show respect in India?**

   (F) Wear your socks outside.
   (G) Bow down and touch an older person's feet.
   (H) Frown at people.
   (J) Talk quietly.

GO ON

## READING: COMPREHENSION
## SAMPLE TEST

● **Directions:** Read or listen to the paragraphs below about sign language. Then answer the questions.

## *Sign Language*

People who may not be able to hear or speak well use sign language. They use their hands instead of their voices to talk. Their hands make signals to show different letters, words, and ideas. For example, to say the word "love," cross your arms over your chest.

Other people use sign language too. Have you ever watched a football game? The referees use hand signals to let you know what has happened in the game, such as a foul or time out. Have you ever been stuck in a traffic jam where there is a police officer? The police can use sign language to tell cars to go and wait.

Guess who else uses sign language? You! You wave your hand when you say hello and good-bye. You nod your head up and down to say "yes" and back and forth to say "no." You use your fingers to point and show which way to go. We use our hands and body to make signals all of the time!

**13. Why do people use sign language?**

- (A) Because they don't feel like talking.
- (B) Because they don't feel like listening.
- (C) Because they cannot ride a bike.
- (D) Because they cannot hear or speak well.

**14. What do people use when signing?**

- (F) their hand and arms
- (G) their eyes, ears, and mouth
- (H) their feet and legs
- (J) their hair and head

**15. Who would be the most likely to use sign language?**

- (A) a boy playing at the park
- (B) a man who cannot hear
- (C) a woman who cannot walk
- (D) a girl learning to tie her shoe

**16. What is the main idea of the story?**

- (F) using sign language
- (G) writing sign language
- (H) playing with children who use sign language
- (J) buying food using sign language

Name _____

# ANSWER SHEET

| STUDENT'S NAME | | SCHOOL |
|---|---|---|

LAST  FIRST  MI  TEACHER

FEMALE ◯   MALE ◯

**BIRTH DATE**

| MONTH | DAY | YEAR |
|---|---|---|

JAN ◯
FEB ◯
MAR ◯
APR ◯
MAY ◯
JUN ◯
JUL ◯
AUG ◯
SEP ◯
OCT ◯
NOV ◯
DEC ◯

DAY: (0)(1)(2)(3) (0)(1)(2)(3)(4)(5)(6)(7)(8)(9)

YEAR: (0)(1)(2)(3)(4)(5)(6)(7)(8)(9)(0) with (5)(6)(7)(8)(9)

**GRADE** ① ② ③

(Student name grid with columns of bubbles A through Z)

## Part 1: WORD ANALYSIS

| A | A B C D | 5 | A B C D | 8 | F G H J | D | F G H | 16 | F G H | 19 | A B C D |
| 1 | A B C D | 6 | F G H J | 9 | A B C D | E | A B C | F | F G H J | 20 | F G H J |
| 2 | F G H J | B | F G H J | 10 | F G H J | 13 | A B C | G | A B C D | 21 | A B C D |
| 3 | A B C D | C | A B C D | 11 | A B C D | 14 | F G H | 17 | A B C D | 22 | F G H J |
| 4 | F G H J | 7 | A B C D | 12 | F G H J | 15 | A B C | 18 | F G H J | | |

## Part 2: VOCABULARY

| A | A B C D | 6 | F G H J | 12 | F G H J | 18 | F G H J | 23 | A B C D | 29 | A B C D |
| 1 | A B C D | 7 | A B C D | 13 | A B C D | 19 | A B C D | 24 | F G H J | 30 | F G H J |
| 2 | F G H J | 8 | F G H J | 14 | F G H J | 20 | F G H J | 25 | A B C D | 31 | A B C D |
| 3 | A B C D | 9 | A B C D | 15 | A B C D | 21 | A B C D | 26 | F G H J | 32 | F G H J |
| 4 | F G H J | 10 | F G H J | 16 | F G H J | 22 | F G H J | 27 | A B C D | 33 | A B C D |
| B | F G H J | C | A B C D | D | F G H J | E | A B C D | 28 | F G H J | 34 | F G H J |
| 5 | A B C D | 11 | A B C D | 17 | A B C D | F | F G H J | G | A B C D | | |

## Part 3: READING COMPREHENSION

| A | A B C D | 4 | F G H J | 8 | F G H J | 12 | F G H J | 16 | F G H J | 20 | F G H J |
| 1 | A B C D | 5 | A B C D | 9 | A B C D | 13 | A B C D | 17 | A B C D | | |
| 2 | F G H J | 6 | F G H J | 10 | F G H J | 14 | F G H J | 18 | F G H J | | |
| 3 | A B C D | 7 | A B C D | 11 | A B C D | 15 | A B C D | 19 | A B C D | | |

Name _____

## READING PRACTICE TEST

● **Part I: Word Analysis**

**Directions:** Choose the best answer to each question.

---

**Example**

A. Which word has the same beginning sound as **small**?

    Ⓐ snow
    Ⓑ smooth
    Ⓒ shown
    Ⓓ something

---

1. Which word has the same vowel sound as **catch**?

    Ⓐ came
    Ⓑ bad
    Ⓒ eat
    Ⓓ clean

2. Which word has the same beginning sound as **block**?

    Ⓕ box
    Ⓖ breeze
    Ⓗ blink
    Ⓙ answer

3. Which word has the same ending sound as **work**?

    Ⓐ yard
    Ⓑ stood
    Ⓒ took
    Ⓓ watch

4. Which word has the same vowel sound as **stood**?

    Ⓕ two
    Ⓖ those
    Ⓗ road
    Ⓙ could

5. Which word has the same ending sound as **with**?

    Ⓐ while
    Ⓑ kiss
    Ⓒ bath
    Ⓓ these

6. Which word has the same beginning sound as **same**?

    Ⓕ ham
    Ⓖ rain
    Ⓗ shall
    Ⓙ sand

GO ON

# READING PRACTICE TEST

● Part 1: Word Analysis (cont.)

Directions: Choose the best answer to each question.

Examples

B.  Which word is a compound word, a word that is made up of two smaller words?

- (F) complete
- (G) certain
- (H) became
- (J) sunlight

C.  Look at the underlined word. Find the answer that tells what the contraction means.
    **that'll**

- (A) that is
- (B) that will
- (C) that all
- (D) that calls

**If an item is too difficult, skip it and come back to it later.**

7.  Which word is a compound word?

- (A) sidewalk
- (B) building
- (C) darkness
- (D) small

8.  Which word is a compound word?

- (F) several
- (G) party
- (H) person
- (J) playground

9.  Which word is a compound word?

- (A) nice
- (B) clothes
- (C) snowball
- (D) picture

10. **needn't**

- (F) need noses
- (G) need not
- (H) need night
- (J) need next

11. **could've**

- (A) could leave
- (B) could have
- (C) could very
- (D) could has

12. **what's**

- (F) what is
- (G) what stinks
- (H) what shakes
- (J) what sees

GO ON

## READING PRACTICE TEST

● **Part 1: Word Analysis (cont.)**

Directions: Choose the word that best fits in the blanks.

**Examples**

Jawan ____(D)____ down at the table. He was hungry and the ____(E)____ looked good.

**D.** F ate
G look
H sat

**E.** A chair
B mom
C food

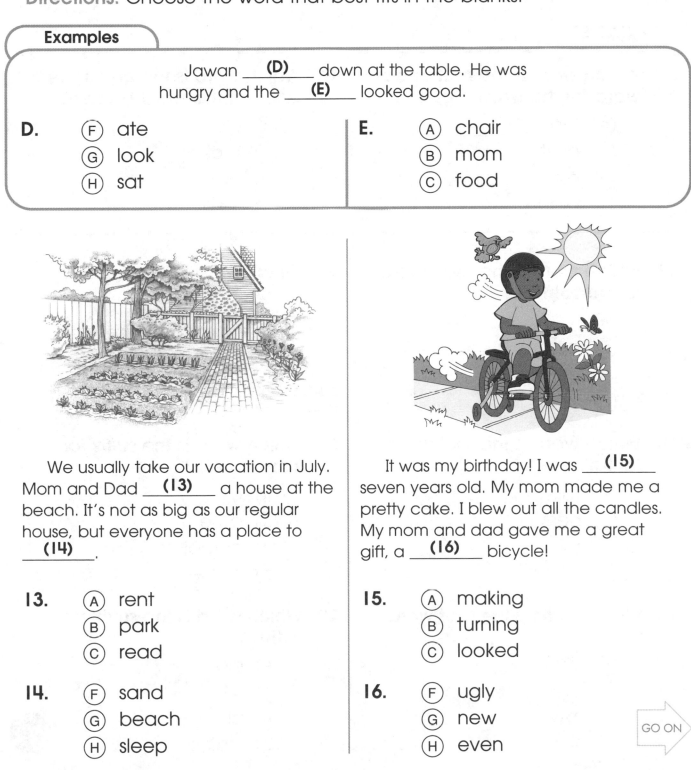

We usually take our vacation in July. Mom and Dad ____(13)____ a house at the beach. It's not as big as our regular house, but everyone has a place to ____(14)____.

It was my birthday! I was ____(15)____ seven years old. My mom made me a pretty cake. I blew out all the candles. My mom and dad gave me a great gift, a ____(16)____ bicycle!

**13.** A rent
B park
C read

**14.** F sand
G beach
H sleep

**15.** A making
B turning
C looked

**16.** F ugly
G new
H even

GO ON

Name _____

## READING PRACTICE TEST

● **Part 1: Word Analysis (cont.)**

Directions: Choose the best answer to each question.

### Example

**F.** Which word is the root or base word for the word **biggest**?

- Ⓕ big
- Ⓖ gest
- Ⓗ est
- Ⓙ bigge

**G.** Which word is the ending or suffix for the word **broken**?

- Ⓐ en
- Ⓑ broke
- Ⓒ bro
- Ⓓ roke

**17.** Which word is the root word for **certainly**?

- Ⓐ ly
- Ⓑ cert
- Ⓒ certain
- Ⓓ change

**18.** Which word is the root word for **fullness**?

- Ⓕ falling
- Ⓖ ness
- Ⓗ full
- Ⓙ fur

**19.** Which word is the root word for **slower**?

- Ⓐ slip
- Ⓑ er
- Ⓒ low
- Ⓓ slow

**20.** Which word is the suffix for **lighter**?

- Ⓕ light
- Ⓖ er
- Ⓗ igh
- Ⓙ lig

**21.** Which word is the suffix for **completely**?

- Ⓐ ly
- Ⓑ pete
- Ⓒ complete
- Ⓓ come

**22.** Which word is the suffix for **listing**?

- Ⓕ ing
- Ⓖ list
- Ⓗ isti
- Ⓙ licking

STOP

# READING PRACTICE TEST

● **Part 2: Vocabulary**

**Directions:** Choose the word that best matches the picture.

**Example**

**A.**

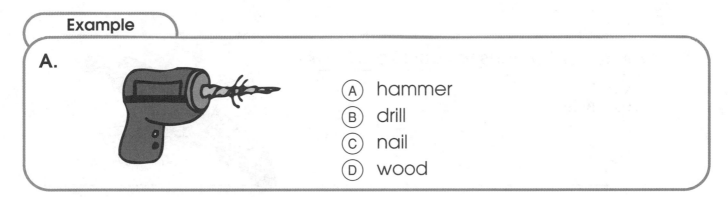

- (A) hammer
- (B) drill
- (C) nail
- (D) wood

**Look at the picture carefully and then read the choices.**

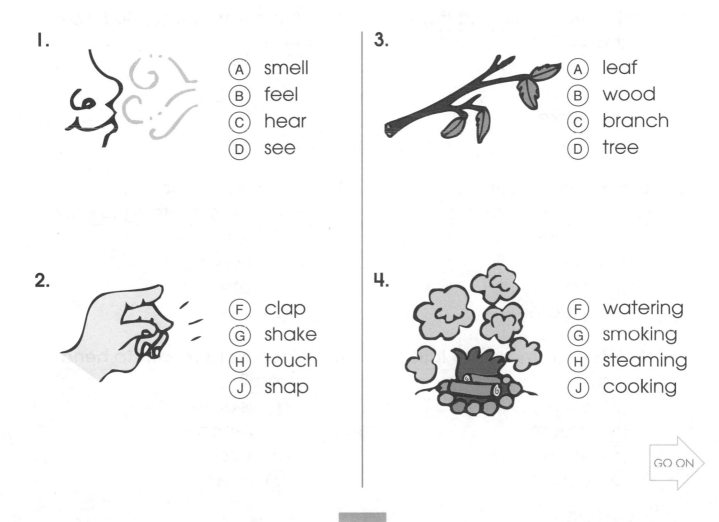

**1.**
- (A) smell
- (B) feel
- (C) hear
- (D) see

**3.**
- (A) leaf
- (B) wood
- (C) branch
- (D) tree

**2.**
- (F) clap
- (G) shake
- (H) touch
- (J) snap

**4.**
- (F) watering
- (G) smoking
- (H) steaming
- (J) cooking

GO ON

Name _____

## READING PRACTICE TEST

● **Part 2: Vocabulary (cont.)**

Directions: Choose the best answer.

> **Example**
>
> B.   Which word means to soar like a bird?
>   - Ⓕ   air
>   - Ⓖ   ride
>   - Ⓗ   run
>   - Ⓙ   fly

**Key words in the question will help you find the answer.**

5.   Which word is something that walks?
   - Ⓐ   cat
   - Ⓑ   worm
   - Ⓒ   snake
   - Ⓓ   fish

6.   Which word means to take air in through your nose?
   - Ⓕ   cough
   - Ⓖ   swim
   - Ⓗ   eat
   - Ⓙ   breathe

7.   Which word means to talk about?
   - Ⓐ   write
   - Ⓑ   dream
   - Ⓒ   enjoy
   - Ⓓ   discuss

8.   Which word means to follow after?
   - Ⓕ   chase
   - Ⓖ   begin
   - Ⓗ   fall
   - Ⓙ   turn

9.   Which word means feeling like you need something to eat?
   - Ⓐ   full
   - Ⓑ   hungry
   - Ⓒ   ate
   - Ⓓ   food

10.   Which word means to bend toward?
   - Ⓕ   lean
   - Ⓖ   reach
   - Ⓗ   sleep
   - Ⓙ   drop

GO ON

Name _____

# READING PRACTICE TEST

● **Part 2: Vocabulary (cont.)**

**Directions:** Look at the underlined word in each sentence. Which word is a synonym for that word?

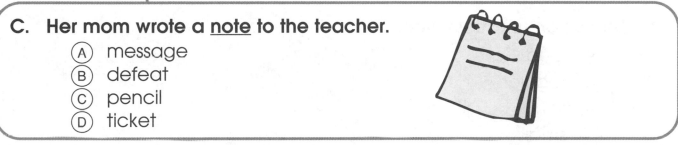

**Example**

C. Her mom wrote a <u>note</u> to the teacher.
- (A) message
- (B) defeat
- (C) pencil
- (D) ticket

**Use the meaning of the sentence to help you find the meaning of the word.**

11. Susan was <u>grateful</u> that her dad drove her to school.
- (A) thankful
- (B) busy
- (C) curious
- (D) finished

12. The brothers <u>yelled</u> for their dog to come home.
- (F) cared
- (G) called
- (H) heard
- (J) whispered

13. Grandma asked me to <u>split</u> the cookies evenly between the children.
- (A) use
- (B) think
- (C) divide
- (D) stand

14. I always keep my room very <u>neat</u>.
- (F) bad
- (G) pretty
- (H) tidy
- (J) dark

15. She likes to eat <u>big</u> oranges.
- (A) huge
- (B) tiny
- (C) ready
- (D) round

16. She watched the cat <u>jump</u> off the chair.
- (F) leap
- (G) lick
- (H) break
- (J) dream

GO ON

Name _____

## READING PRACTICE TEST

● **Part 2: Vocabulary (cont.)**

**Directions:** Look at the underlined word in each sentence. Choose the word that is the antonym of the underlined word.

| Example |
| --- |

D.  He has an <u>unusual</u> voice.

 Ⓕ loud

 Ⓖ regular

 Ⓗ soft

 Ⓙ small

17.  They drove down the <u>narrow</u> road.

 Ⓐ long

 Ⓑ new

 Ⓒ bumpy

 Ⓓ wide

18.  She picked her <u>fancy</u> dress to wear to the party.

 Ⓕ best

 Ⓖ plain

 Ⓗ small

 Ⓙ little

19.  She made sure the knot was good and <u>tight</u>.

 Ⓐ clean

 Ⓑ different

 Ⓒ loose

 Ⓓ last

20.  After granting our three wishes, the kind fairy <u>vanished</u> from sight.

 Ⓕ appeared

 Ⓖ asked

 Ⓗ going

 Ⓙ got

21.  He thought his bike was <u>fast</u>.

 Ⓐ funny

 Ⓑ food

 Ⓒ last

 Ⓓ slow

22.  On Thursday, Daniel was <u>absent</u>.

 Ⓕ giving

 Ⓖ present

 Ⓗ hurt

 Ⓙ gone

GO ON

Name _____

# READING PRACTICE TEST

## ● Part 2: Vocabulary (cont.)

**Directions:** Choose the word that best fits in each blank.

> **Examples**
>
> Mr. Jennings went _____(E)_____ after work. He bought food for dinner and then he went _____(F)_____.
>
> **E.**
> - Ⓐ shopping
> - Ⓑ walking
> - Ⓒ driving
>
> **F.**
> - Ⓕ soon
> - Ⓖ fast
> - Ⓗ home

**When deciding which answer is best, try each answer choice in the blank.**

Our neighbor is a gardener. One of her _____(23)_____ trees recently died. She said it was because of a bug that likes to eat _____(24)_____.

**23.**
- Ⓐ girl
- Ⓑ half
- Ⓒ small

**24.**
- Ⓕ each
- Ⓖ leaves
- Ⓗ dirt

One sunny June day, a man _____(25)_____ too fast down the road. A police officer stopped him and gave him a _____(26)_____.

**25.**
- Ⓐ drove
- Ⓑ paced
- Ⓒ ran

**26.**
- Ⓕ picture
- Ⓖ ticket
- Ⓗ rest

**27.** There are many different _____(27)_____ of bats. One kind is the brown bat.
- Ⓐ only
- Ⓑ paper
- Ⓒ kinds

**28.** _____(28)_____ brown bats eat insects. One bat can eat 600 mosquitoes in just an hour.
- Ⓕ second
- Ⓖ little
- Ⓗ sleep

GO ON ▷

Name _____

# READING PRACTICE TEST

● **Part 2: Vocabulary (cont.)**

**Directions:** Some words have more than one meaning. Choose the word that will make sense in both blanks.

**Example**

G. My mom gets to take _____ at work.
I get mad when my brother _____ my toys.

- (A) misses
- (B) breaks
- (C) picks
- (D) walks

29. He carried his _____ to the baseball field.
The _____ was hanging in the cave.
- (A) bat
- (B) men
- (C) ball
- (D) sheep

30. In the _____ my mom plants all of her flowers.
The _____ next to the mountain had fresh water.
- (F) picnic
- (G) fall
- (H) spring
- (J) snow

31. Did you go to the _____ with your friends?
Where should I _____ the car?
- (A) party
- (B) school
- (C) park
- (D) drive

32. A bear has a heavy _____.
My mom bought me a new _____ for winter.
- (F) hat
- (G) fur
- (H) enjoy
- (J) coat

33. The river _____ into two separate streams.
The _____ on the tree swayed in the wind.
- (A) leaves
- (B) branches
- (C) wanted
- (D) goes

34. Cinderella was the most beautiful girl at the _____.
Hunter's grandma bought him a red _____ for his birthday.
- (F) party
- (G) gift
- (H) ball
- (J) bike

STOP

Name _____

# READING PRACTICE TEST

● **Part 3: Story Comprehension**

**Example**

Bigfoot is a creature that may be real or make-believe. Although many people say they have seen this creature, scientists want more proof. Is there a man-like beast lurking around the woods in countries all over the world?

A.  **What is Bigfoot?**
  - (A) a huge foot
  - (B) a giant sock
  - (C) a creature
  - (D) a country

**Read or listen to the paragraph below that tells about horses. Then, answer the questions.**

## Horses

Horses are beautiful animals. Most horses have smooth, shiny coats. They have long manes and tails. Their hair may be brown, black, white, yellow, or spotted. Sometimes horses neigh, or make a loud, long cry. Horses need to be brushed every day. This helps keep them clean. Many people keep horses as pets or to work on farms. Some people enjoy riding them for fun. Horses are wonderful animals.

1.  **What does the word neigh mean?**
  - (A) to smile
  - (B) to be different colors
  - (C) to keep clean by brushing
  - (D) to make a loud, long cry

2.  **How often should horses be brushed?**
  - (F) every day
  - (G) every week
  - (H) every month
  - (J) every year

3.  **What do you know about horses?**
  - (A) Horses are the same color.
  - (B) Horses never make noise.
  - (C) Some people enjoy riding horses for fun.
  - (D) Horses have feathers.

4.  **If you had a horse for a pet, what might happen?**
  - (F) You would have to feed it.
  - (G) You would have to brush its mane and tail.
  - (H) You would have to have a place for the horse to stay.
  - (J) All of the above

GO ON

Name _____

# READING PRACTICE TEST

● **Part 3: Story Comprehension (cont.)**

**Directions:** Read or listen to the paragraphs below that tell about stars. Then, answer the questions.

## Stars

**(1)** When you look up on a clear, dark night, you can see small points of light called stars. Actually, stars are not small at all. Some stars may be 50 million miles across! Stars just look like points of light because they are so far from Earth. Our sun is a star. It looks bigger than other stars in the sky because it is closer to us. A star's brightness depends on its mass and distance from Earth. Bigger stars are brighter than smaller ones. Stars also look brighter when they are closer.

**(2)** To make it easier to study, people have grouped stars into patterns. The patterns are called constellations. They may be large or small. They may have bright or dim stars. Sometimes in a constellation, the bright stars may be in the shape of a person or animal.

**(3)** Stars, unlike planets, make their own heat and light. The color of a star's light can tell us how much heat it has. The cooler stars give off a reddish light. The hottest stars look blue or blue-white in color. Stars do not last the same amount of time. They all will eventually burn out.

5. **What does the word constellation mean?**
   - (A) large and in space
   - (B) different stars people see from Mars
   - (C) different color stars we can see from the earth
   - (D) a pattern of stars that are grouped together

6. **Which of the following is an opinion?**
   - (F) Stars are fun to look at every night.
   - (G) Our sun is a star.
   - (H) Stars look brighter when they are closer.
   - (J) Cooler stars give off a reddish light.

7. **What is a supporting detail for paragraph 2?**
   - (A) Colors of stars help us to know how hot they are.
   - (B) Our sun is a star.
   - (C) It takes imagination to find when different patterns in the sky look like people or animals.
   - (D) When stars burn out they turn into new kinds of stars.

8. **What would happen if you traveled through space and got closer and closer to a star?**
   - (F) You would see it get smaller.
   - (G) It would look like a rainbow.
   - (H) It would get brighter.
   - (J) All of the above

GO ON

Name _____

## READING PRACTICE TEST

● **Part 3: Story Comprehension (cont.)**

**Directions:** Read or listen to the paragraph below. It tells about honey and bees. Then, answer the questions.

## *Sweet as Honey*

Honey is sweet and thick. Honeybees make it. First, they fly from flower to flower. At each flower, they collect nectar. Nectar is watery. It is found inside flower blossoms. The bees sip the nectar from flowers. Next, they store it in their bodies. It is kept in their honey bags. Then, the nectar in the honey bags changes. It changes into two kinds of sugars. The bees fly back to their hives. Finally, they put the nectar into their hives. While it is there, most of the water leaves or evaporates. All that is left is the sweet, thick honey inside the honeycomb. People who collect honey remove the combs. Last, the sweet honey is sold for us to eat.

9. **What is nectar?**
   - (A) a flower
   - (B) a watery substance that bees sip from flowers
   - (C) another name for honey
   - (D) a part of a bee's body that makes honey

10. **What would happen if the bees didn't have honey bags?**
    - (F) They couldn't make honey.
    - (G) They would fly in circles.
    - (H) They couldn't find flowers.
    - (J) They wouldn't be able to see.

11. **What happens after the bees put the nectar into their hives?**
    - (A) They fly from flower to flower.
    - (B) They collect the nectar.
    - (C) The bees sip the nectar from flowers.
    - (D) Most of the water leaves or evaporates.

12. **If you were a honey collector, where would you go to find honey?**
    - (F) in the store
    - (G) in the honeybees' hive
    - (H) in your house
    - (J) in the sand

GO ON

## READING PRACTICE TEST

● **Part 3: Story Comprehension (cont.)**

**Directions:** Read or listen to the paragraphs below that tell about a mom who lost her spaghetti. Then, answer the questions.

# *The Investigation*

The bowl sat empty. "Oh, no! My spaghetti is missing!" shrieked Mom. "I was supposed to take it to the school potluck tonight. What am I going to do?"

I decided to help my mom find her lost spaghetti. "Don't panic Mom, I'll look for clues," I said as I started looking around. The spaghetti had been in the bowl, on the counter, near the sink. First, I ran outside to check for footprints. There were none! It must have been an inside job.

Who would be my first suspect? I went to my baby sister Laurie's room. I checked in her crib, in her toy box, and in the closet. There was no sign of the spaghetti.

Next, I went to question my second suspect. I asked Dad if he had seen anything unusual. He had been mowing the lawn and didn't know anything about the case.

My leads seemed to be vanishing. Could a thief have come into our house and helped himself to dinner? Had aliens zapped it aboard their spaceship?

I looked around. Suddenly, I noticed through the open window two birds carrying long, red-and-white worms in their beaks. The Case of the Missing Spaghetti was closed!

13. **What is the solution to The Case of the Missing Spaghetti?**
   - (A) Dad took the spaghetti.
   - (B) Laurie ate the spaghetti.
   - (C) Birds took the spaghetti.
   - (D) Mom had put the spaghetti in the fridge.

14. **Who was the second suspect?**
   - (F) baby Laurie
   - (G) Mom
   - (H) Dad
   - (J) the birds

15. **How do you know Dad didn't take the spaghetti?**
   - (A) He was mowing the lawn.
   - (B) He was watching Laurie.
   - (C) He liked pizza better.
   - (D) Dad didn't like to investigate.

16. **Why might the birds have taken the spaghetti?**
   - (F) They liked Italian food.
   - (G) They thought they were worms.
   - (H) They wanted to try something different.
   - (J) They needed to make a nest.

GO ON

Name _____

## READING PRACTICE TEST

● **Part 3: Story Comprehension (cont.)**

**Directions:** Read or listen to the paragraphs below that tell about a boy who builds a robot. Then, answer the questions.

# *Bert, the Inventor*

Every day after school, Bert locked himself in his bedroom. He was working on a secret project. He didn't tell anyone what he was doing. Not even his best friend Larry.

Bert finally finished. He had made a robot that looked exactly like himself. The robot had orange hair, freckles, and glasses. The robot and Bert both talked in a squeaky voice. "Life is going to be easy now!" exclaimed Bert. "I'm going to send my robot to school while I stay home and play."

The next morning the robot ate breakfast. Then, he rode the bus to school. After school the bus dropped the robot back home. The robot knocked on the door.

"Sweetie, I am so glad you're home. I really missed you!" said Mom. Then, she took the robot into the kitchen and gave him a snack before dinner.

"We had lots of fun at school today," said the robot. "We went to the space museum. I got to try on a real space suit. It was too big for me but the teacher took my picture."

Bert was listening outside the kitchen. He was sad. He wanted to be an astronaut someday. He decided this wasn't a good idea. So the next day, Bert went to school himself.

**17. What did Bert look like?**

Ⓐ He had curly hair and was tall.

Ⓑ He had red hair and wore a cap.

Ⓒ He was short with blonde hair.

Ⓓ He had orange hair, freckles, and glasses.

**18. Why did Bert decide to go to school himself?**

Ⓕ He missed his mom's smile.

Ⓖ He missed going to the space museum.

Ⓗ He missed his friend Larry.

Ⓙ He missed eating breakfast and going to school.

**19. Where does this story take place?**

Ⓐ at school

Ⓑ at the grocery store

Ⓒ at Larry's house

Ⓓ at Bert's house

**20. Why did Bert create the robot?**

Ⓕ He wanted to make life easier and have the robot go to school for him.

Ⓖ His mom was feeling sick and needed help cleaning.

Ⓗ He didn't want to be friends with Larry anymore.

Ⓙ He was sad that he didn't have any brothers.

STOP

# ANSWER KEY

**READING: WORD ANALYSIS**
Lesson 1: Word Sounds
• Page 262
A. B
1. A
2. H
3. C
4. F
5. B
6. F

**READING: WORD ANALYSIS**
Lesson 2: Rhyming Words
• Page 263
A. A
1. A
2. G
3. B
4. H

**READING: WORD ANALYSIS**
Lesson 3: Word Sounds
• Page 264
A. C
B. G
1. A
2. J
3. B
4. H
5. B
6. F

**READING: WORD ANALYSIS**
Lesson 4: Word Study
• Page 265
1. C
2. H
3. D
4. F
5. D
6. F

**READING: WORD ANALYSIS**
Lesson 5: Contractions and Compound Words
• Page 266
A. A
B. F
1. D
2. G
3. D
4. J
5. B
6. H

**READING: WORD ANALYSIS**
Lesson 6: Root Words and Suffixes
• Page 267
A. D
B. H
1. C
2. F
3. B
4. H
5. D
6. H

**READING: WORD ANALYSIS**
Sample Test
• Pages 268–271
A. B
1. B
2. F
3. B
4. H
5. B
6. G
B. H
7. C
8. G
9. C
10. F
C. B
D. H
11. A
12. H
13. D
14. G

15. C
16. J
E. D
F. G
17. B
18. F
19. D
20. F
21. B
22. J

**READING: VOCABULARY**
Lesson 7: Picture Vocabulary
• Page 272
A. B
B. F
1. C
2. F
3. D
4. H

**READING: VOCABULARY**
Lesson 8: Word Meaning
• Page 273
A. D
1. A
2. H
3. D
4. G
5. B
6. F

**READING: VOCABULARY**
Lesson 9: Synonyms
• Page 274
A. D
1. C
2. J
3. B
4. F
5. A
6. J

**READING: VOCABULARY**
Lesson 10: Antonyms
• Page 275
A. C
1. D
2. H
3. B
4. F
5. C
6. H

**READING: VOCABULARY**
Lesson 11: Words in Context
• Page 276
A. B
B. F
1. B
2. H
3. A
4. H

**READING: VOCABULARY**
Lesson 12: Multiple Meaning Words
• Page 277
A. D
1. A
2. H
3. B
4. J
5. C

**READING: VOCABULARY**
Sample Test
• Pages 278–281
A. D
1. A
2. H
3. D
4. F
B. H
5. B
6. G
7. A
8. H
9. D

# ANSWER KEY

10. F
C. B
D. F
11. B
12. G
13. D
12. G
13. D
14. F
15. C
16. G
E. C
F. G
17. A
18. H
19. A
20. F

**READING:
COMPREHENSION**
Lesson 13: Picture
Comprehension
• Page 282
A. B
1. A
2. H
3. D
4. F

**READING:
COMPREHENSION**
Lesson 14: Critical
Reading
• Page 283
A. D
1. B
2. J

**READING:
COMPREHENSION**
Lesson 15: Fiction
• Pages 284–285
A. A
1. D
2. H
3. B
4. J
5. C
6. H
7. D
8. J

**READING:
COMPREHENSION**
Lesson 16: Nonfiction
• Pages 286–287
1. C
2. J
3. B
4. H
5. A
6. H
7. C
8. J

**READING:
COMPREHENSION**
Sample Test
• Pages 288–291
A. A
1. B
2. F
3. D
4. J
5. B
6. J
7. A
8. H
9. C
10. J
11. C
12. G
13. D
14. F
15. B
16. F

**READING PRACTICE
TEST**
Part 1: Word Analysis
• Pages 293–296
A. B
1. B
2. H
3. C
4. J
5. C
6. J
B. J
C. B
7. A
8. J

9. C
10. G
11. B
12. F
D. H
E. C
13. A
14. H
15. B
16. G
F. F
G. A
17. C
18. H
19. D
20. G
21. A
22. F

**READING PRACTICE
TEST**
Part 2: Vocabulary
• Pages 297–302
A. B
1. A
2. J
3. C
4. G
B. J
5. A
6. J
7. D
8. F
9. B
10. F
C. A
11. A
12. G
13. C
14. H
15. A
16. F
D. G
17. D
18. G
19. C
20. F
21. D
22. G
E. A

F. H
23. C
24. G
25. A
26. G
27. C
28. G
G. B
29. A
30. H
31. C
32. J
33. B
34. H

**READING PRACTICE
TEST**
Part 3: Story
Comprehension
• Pages 303–307
A. C
1. D
2. F
3. C
4. J
5. D
6. F
7. C
8. H
9. B
10. F
11. D
12. G
13. C
14. H
15. A
16. G
17. D
18. G
19. D
20. F

# Answer Key

## Batter Up!

What did Bobby yell to the batter?

**Directions:** To find out, say the name of each picture. On the line, write the letter that you hear at the beginning of each picture.

h i t    a

h o m e   r u n !

**5**

## Bats and Balls

**Directions:** Look at the baseball words below. Use the letters from the word box to make new words. **Hint:** Some letters can be used for both sets of words.

**Word Box**
c
f
h
m
p
r
s
t
v
w
ch
sm

bat

_c_ at    _m_ at    _s_ at
_f_ at    _p_ at    _v_ at
_h_ at    _r_ at    _ch_ at

ball

_c_ all    _m_ all    _w_ all
_f_ all    _t_ all    _sm_ all
_h_ all

**6**

## What Does That Spell?

**Directions:** Write the letters from the word box to make new words. Some letters can be used for both sets of words.

f   b   c   n   p   sk   s   t   fl

win

_f_ in    _p_ in
_b_ in    _sk_ in
_s_ in    _t_ in

game

_f_ ame    _s_ ame
_c_ ame    _t_ ame
_n_ ame    _fl_ ame

**7**

## Sounds the Same

Different words may begin with the same sound.

**Example: Box** and **boy** begin with the same sound. **Cat** and **dog** do not.

**Directions:** Say each picture's name. Color the pictures in the box if their names begin with the same sound.

**8**

## Tic-Tac-Toe

**Directions:** Find the three pictures in each game whose names begin with the same sound. Draw a line through them.

**9**

## Beginning Consonants: b, c, d, f, g, h, j

**Directions:** Fill in the beginning consonant for each word.

Example: _c_ at

_f_ ox

_j_ acket

_g_ oat

_h_ ouse

_d_ og

_f_ ire

**10**

### Beginning Consonants: k, l, m, n, p, q, r
Directions: Directions: Write the letter that makes the beginning sound for each picture.

k    q    r    n

m    l    k    r

q    p    n    m

l    k    r    p

**11**

### Beginning Consonants: k, l, m, n, p, q, r
Directions: Fill in the beginning consonant for each word.

Example: __r__ ose

__m__ oney

__q__ uilt

__l__ ion

__p__ an

__k__ ey

__n__ ose

**12**

### Beginning Consonants: s, t, v, w, x, y, z
Directions: Directions: Write the letter under each picture that makes the beginning sound.

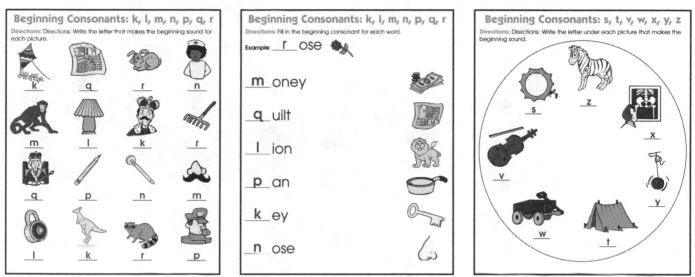

s    z

v    x

w    t    y

**13**

### Beginning Consonants: s, t, v, w, x, y, z
Directions: Fill in the beginning consonant for each word.

Example: __s__ ock

__z__ ipper

__t__ able

__x__ ray

__v__ ase

__y__ olk

__w__ and

**14**

### Ending Consonants: b, d, f, g
Directions: Fill in the ending consonant for each word.

ma __n__

cu __b__

roo __f__

do __g__

be __d__

bi __b__

**15**

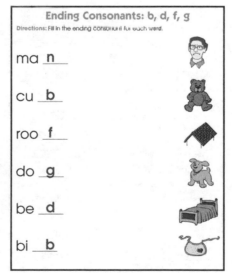

### Ending Consonants: k, l, m, n, p, r
Directions: Fill in the ending consonant for each word.

nai __l__

ca __n__

gu __m__

ca __r__

truc __k__

ca __p__

pai __l__

**16**

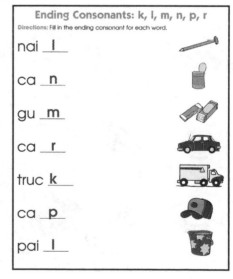

## Ending Consonants: s, t, x

**Directions:** Fill in the ending consonant for each word.

ca __t__

bo __x__

bu __s__

fo __x__

boa __t__

ma __t__

**17**

## Consonant Blends

**Consonant blends** are two or three consonant letters in a word whose sounds combine, or blend. **Examples: br, fr, gr, pr, tr**

**Directions:** Look at each picture. Say its name. Write the blend you hear at the beginning of each word.

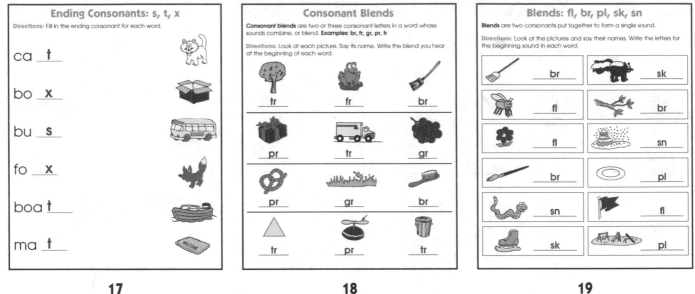

| | | |
|---|---|---|
| tr | fr | br |
| pr | tr | gr |
| pr | gr | br |
| tr | pr | tr |

**18**

## Blends: fl, br, pl, sk, sn

**Blends** are two consonants put together to form a single sound.

**Directions:** Look at the pictures and say their names. Write the letters for the beginning sound in each word.

| | |
|---|---|
| br | sk |
| fl | br |
| fl | sn |
| br | pl |
| sn | fl |
| sk | pl |

**19**

## Blends: bl, sl, cr, cl

**Directions:** Look at the pictures and say their names. Write the letters for the beginning sound in each word.

__cl__ own    __bl__ anket    __cr__ ayon

__cl__ ock    __sl__ ide    __cl__ oud

__sl__ ed    __cr__ ab    __cr__ ocodile

**20**

## Consonant Blends

**Directions:** Write a word from the word box to answer each riddle.

| clock | glass | blow | climb | slipper |
|---|---|---|---|---|
| sleep | gloves | clap | blocks | flashlight |

1. You need me when the lights go out. **What am I?** — flashlight

2. People use me to tell the time. **What am I?** — clock

3. You put me on your hands in the winter to keep them warm. **What am I?** — gloves

4. Cinderella lost one like me at midnight. **What am I?** — slipper

5. This is what you do with your hands when you are pleased. **What is it?** — clap

6. You can do this with a whistle or with bubble gum. **What is it?** — blow

7. These are what you might use to build a castle when you are playing. **What are they?** — blocks

8. You do this to get to the top of a hill. **What is it?** — climb

9. This is what you use to drink water or milk. **What is it?** — glass

10. You do this at night with your eyes closed. **What is it?** — sleep

**21**

## Nothing But Net

**Directions:** Write the missing consonant blends.

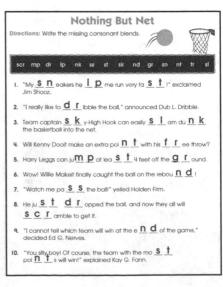

| scr | mp | dr | lp | nk | ss | st | sk | nd | gr | sn | nt | fr | sl |
|---|---|---|---|---|---|---|---|---|---|---|---|---|---|

1. "My __s n__ eakers he __l p__ me run very fa __s t__ !" exclaimed Jim Shooz.

2. "I really like to __d r__ ibble the ball," announced Dub L. Dribble.

3. Team captain __s k__ y-High Hook can easily __s l__ am du __n k__ the basketball into the net.

4. Will Kenny Dooit make an extra poi __n t__ with his __f r__ ee throw?

5. Harry Leggs can ju __m p__ at lea __s t__ 4 feet off the __g r__ ound.

6. Wow! Willie Makeit finally caught the ball on the rebou __n d__ !

7. "Watch me pa __s s__ the ball!" yelled Holden Firm.

8. He ju __s t__ __d r__ opped the ball, and now they all will __s c r__ amble to get it.

9. "I cannot tell which team will win at the e __n d__ of the game," decided Ed G. Nerves.

10. "You silly boy! Of course, the team with the mo __s t__ poi __n t__ s will win!" explained Kay G. Fann.

**22**

## Consonant Digraph th

Some consonants work together to stand for a new sound. They are called **consonant digraphs**. Listen for the sound of consonant digraph **th** in **think**.

think

**Directions:** Print **th** under the pictures whose names begin with the sound of **th**. Color the **th** pictures.

th

th    th

30
th

**23**

## Think About th

**Directions:** Say the name of each picture. Fill in the missing letter or letters.

think    horn    thorn
10
ten    thumb    thirty

**Directions:** Find and circle these **th** words in the puzzle. The words may go **across** or **down**.

think    thorn    thumb    thirty

**24**

## Consonant Digraph sh

Listen for the sound of consonant digraph **sh** in **sheep**.

**Directions:** Color the pictures whose names begin with the sound of **sh**.

sheep

**25**

## Change a Word

**Directions:** Make a new word by changing the beginning sound to **sh**. Write the new word on the line.

made - m
+ sh = shade

| zip | sell | beep |
|-----|------|------|
| ship | shell | sheep |
| tin | line | lift |
| shin | shine | shift |
| red | cape | cave |
| shed | shape | shave |
| top | bake | feet |
| shop | shake | sheet |

**26**

## Consonant Digraph wh

**Directions:** Write **wh**, **th**, or **sh** to complete each word.

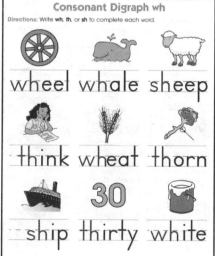

wheel    whale    sheep
think    wheat    thorn
30
ship    thirty    white

**27**

## Wheel of Fortune

Listen for the sound of consonant digraph **wh** in **whale**.

whale

**Directions:** Color the pictures whose names begin with consonant digraph **wh**.

wh
30

**28**

## Consonant Digraph ch

Listen for the sound of consonant digraph **ch** in **cherry**.

cherry

**Directions:** Trace the cherry if the name of the picture begins with the **ch** sound. Use a red crayon.

**29**

## Read and Write Digraphs

**Directions:** Write a word from the box to label each picture.

| chest | check | sheep |
| chimp | cherry | thirty |
| chain | cheese | wheel |

cherry    sheep    chain

chest    wheel    cheese

chimp    thirty    check

**30**

## Consonant Digraph kn

Listen for the sound of consonant digraph **kn** in **knot**.
The **k** is silent.

knot

**Directions:** Color the pictures whose names begin with the **kn** sound. Connect all the colored pictures from the knight to his horse.

**31**

## Knocking Around in Knickers

A long time ago, golfers wore knickers when they played. **Knickers** are short, loose trousers gathered just below the knee. **Kn** at the beginning of a word makes the same sound as **n**.

**Directions:** Look at each picture and write **kn** or **k** at the beginning to complete the words.

kn_ife    k_ite    kn_ock

kn_ot    kn_uckle    kn_ight

k_ing    kn_ee    k_ey

**32**

## Consonant Digraph wr

Listen for the sound of consonant digraph **wr** in **wren**. The **w** is silent.

wren

**Directions:** Write a word from the box to label each picture. Color the pictures whose names begin with **wr**.

| web | wrist | wring | wrap |
| worm | write | wreath | wink | wrench |

wreath    wrap    worm

wrist    wrench    web

wink    write    wring

**33**

## Ending Digraphs

Some words end with consonant digraphs. Listen for the ending digraphs in **duck**, **moth**, **dish**, and **branch**.

duck    moth    dish    branch

**Directions:** Say the name of each picture. Circle the letters that stand for the ending sound.

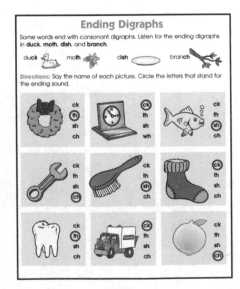

**34**

## Hear and Write Digraphs

**Directions:** The name of each picture below ends with **ck**, **th**, **sh**, or **ch**. Write each word on the lines below.

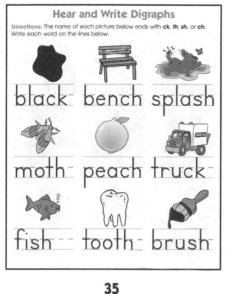

black    bench    splash

moth    peach    truck

fish    tooth    brush

**35**

## Missing Digraphs

**Directions:** Fill in the circle beside the missing digraph in each word.

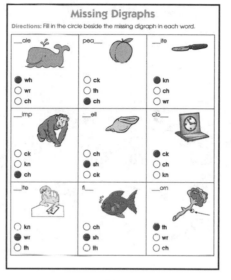

| __ale | pea__ | __ife |
|---|---|---|
| ● wh | ○ ck | ● kn |
| ○ wr | ○ th | ○ ch |
| ○ ch | ● ch | ○ wr |

| __imp | __ell | clo__ |
|---|---|---|
| ○ ck | ○ ch | ● ck |
| ○ kn | ● sh | ○ ch |
| ● ch | ○ ck | ○ kn |

| __ife | fi__ | __orn |
|---|---|---|
| ○ kn | ○ ch | ● th |
| ● wr | ● sh | ○ wr |
| ○ th | ○ th | ○ ch |

**36**

## Missing Digraphs

**Directions:** Fill in the circle beside the missing digraph in each word.

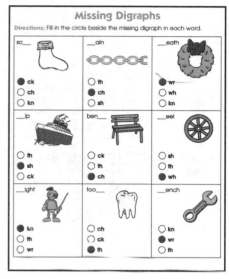

| so__ | __ain | __eath |
|---|---|---|
| ● ck | ○ th | ● wr |
| ○ ch | ● ch | ○ wh |
| ○ kn | ○ sh | ○ kn |

| __ip | ben__ | __eel |
|---|---|---|
| ○ th | ○ ck | ○ sh |
| ● sh | ○ th | ○ th |
| ○ ck | ● ch | ● wh |

| __ight | too__ | __ench |
|---|---|---|
| ● kn | ○ ch | ○ kn |
| ○ th | ○ ck | ● wr |
| ○ wr | ● th | ○ th |

**37**

## At the Pool

**Directions:** Write the correct letters from the word box to complete the word for each picture.

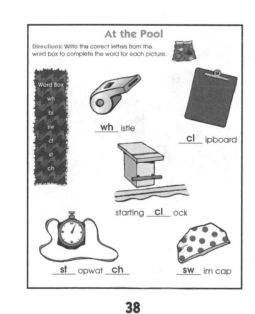

Word Box
wh
bl
sw
cl
st
ch

**wh** istle

**cl** ipboard

starting **cl** ock

**st** opwat **ch**

**sw** im cap

**38**

## Silent Letters

Some words have letters you cannot hear at all, such as the **gh** in **night**, the **w** in **wrong**, the **l** in **walk**, the **k** in **knee**, the **b** in **climb**, and the **t** in **listen**.

**Directions:** Look at the words in the word box. Write the word under its picture. Underline the silent letters.

| knife | light | calf | wrench | lamb | eight |
|---|---|---|---|---|---|
| wrist | whistle | comb | thumb | knob | knee |

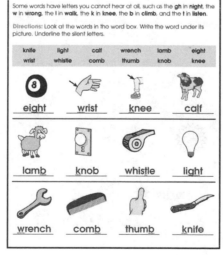

ei**gh**t    **w**rist    **k**nee    cal**f**

lam**b**    **k**nob    **wh**is**t**le    li**gh**t

**w**rench    com**b**    thum**b**    **k**nife

**39**

## A Flying Saucer?

A **discus** is a flat circle made mostly of wood with a metal center and edge that looks a bit like a plate. A men's discus is about 9 inches across and weighs a little over 4 pounds. A women's discus is about 2 inches smaller and about 2 pounds lighter. The men's world record throw is 243 feet, but the women's world record is even greater—252 feet!

**Directions:** Read the word in each discus. Write its silent consonant in the center.

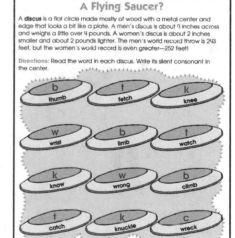

| b thumb | t fetch | k knee |
|---|---|---|
| w wrist | b limb | t watch |
| k know | w wrong | b climb |
| t catch | k knuckle | c wreck |

**40**

Answer Key      315      Total Reading Grade 2

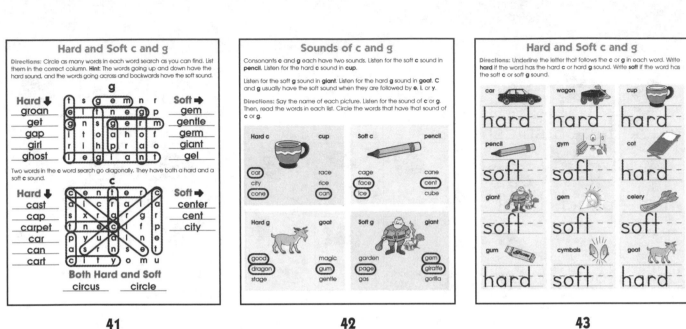

**Hard and Soft c and g**

Directions: Circle as many words in each word search as you can find. List them in the correct column. **Hint:** The words going up and down have the hard sound, and the words going across and backwards have the soft sound.

**g**

| Hard ↓ | Soft → |
|--------|--------|
| groan | gem |
| get | gentle |
| gap | germ |
| girl | giant |
| ghost | gel |

Two words in the **c** word search go diagonally. They have both a hard and a soft **c** sound.

**c**

| Hard ↓ | Soft → |
|--------|--------|
| cast | center |
| cap | cent |
| carpet | city |
| car | |
| can | |
| cart | |

**Both Hard and Soft**
circus    circle

41

**Sounds of c and g**

Consonants **c** and **g** each have two sounds. Listen for the soft **c** sound in **pencil**. Listen for the hard **c** sound in **cup**.

Listen for the soft **g** sound in **giant**. Listen for the hard **g** sound in **goat**. C and **g** usually have the soft sound when they are followed by **e**, **i**, or **y**.

Directions: Say the name of each picture. Listen for the sound of **c** or **g**. Then, read the words in each list. Circle the words that have that sound of **c** or **g**.

Hard c — cup
car, race
city, rice
cone, can

Soft c — pencil
cage, cane
face, cent
ice, cube

Hard g — goat
good, magic
dragon, gum
stage, gentle

Soft g — giant
garden, gem
page, giraffe
gas, gorilla

42

**Hard and Soft c and g**

Directions: Underline the letter that follows the **c** or **g** in each word. Write **hard** if the word has the hard **c** or hard **g** sound. Write **soft** if the word has the soft **c** or soft **g** sound.

| car | wagon | cup |
|-----|-------|-----|
| hard | hard | hard |
| pencil | gym | cot |
| soft | soft | hard |
| giant | gem | celery |
| soft | soft | soft |
| gum | cymbals | goat |
| hard | soft | hard |

43

**Kick It In!**

Directions: Write a vowel to complete each word below.

a  e  i  o  u

n e t

s o cks

p a ss

r u n

k i ck

44

**Short a Picture Match**

Directions: Cut out the cards. Read the words. Match the words and the pictures.

hat    van    bat    ham

bag    man    map    fan

45

**The Donkey's Tail**

Directions: Find the donkey tails with pictures whose names have the short **i** sound. Cut them out. Glue those tails onto the donkeys.

47

### Feed the Pup

**Directions:** Cut out the picture cards. Say the name of each picture. If the name has the sound of short **u**, glue the card in the pup's bowl.

**49**

### Short o Puzzles

**Directions:** Cut out the puzzle pieces. Match each picture with its name.

box

log

top

mop

fox

dog

**51**

### Super Silent e

Long vowel sounds have the same sound as their names. When a **Super Silent e** appears at the end of a word, you cannot hear it, but it makes the other vowel have a long sound. For example: **tub** has a **short** vowel sound, and **tube** has a **long** vowel sound.

**Directions:** Look at the following pictures. Decide if the word has a short or long vowel sound. Circle the correct word. Watch for the **Super Silent e!**

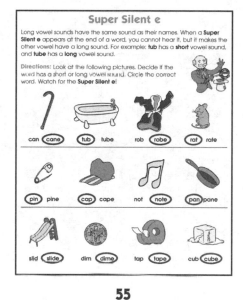

can (cane)   tub (tube)   rob (robe)   rat rate

(pin) pine   (cap) cape   not (note)   pan pane

slid (slide)   dim (dime)   tap (tape)   cub (cube)

**55**

### Long Vowels

Long vowel sounds have the same sound as their names. When a **Super Silent e** comes at the end of a word, you cannot hear it, but it changes the short vowel sound to a long vowel sound.

**Examples:** rope, skate, bee, pie, cute

**Directions:** Say the name of the pictures. Listen for the long vowel sounds. Write the missing long vowel sound under each picture.

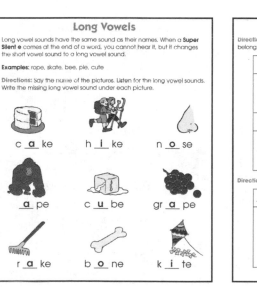

c **a** ke     h **i** ke     n **o** se

**a** pe     c **u** be     gr **a** pe

r **a** ke     b **o** ne     k **i** te

**56**

### Review

**Directions:** Read the words in each box. Cross out the word that does **not** belong.

| long vowels | short vowels |
|---|---|
| cube | man |
| rake | pet |
| me | fix |

| long vowels | short vowels |
|---|---|
| soap | cat |
| seed | pin |
| read | frog |

**Directions:** Write **short** or **long** to label the words in each box.

| **long** vowels | **short** vowels |
|---|---|
| hose | frog |
| take | hot |
| bead | sled |
| cube | lap |
| eat | block |
| see | sit |

**57**

### Tricky ar

When **r** follows a vowel, it changes the vowel's sound. Listen for the **ar** sound in **star**.

**Directions:** Color the pictures whose names have the **ar** sound.

star

**58**

## Write ar or or

Listen for the **or** sound in **horn**.

horn

**Directions:** Write **ar** or **or** to complete each word.

| | | |
|---|---|---|
| thorn | cart | forty **40** |
| stork | corn | harp |
| arm | star | porch |

**59**

## Mix and Match

The letters **ur**, **er**, and **ir** all have the same sound. Listen for the vowel sound in **surf**, **fern**, and **girl**.

surf    fern    girl

**Directions:** Draw a line from each word in the circle to the picture it names.

**30**

herd
turkey
clerk
thirty
purse
bird

**60**

## Rhyme Time

**Directions:** Cut out the words at the bottom of the page. Glue them beside the words they rhyme with.

| | | | |
|---|---|---|---|
| barn | yarn | corn | horn |
| purse | nurse | skirt | shirt |
| bird | herd | girl | curl |
| star | car | cork | fork |

**61**

## Write ur, er, and ir

**Directions:** Find a word from the box to name each picture. Write it on the line below the picture.

| turkey | clerk | dirt | fern |
|---|---|---|---|
| girl | herd | purple | surf | thirty |

| | | |
|---|---|---|
| fern | girl | surf |
| turkey | clerk | herd |
| dirt | purple | thirty **30** |

**63**

## Vowel Pairs ai and ay

You know that the letters **a__e** usually stand for the long **a** sound. The vowel pairs **ai** and **ay** can stand for the long **a** sound, too. Listen for the long **a** sound in **train** and **hay**.

**Directions:** Say the name of each picture below. Look at the vowel pair that stands for the long **a** sound. Under each picture, write the words from the box that have the same long **a** vowel pair.

| cage | chain | gate | gray |
|---|---|---|---|
| mail | pay | snail | skate |
| play | snake | stay | tail |

cake    train    hay

| cage | chain | gray |
|---|---|---|
| gate | mail | pay |
| skate | snail | play |
| snake | tail | stay |

**64**

## Vowel Pairs oa and ow

You know that the letters **o__e** and **oe** usually stand for the long **o** sound. The vowel pairs **oa** and **ow** can stand for the long **o** sound, too. Listen for the long **o** sound in **road** and **snow**.

**Directions:** Find and circle eight long **o** words. The words may go **across** or **down**. Beside each picture, write the words that use the same long **o** vowel pair.

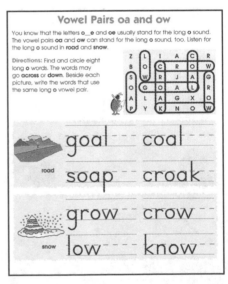

```
Z  L  I  A  C  R
B  O  W  C  R  O  W
S  O  G  R  J  A  G  R
O  A  P  A  G  X  O
P  A  K  N  O  W
```

road

| goal | coal |
|---|---|
| soap | croak |

snow

| grow | crow |
|---|---|
| low | know |

**65**

## Vowel Pair ui

You know that the letters **u_e** and **ue** usually stand for the long **u** sound. The vowel pair **ui** can stand for the long **u** sound, too. Listen for the long **u** sound in **cruise**.

**Directions:** Circle the name of the picture. Then, write the name on the line.

cruise

| mall, male, **mule** | sun, **Sue**, say | **fruit**, flat, frame |
|---|---|---|
| **mule** | **Sue** | **fruit** |
| sun, sit, **suit** | **cubes**, cubs, caves | **juice**, juice, just |
| **suit** | **cubes** | **juice** |
| fly, **flute**, fleece | globe, gull, **glue** | **blue**, black, ball |
| **flute** | **glue** | **blue** |

**66**

## Vowel Pair ie

You know that the letters **i_e** usually stand for the long **i** sound. The vowel pair **ie** can stand for the long **i** sound, too. Listen for the long **i** sound in **butterflies**.

**Directions:** Write **i_e** or **ie** to complete each word. Draw a picture for one **i_e** word and one **ie** word.

butterflies

| dime | tie | flies |
|---|---|---|
| five | knife | tried |
| pie | tie | kite |

i_e picture | ie picture

**Pictures will vary.**

**67**

## Missing Vowel Pairs

**Directions:** Fill in the circle beside the missing vowel pair in each word.

| t__ | tr__ | sn__ |
|---|---|---|
| ● ie  ○ ay  ○ oa | ○ ow  ○ ui  ● ay | ● ow  ○ ie  ○ ay |
| ch__n | gr__ | r__d |
| ○ ie  ○ ui  ● ai | ○ oa  ● ay  ○ ie | ● oa  ○ ay  ○ ui |
| b__ | fl__s | s__t |
| ○ ai  ● ow  ○ ui | ● ai  ○ oa  ● ie | ● ui  ○ ay  ○ ie |

**68**

## Missing Vowel Pairs

**Directions:** Fill in the circle beside the missing vowel pair in each word.

| h__ | tr__n | s__p |
|---|---|---|
| ○ ui  ○ ow  ● ay | ○ oa  ● ai  ○ ie | ● oa  ○ ai  ○ ui |
| j__ce | p__ | cr__ |
| ○ ai  ● ui  ○ ie | ○ ui  ○ oa  ● ie | ○ ui  ○ ay  ● ow |
| g__t | fr__t | sn__l |
| ○ ai  ● oa  ○ ui | ● ai  ○ ow  ○ ui | ○ ow  ● ai  ○ ie |

**69**

## Vowel Pair ea

Some vowel pairs can stand for more than one sound. The vowel pair **ea** has the sound of long **e** in **team** and short **e** in **head**.

team          head

**Directions:** Say the name of each picture. Listen for the sound that **ea** stands for. Circle **Long e** or **Short e**. Then, color the pictures whose names have the short **e** sound.

| Long e / (Short e) | Long e / (Short e) | (Long e) / Short e |
|---|---|---|
| Long e / (Short e) | Long e / (Short e) | (Long e) / Short e |
| Long e / (Short e) | (Long e) / Short e | Long e / (Short e) |

**70**

## Vowel Pair oo

Listen for the difference between the sound of the vowel pair **oo** in **moon** and its sound in **book**.

moon          book

**Directions:** Say the name of the picture. Circle the picture of the moon or the book to show the sound of vowel pair **oo**.

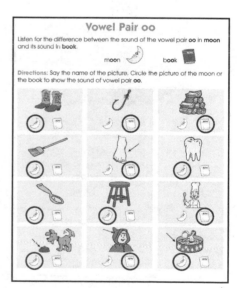

**71**

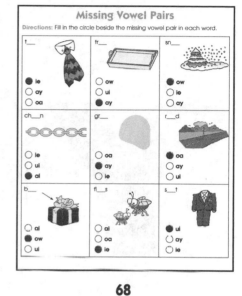

## Y as a Vowel

Y as a vowel can make two sounds. Y can make the long sound of **e** or the long sound of **i**.

**Directions:** Color the spaces:
**purple** – y sounds like **i**.
**yellow** – y sounds like **e**.

What is the picture? __Y__

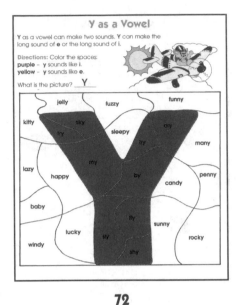

jelly · fuzzy · funny
kitty · sky · cry
try · sleepy · many
lazy · by · my
happy · by · penny
baby · candy
fly · sunny
windy · lucky · sly · rocky
shy

**72**

## A Fork in the Road

**Directions:** Write the words below on the correct "road."

sky    jelly    try    kitty    fly    my
fry    cry    funny    dry    penny
candy    by    sleepy    happy    lazy    baby
sly    fuzzy    shy    many    why

| | |
|---|---|
| jelly | sky |
| kitty | try |
| funny | fly |
| penny | my |
| candy | fry |
| sleepy | cry |
| happy | dry |
| lazy | by |
| baby | sly |
| fuzzy | shy |
| many | why |

Y sounds like **long e**.          Y sounds like **long i**.

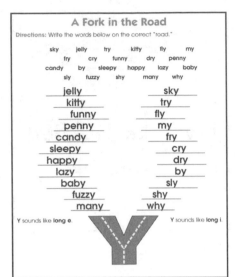

**73**

## Short and Long a e i o u

**Directions:** Color the correct pictures in each box.
˘ means short vowel sound     ¯ means long vowel sound

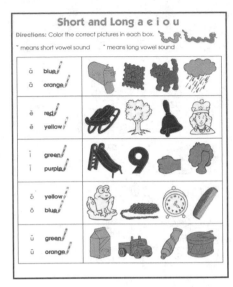

| ă blue | ā orange |
| ĕ red | ē yellow |
| ĭ green | ī purple |
| ŏ yellow | ō blue |
| ŭ green | ū orange |

**74**

## Review

**Directions:** Read the story. Fill in the blanks with words from the word box.

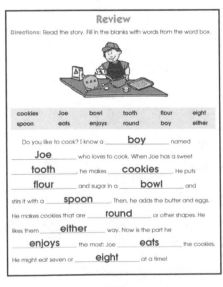

| cookies | Joe | bowl | tooth | flour | eight |
| spoon | eats | enjoys | round | boy | either |

Do you like to cook? I know a __boy__ named
__Joe__ who loves to cook. When Joe has a sweet
__tooth__, he makes __cookies__. He puts
__flour__ and sugar in a __bowl__ and
stirs it with a __spoon__. Then, he adds the butter and eggs.
He makes cookies that are __round__ or other shapes. He
likes them __either__ way. Now is the part he
__enjoys__ the most: Joe __eats__ the cookies.
He might eat seven or __eight__ at a time!

**75**

## Compound Your Effort

A **compound word** is made from two shorter words. An example of a compound word is **sandbox**, made from **sand** and **box**.

**Directions:** Find one word in the word box that goes with each of the words below to make a compound word. Write the compound words on the lines. Cross out each word that you use.

**Word Box**

board · room · thing · side · bag
writing · book · hopper · toe · ball
class · where · work · out · basket

1. coat __coatroom__
2. snow __snowball__
3. home __homework__
4. waste __wastebasket__
5. tip __tiptoe__
6. chalk __chalkboard__
7. note __notebook__
8. grass __grasshopper__
9. school __schoolbag__
10. with __without__

Look at the words in the word box that you did **not** use. Use those words to make your own compound words.

1. __outside__
2. __something__
3. __nowhere__
4. __classroom__
5. __handwriting__

**76**

## Word Magic

Maggie Magician announced, "One plus one equals one!" The audience giggled. So, Maggie put two words into a hat and waved her magic wand. When she reached into the hat, Maggie pulled out one word and a picture. "See," said Maggie. "I was right!"

**Directions:** Use the word box to help you write a compound word for each picture below.

ball · door · rain · star · shirt · bell · fish · shoe · book · foot · basket
bow · lace · box · stool · light · sun · cup · mail · tail · cake · worm

__shoelace__     __cupcake__     __doorbell__
__basketball__   __mailbox__     __footstool__
__rainbow__      __shirttail__   __starfish__
__bookworm__     __sunlight__

**77**

## Mixing a Compound

| sometimes | downtown | girlfriend |
| everybody | maybe | myself | lunchbox |
| baseball | outside | today |

**Directions:** Write the correct compound word on the line. Then, use the numbered letters to solve the code.

1. Opposite of inside — o u t s i d e
2. Another word for *me* — m y s e l f
3. A girl who is a friend — g i r l f r i e n d
4. Not yesterday or tomorrow, but . . . — t o d a y
5. All of the people — e v e r y b o d y
6. A sport — b a s e b a l l
7. The main part of a town — d o w n t o w n
8. Not always, just . . . — s o m e t i m e s
9. A box for carrying your lunch — l u n c h b o x
10. Perhaps or might — m a y b e

W o n d e r f u l   Y o u
f o u n d   t h e
r i g h t   s o l u t i o n !

**78**

## Prefix re

A **prefix** is a word part. It is added to the beginning of a base word to change the base word's meaning. The prefix **re** means "again."

**Example:** **Refill** means "to fill again."

**Directions:** Look at the pictures. Read the base words. Add the prefix **re** to the base word to show that the action is being done again. Write your new word on the line.

read — reread
write — rewrite
paint — repaint
use — reuse
build — rebuild
pay — repay

**79**

## Prefixes un and dis

The prefixes **un** and **dis** mean "not" or "the opposite of."

**Unlocked** means "not locked."

**Dismount** is the opposite of "mount."

**Directions:** Look at the pictures. Circle the word that tells about the picture. Then, write the word on the line.

tied — (untied) / untied
like — (dislike) / dislike
happy — unhappy / (happy)
obey — (obey) / disobey
safe — (unsafe) / unsafe
honest — (dishonest) / dishonest

**80**

## Suffixes ful, less, ness, ly

A **suffix** is a word part that is added at the end of a base word to change the base word's meaning. Look at the suffixes below.

The suffix **ful** means "full of." **Cheerful** means "full of cheer."

The suffix **less** means "without." **Cloudless** means "without clouds."

The suffix **ness** means "a state of being." **Darkness** means "being dark."

The suffix **ly** means "in this way." **Slowly** means "in a slow way."

**Directions:** Add the suffixes to the base words to make new words.

care + ful = careful
pain + less = painless
brave + ly = bravely
sad + ly = sadly
sick + ness = sickness

**81**

## Suffixes and Meanings

**Remember:** The suffix **ful** means "full of."

The suffix **less** means "without."

The suffix **ness** means "a state of being."

The suffix **ly** means "in this way." The sun shines **brightly**.

**Directions:** Write the word that matches the meaning.

without pain — painless
in a quick way — quickly
in a neat way — neatly
without fear — fearless
full of grace — graceful
the state of being soft — softness
the state of being sick — sickness
in a glad way — gladly

**82**

## Suffixes er and est

Suffixes **er** and **est** can be used to compare. Use **er** when you compare two things. Use **est** when you compare more than two things.

**Example:** The puppy is smaller than its mom.
This puppy is the smallest puppy in the litter.

**Directions:** Add the suffixes to the base words to make words that compare.

| Base Word | + er | + est |
| --- | --- | --- |
| 1. loud | louder | loudest |
| 2. old | older | oldest |
| 3. neat | neater | neatest |
| 4. fast | faster | fastest |
| 5. kind | kinder | kindest |
| 6. tall | taller | tallest |

**83**

## Scale the Synonym Slope

**Synonyms** are words that have almost the same meaning. **Tired** and **sleepy** are synonyms. **Talk** and **speak** are synonyms.

**Directions:** Read the word. Find its synonym on the hill. Write the synonym on the line.

1. glad — happy
2. little — small
3. begin — start
4. above — over
5. damp — wet
6. large — big

(hill words: wet, big, happy, over, small, start)

**84**

## Synonym Match

**Directions:** Look at the pictures. Read the words in the box. Write two synonyms you could use to tell about each picture.

rocks  start  road  begin  street  stones  sad  unhappy

sad
unhappy
road
street

rocks
stones
start
begin

**85**

## Almost the Same!

**Directions:** Write a word that has almost the same meaning as the **boldfaced** word. Use the word list for clues.

Hey, you're *large!*
And you're *big!*

| Word List | | |
|---|---|---|
| itchy | fortress | phantom |
| instructor | job | difficult |

1. My **teacher** is very smart!  instructor
2. I don't like that sweater. It is too **scratchy**.  itchy
3. My teacher gave a very **hard** test in math.  difficult
4. The prince lived in a **castle**.  fortress
5. Everyone has a **task** to do in my house.  job
6. The **ghost** at the fun house was so scary!  phantom

**86**

## Bored Belinda!

Belinda is bored with using the same words all the time. Help her figure out a new word for the **boldfaced** words in each sentence.

**Directions:** Read each sentence and then circle the correct new word below.

I hope my grandma will like this **gift**.
(present)  toaster

I always **laugh** when I watch my silly kitten.
(chuckle)  worry

My friend loves to **talk** on the telephone.
draw  (chat)

The little boy was **charming** to his grandparents.
(delightful)  naughty

Can you please **sew** this fabric together?
hitch  (stitch)

**87**

## We Go Together!

**Directions:** Circle the two words in each line that have almost the same meaning.

1. (gooey)  (sticky)  hard
2. slow  (hurry)  (rush)
3. (slope)  (hill)  sled
4. (stop)  red  (end)
5. treat  (pledge)  (promise)
6. (piece)  (bit)  pie
7. excuse  (easy)  (simple)
8. (complete)  (whole)  pile

**88**

## Amazing Antonyms

**Antonyms** are words that have opposite meanings. **Old** and **new** are antonyms. **Laugh** and **cry** are antonyms, too.

**Directions:** Below each word, write its antonym. Use words from the word box.

down  go  left  sad  dry

stop — go
happy — sad
right — left
up — down
wet — dry

**89**

## Who's Afraid?

Help Frog and Toad escape from the snake.

**Directions:** Read the two words in each space. If the words are antonyms, color the space **green**. Do not color the other spaces.

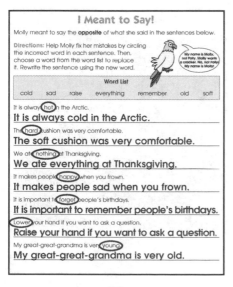

---

## Antonyms Are Opposites!

**Directions:** Look at the words on the balloons. Write an antonym to replace the word in the box for each sentence.

| cold | Summers in California are _____ **hot** _____. |
| slow | Cheetahs run very _____ **fast** _____. |
| tame | The gorillas in the jungle are _____ **wild** _____. |
| off | If you are cold, turn the heat _____ **on** _____. |
| good | Screaming in class is _____ **bad** _____. |
| pretty | The green troll was very _____ **ugly** _____. |
| huge | An ant is _____ **little** _____. |
| wet | The desert is very _____ **dry** _____. |

**91**

---

## Trading Places

**Directions:** In each sentence below, circle the incorrect word. Then, rewrite the sentence replacing the circled word with its **antonym** from the word list. The first one has been done for you.

| Word List | |
|---|---|
| happy | tall |
| full | tie |
| loud | lock |
| dangerous | |

Swimming in the dark was (safe).
**Swimming in the dark was dangerous.**

The gorilla's scream sounded very (quiet).
**The gorilla's scream sounded very loud.**

The packed room was (empty).
**The packed room was full.**

My 6-foot brother is very (short).
**My 6-foot brother is very tall.**

George, the funny clown, makes me very (unhappy). George, the **funny clown, makes me very happy.**

In an unsafe place, you should always (unlock) the door. **In a unsafe place, you should always lock the door.**

You need to (untie) your shoes before you run.
**You need to tie your shoes before you run.**

**92**

---

## I Meant to Say!

Molly meant to say the **opposite** of what she said in the sentences below.

**Directions:** Help Molly fix her mistakes by circling the incorrect word in each sentence. Then, choose a word from the word list to replace it. Rewrite the sentence using the new word.

| Word List | | | | | | |
|---|---|---|---|---|---|---|
| cold | sad | raise | everything | remember | old | soft |

It is always (hot) in the Arctic.
**It is always cold in the Arctic.**

The (hard) cushion was very comfortable.
**The soft cushion was very comfortable.**

We ate (nothing) at Thanksgiving.
**We ate everything at Thanksgiving.**

It makes people (happy) when you frown.
**It makes people sad when you frown.**

It is important to (forget) people's birthdays.
**It is important to remember people's birthdays.**

(Lower) your hand if you want to ask a question.
**Raise your hand if you want to ask a question.**

My great-great-grandma is very (young).
**My great-great-grandma is very old.**

**93**

---

## Antonym or Synonym?

**Directions:** Use **yellow** to color the spaces that have word pairs that are **antonyms**. Use **blue** to color the spaces that have word pairs that are **synonyms**.

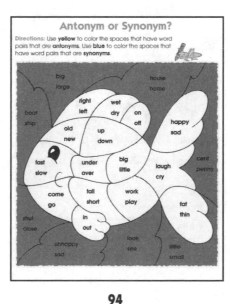

**94**

---

## Contractions

A **contraction** is a word made up of two words joined together with one or more letters left out. An **apostrophe** is used in place of the missing letters.

**Examples:** I am—**I'm**
do not—**don't**
that is—**that's**

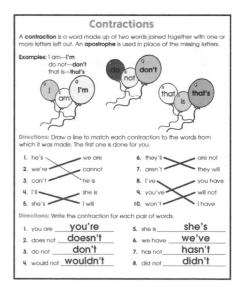

**Directions:** Draw a line to match each contraction to the words from which it was made. The first one is done for you.

| | | | | | |
|---|---|---|---|---|---|
| 1. he's | we are | 6. they'll | are not |
| 2. we're | cannot | 7. aren't | they will |
| 3. can't | he is | 8. I've | you have |
| 4. I'll | she is | 9. you've | will not |
| 5. she's | I will | 10. won't | I have |

**Directions:** Write the contraction for each pair of words.

| | | | | |
|---|---|---|---|---|
| 1. you are | **you're** | 5. she is | **she's** |
| 2. does not | **doesn't** | 6. we have | **we've** |
| 3. do not | **don't** | 7. has not | **hasn't** |
| 4. would not | **wouldn't** | 8. did not | **didn't** |

**95**

---

## Something Is Missing!

doesn't · it's · she's
don't · aren't · who's · he's
didn't · that's · isn't

**Directions:** Write the correct contraction for each set of words. Then, circle the letter that was left out when the contraction was made.

1. he is — **he's**
2. are not — **aren't**
3. do not — **don't**
4. who is — **who's**
5. is not — **isn't**
6. did not — **didn't**
7. it is — **it's**
8. she is — **she's**
9. does not — **doesn't**
10. that is — **that's**

**Directions:** Write the missing contraction on the line.

1. **She's** on her way to school.
2. There **isn't** enough time to finish the story.
3. Do you think **it's** too long?
4. We **aren't** going to the party.
5. Donna **doesn't** like the movie.
6. **Who's** going to try for a part in the play?
7. Bob said **he's** going to run in the big race.
8. They **don't** know how to bake a cake.
9. Tom **didn't** want to go skating on Saturday.
10. Look. **that's** where they found the lost watch.

**96**

## Highlight Happy!

**Highlighting** is a strategy that will help you with your reading. When you highlight something, you use a light-colored marker to color over a special word or words that you want to remember.

### Highlighting means you...

**Directions:** Follow the directions to highlight words in the sentences below.

1. Highlight three things you might find in the ocean.

   There are many creatures that live in the ocean. If you are lucky, you might see a whale or a dolphin in the ocean. If you are unlucky, you might find a stingray or even a shark.

2. Highlight five things you should bring to the beach.

   Spending the day at the beach can be lots of fun. However, you must remember to bring sun block and a towel, a hat, sandals, a towel and a snack.

**97**

## Tooth Tales, cont.

**Directions:** Answer the questions from the story about your teeth.

What are your teeth made of? **enamel**

What is the hardest material in your body? **enamel**
Highlight where you found the answer.

How many different types of teeth are in your mouth? **four**
Highlight where you found the answer.

What are your two very pointy teeth called? **canines**
Highlight where you found the answer.

What teeth are used for grinding food? **molars**
(Hint: The Tooth Fairy likes this type of tooth!)
Highlight where you found the answer.

How many teeth do adults have? **thirty-two**
Highlight where you found the answer.

What teeth are used for biting? **incisors**
Highlight where you found the answer.

How many molars do people have? **twelve**
Highlight where you found the answer.

**99**

## The World's Greatest Tree House!

**Directions:** Create the world's greatest tree house by following the directions below to finish the picture. Use crayons to draw or color each part as indicated.

**Pictures will vary.**

1. Draw a super cool clubhouse door with a special doorknocker.
2. Draw windows (any shape!) and curtains for the windows.
3. Draw a ladder leading up to the tree house.
4. Draw a sign over the door of the tree house.
5. Draw a swing hanging from the tree.
6. Draw two children using the tree house.

**Extra! Extra! Read All About It!**

Write a story about this tree house. Does anyone live there? Was it hard to build? Is it used for a secret club or does an entire family live there?

**Answers will vary.**

**100**

## Clue Caper!

**Directions:** Read the clues below. Write each child's name under the correct picture. Color the hats using the following clues.

Anna · Talia · Sara · Kessia

- Anna is tall and wearing a green top hat. There is a red baseball cap on top of her top hat!
- Sara is short and wearing a blue polka dotted hat.
- Talia has long hair and is standing between Anna and Sara. Talia is wearing a pretty ribbon in her hair with a flower on it.
- Kessia is standing next to Sara. She is wearing a white baker's hat with a purple veil!

How many hats do you count on the page? **4**

**101**

## Something's Fruity!

**Directions:** Find and circle **twelve** things that are wrong with this picture.

**102**

## Make the Touchdown!

**Directions:** Read the directions. Draw a line as you move from space to space.

1. Start at the football player running with the football.
2. Go up 2 spaces.
3. Go right 3 spaces. Oops!
4. Now, go down 3 spaces.
5. Hurry and go left 1 space.
6. Turn and go down 2 spaces.
7. Now, quickly turn right and go 3 spaces.
8. You were almost tackled. Go up 3 spaces.
9. Move quickly to the right 1 space.
10. Hurray! You made the touchdown!

**Directions:** Draw a brown football under the goalpost.

**103**

## Coach's Call

**Directions:** Follow the directions to draw and color the football player's uniform.

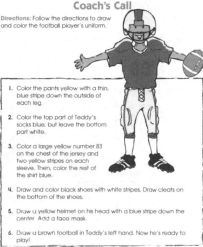

1. Color the pants yellow with a thin, blue stripe down the outside of each leg.
2. Color the top part of Teddy's socks blue, but leave the bottom part white.
3. Color a large yellow number 83 on the chest of the jersey and two yellow stripes on each sleeve. Then, color the rest of the shirt blue.
4. Draw and color black shoes with white stripes. Draw cleats on the bottom of the shoes.
5. Draw a yellow helmet on his head with a blue stripe down the center. Add a face mask.
6. Draw a brown football in Teddy's left hand. Now he's ready to play!

**104**

## Game Story

**Directions:** Put the basketball story in order. Write the numbers 1–5 on the blanks to show when each event happened.

4. At the end of the regulation game, the score was tied.
1. The teams warmed up before the game.
3. The score at the half was Cougars, 25; Lions, 20.
2. Kim made the first basket of the game.
5. When the overtime ended, the Lions had won the game 50–49.

**105**

## Story Sequence

Look at picture number 4. What do you think happened before Donna went to the beach? What might happen when she is at the beach?

**Directions:** You get to decide how the story will go from beginning to end. Write a number in the empty square in each of the other pictures. Choose any number from 1 through 7 (except 4). Number 1 will be what happened first. Number 7 will be what you think happened last.

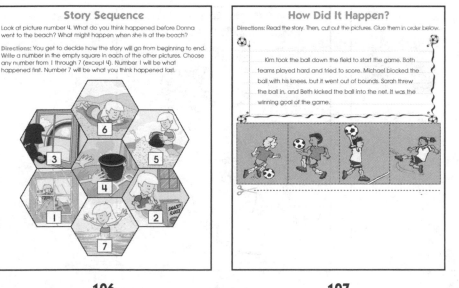

**106**

## How Did It Happen?

**Directions:** Read the story. Then, cut out the pictures. Glue them in order below.

Kim took the ball down the field to start the game. Both teams played hard and tried to score. Michael blocked the ball with his knees, but it went out of bounds. Sarah threw the ball in, and Beth kicked the ball into the net. It was the winning goal of the game.

**107**

## Story Sequence

Look at picture number 4. What do you think happened before Danny went to the amusement park? What might happen when he is at the amusement park?

**Directions:** You get to decide how the story will go from beginning to end. Write a number in the empty square in each of the other pictures. Choose any number from 1 through 7 (except 4). Number 1 will be what happened first. Number 7 will be what you think happened last.

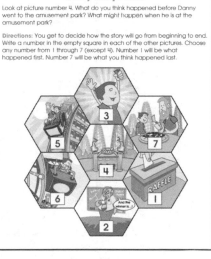

**109**

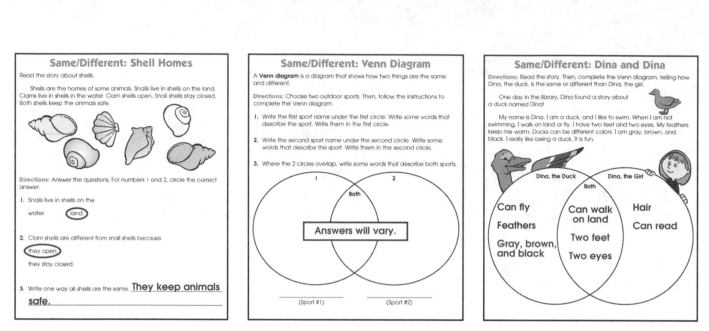

### Same/Different: Shell Homes

Read the story about shells.

Shells are the homes of some animals. Snails live in shells on the land. Clams live in shells in the water. Clam shells open. Snail shells stay closed. Both shells keep the animals safe.

**Directions:** Answer the questions. For numbers 1 and 2, circle the correct answer.

1. Snails live in shells on the
   water.  (land.)

2. Clam shells are different from snail shells because
   (they open.)
   they stay closed.

3. Write one way all shells are the same. **They keep animals safe.**

**110**

### Same/Different: Venn Diagram

A **Venn diagram** is a diagram that shows how two things are the same and different.

**Directions:** Choose two outdoor sports. Then, follow the instructions to complete the Venn diagram.

1. Write the first sport name under the first circle. Write some words that describe the sport. Write them in the first circle.

2. Write the second sport name under the second circle. Write some words that describe the sport. Write them in the second circle.

3. Where the 2 circles overlap, write some words that describe both sports.

|   1   | Both |   2   |

**Answers will vary.**

(Sport #1)        (Sport #2)

**111**

### Same/Different: Dina and Dina

**Directions:** Read the story. Then, complete the Venn diagram, telling how Dina, the duck, is the same or different than Dina, the girl.

One day in the library, Dina found a story about a duck named Dina!

My name is Dina. I am a duck, and I like to swim. When I am not swimming, I walk on land or fly. I have two feet and two eyes. My feathers keep me warm. Ducks can be different colors. I am gray, brown, and black. I really like being a duck. It is fun.

Dina, the Duck        Both        Dina, the Girl

Can fly | Can walk on land | Hair
Feathers | Two feet | Can read
Gray, brown, and black | Two eyes |

**112**

### Same/Different: Ann and Lee Have Fun

**Directions:** Read about Ann and Lee. Then, write how they are the same and different in the Venn diagram.

Ann and Lee like to play ball. They like to jump rope. Lee likes to play a card game called "Old Maid." Ann likes to play a card game called "Go Fish."

Ann | Both | Lee

Play "Go Fish" | Jump rope / Play ball | Play "Old Maid"

**113**

### Same/Different: Cats and Tigers

**Directions:** Read about cats and tigers. Then, complete the Venn diagram, telling how they are the same and different.

Tigers are a kind of cat. Pet cats and tigers both have fur. Pet cats are small and tame. Tigers are large and wild.

Pet Cats | Both | Tigers

Small | Cats | Large Wild
Tame | Fur |

**114**

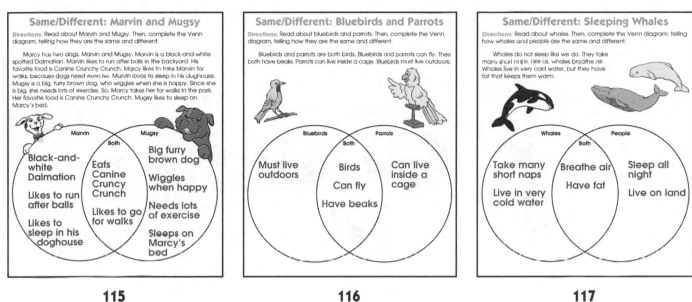

### Same/Different: Marvin and Mugsy

**Directions:** Read about Marvin and Mugsy. Then, complete the Venn diagram, telling how they are the same and different.

Marcy has two dogs, Marvin and Mugsy. Marvin is a black-and-white spotted Dalmatian. Marvin likes to run after balls in the backyard. His favorite food is Canine Crunchy Crunch. Marcy likes to take Marvin for walks, because dogs need exercise. Marvin loves to sleep in his doghouse. Mugsy is a big, furry brown dog, who wiggles when she is happy. Since she is big, she needs lots of exercise. So, Marcy takes her for walks in the park. Her favorite food is Canine Crunchy Crunch. Mugsy likes to sleep on Marcy's bed.

**Marvin**
- Black-and-white Dalmation
- Likes to run after balls
- Likes to sleep in his doghouse

**Both**
- Eats Canine Cruncy Crunch
- Likes to go for walks

**Mugsy**
- Big furry brown dog
- Wiggles when happy
- Needs lots of exercise
- Sleeps on Marcy's bed

**115**

### Same/Different: Bluebirds and Parrots

**Directions:** Read about bluebirds and parrots. Then, complete the Venn diagram, telling how they are the same and different.

Bluebirds and parrots are both birds. Bluebirds and parrots can fly. They both have beaks. Parrots can live inside a cage. Bluebirds must live outdoors.

**Bluebirds**
- Must live outdoors

**Both**
- Birds
- Can fly
- Have beaks

**Parrots**
- Can live inside a cage

**116**

### Same/Different: Sleeping Whales

**Directions:** Read about whales. Then, complete the Venn diagram, telling how whales and people are the same and different.

Whales do not sleep like we do. They take many short naps. Like us, whales breathe air. Whales live in very cold water, but they have fat that keeps them warm.

**Whales**
- Take many short naps
- Live in very cold water

**Both**
- Breathe air
- Have fat

**People**
- Sleep all night
- Live on land

**117**

### Running! Jumping! Throwing!

To be a strong athlete in track and field events you must be good at running, jumping, and throwing. Many track and field words are listed below.

**Directions:** Write the words under the correct track and field event.

| Running | Jumping | Throwing |
|---|---|---|
| lap | pole vault | discus |
| track | broad jump | javelin |
| cross country | hurdles | shot put |
| running | triple jump | hammer |
| relay | long jump | |
| baton | | |

lap    javelin    high jump    baton    relay    long jump
discus    cross country    broad jump    shot put
track    pole vault    hurdles    triple jump    hammer

**118**

### Classifying

Sometimes, you want to put things in groups. One way to put things in groups is to sort them by how they are alike. When you put things together that are alike in some way, you classify them.

You can classify the things in your room. In one group, you can put toys and fun things. In the other group, you can put things that you wear.

**Directions:** Look at the words on the bedroom door. Put the toys and playthings in the toy box. Put the things you wear in the dresser drawers.

doll
truck
ball
paints
book
teddy bear

hat
shirt
mitten
shoe
shorts
sock

hat
doll
shirt
truck
mitten
shoe
ball
paints
shorts
sock
book
teddy bear

**119**

## Shrews

A shrew (*shroo*) is a small animal. It looks like a mouse with a sharp, pointed nose. This animal is sometimes mistaken for a mouse. It has tiny eyes and ears. Its body is covered with short, dark hair. A shrew moves very fast. A shrew eats all day. The shrew's long, pointed nose can fit into tiny holes to find the insects and worms it eats.

The shrew lives in fields, woodlands, gardens, and marshes. Shrews are harmless to humans. They are helpful in gardens because they eat grubs and other insects. The smallest shrew weighs as little as a United States penny.

**Directions:** After reading about the shrew, put an **X** on one word that does **not** belong in each group.

1. small ~~large~~ tiny
2. bugs ~~corn~~ insects
3. move run ~~sleep~~
4. bird mouse ~~dig~~
5. fast quick ~~water~~
6. sharp pointed ~~hair~~
7. nickel penny ~~run~~
8. garden fields ~~sit~~

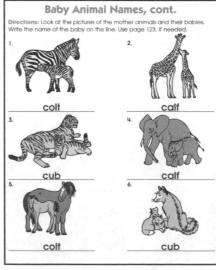

## Birds

There are <u>many</u> kinds of birds. The cardinal is a <u>red</u> bird. The cardinal lays <u>three</u> or <u>four</u> eggs. The brown-headed cowbird is <u>black</u> with a <u>brown</u> head. The hummingbird is a very <u>small</u> bird. It lays <u>two</u> eggs. The bald eagle is a <u>large</u> bird. It is brown with a <u>white</u> head. The bald eagle lays from <u>one</u> to <u>four</u> eggs. Bluebirds are <u>blue</u> with <u>orange</u> or light <u>blue</u> breasts. The bluebird lays up to <u>six</u> eggs.

**Directions:** In the story above, the underlined words are called **adjectives**. Put these describing words in the nests where they belong.

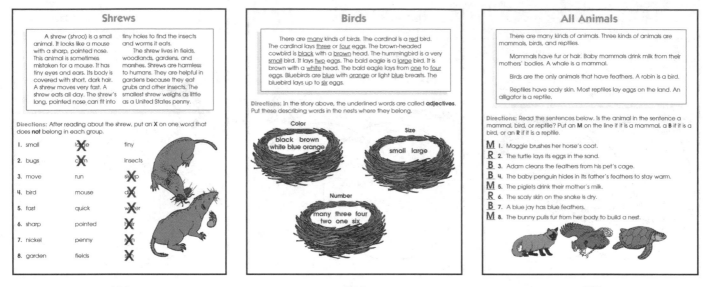

Color: black brown white blue orange

Size: small large

Number: many three four two one six

## All Animals

There are many kinds of animals. Three kinds of animals are mammals, birds, and reptiles.

Mammals have fur or hair. Baby mammals drink milk from their mothers' bodies. A whale is a mammal.

Birds are the only animals that have feathers. A robin is a bird.

Reptiles have scaly skin. Most reptiles lay eggs on the land. An alligator is a reptile.

**Directions:** Read the sentences below. Is the animal in the sentence a mammal, bird, or reptile? Put an **M** on the line if it is a mammal, a **B** if it is a bird, or an **R** if it is a reptile.

**M** 1. Maggie brushes her horse's coat.
**R** 2. The turtle lays its eggs in the sand.
**B** 3. Adam cleans the feathers from his pet's cage.
**B** 4. The baby penguin hides in its father's feathers to stay warm.
**M** 5. The piglets drink their mother's milk.
**R** 6. The scaly skin on the snake is dry.
**B** 7. A blue jay has blue feathers.
**M** 8. The bunny pulls fur from her body to build a nest.

## Baby Animal Names

Many animals are called special names when they are young. A baby deer is called a fawn. A baby cat is called a kitten.

Some young animals have the same name as other kinds of baby animals. A baby elephant is a calf. A baby whale is a calf. A baby giraffe is a calf. A baby cow is a calf.

Some baby animals are called cubs. A baby lion, a baby bear, a baby tiger, and a baby fox are all called cubs.

Some baby animals are called colts. A young horse is a colt. A baby zebra is a colt. A baby donkey is a colt.

**Directions:** Use the story about baby animal names to complete the chart below. Write the kind of animal that belongs with each special baby name.

| calf | cub | colt |
|------|------|------|
| elephant | lion | horse |
| whale | bear | zebra |
| giraffe | tiger | donkey |
| cow | fox | |

## Baby Animal Names, cont.

**Directions:** Look at the pictures of the mother animals and their babies. Write the name of the baby on the line. Use page 123. If needed.

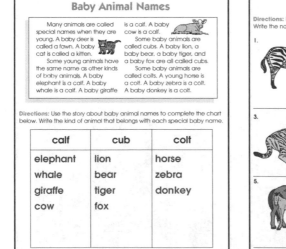

1. colt
2. calf
3. cub
4. calf
5. colt
6. cub

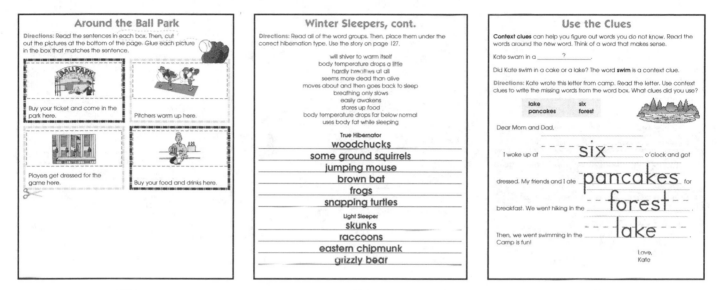

## Around the Ball Park

**Directions:** Read the sentences in each box. Then, cut out the pictures at the bottom of the page. Glue each picture in the box that matches the sentence.

Buy your ticket and come in the park here.

Pitchers warm up here.

Players get dressed for the game here.

Buy your food and drinks here.

**125**

## Winter Sleepers, cont.

**Directions:** Read all of the word groups. Then, place them under the correct hibernation type. Use the story on page 127.

will shiver to warm itself
body temperature drops a little
hardly breathes at all
seems more dead than alive
moves about and then goes back to sleep
breathing only slows
easily awakens
stores up food
body temperature drops far below normal
uses body fat while sleeping

**True Hibernator**
woodchucks
some ground squirrels
jumping mouse
brown bat
frogs
snapping turtles

**Light Sleeper**
skunks
raccoons
eastern chipmunk
grizzly bear

**128**

## Use the Clues

**Context clues** can help you figure out words you do not know. Read the words around the new word. Think of a word that makes sense.

Kate swam in a _____?_____.

Did Kate swim in a cake or a lake? The word **swim** is a context clue.

**Directions:** Kate wrote this letter from camp. Read the letter. Use context clues to write the missing words from the word box. What clues did you use?

| lake | six |
| pancakes | forest |

Dear Mom and Dad,

I woke up at **six** o'clock and got

dressed. My friends and I ate **pancakes** for

breakfast. We went hiking in the **forest**

Then, we went swimming in the **lake**
Camp is fun!

Love,
Kate

**129**

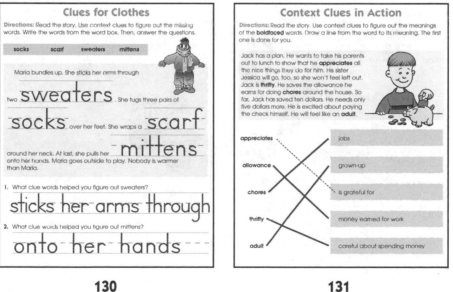

## Clues for Clothes

**Directions:** Read the story. Use context clues to figure out the missing words. Write the words from the word box. Then, answer the questions.

| socks | scarf | sweaters | mittens |

Maria bundles up. She sticks her arms through

two **sweaters**. She tugs three pairs of

**socks** over her feet. She wraps a **scarf**

around her neck. At last, she pulls her **mittens**
onto her hands. Maria goes outside to play. Nobody is warmer than Maria.

1. What clue words helped you figure out sweaters?

**sticks her arms through**

2. What clue words helped you figure out mittens?

**onto her hands**

**130**

## Context Clues in Action

**Directions:** Read the story. Use context clues to figure out the meanings of the **boldfaced** words. Draw a line from the word to its meaning. The first one is done for you.

Jack has a plan. He wants to take his parents out to lunch to show that he **appreciates** all the nice things they do for him. His sister Jessica will go, too, so she won't feel left out. Jack is **thrifty**. He saves the allowance he earns for doing **chores** around the house. So far, Jack has saved ten dollars. He needs only five dollars more. He is excited about paying the check himself. He will feel like an **adult**.

appreciates          jobs

allowance           grown-up

chores            is grateful for

thrifty           money earned for work

adult          careful about spending money

**131**

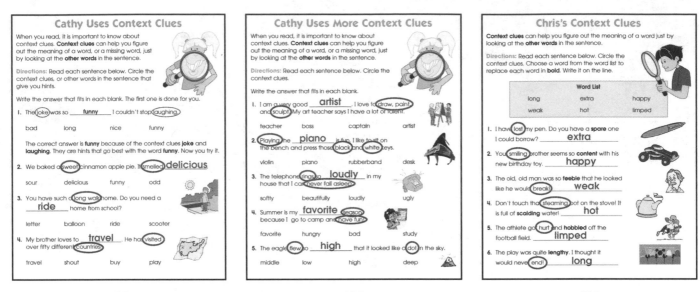

### Cathy Uses Context Clues

When you read, it is important to know about context clues. **Context clues** can help you figure out the meaning of a word, or a missing word, just by looking at the **other words** in the sentence.

**Directions:** Read each sentence below. Circle the context clues, or other words in the sentence that give you hints.

Write the answer that fits in each blank. The first one is done for you.

1. The ⟨joke⟩ was so ___funny___ I couldn't stop ⟨laughing⟩.

    bad          long          nice          funny

The correct answer is **funny** because of the context clues **joke** and **laughing**. They are hints that go best with the word **funny**. Now you try it.

2. We baked a ⟨sweet⟩ cinnamon apple pie. It ⟨smelled⟩ ___delicious___.

    sour       delicious       funny       odd

3. You have such a ⟨long walk⟩ home. Do you need a ___ride___ home from school?

    letter       balloon       ride       scooter

4. My brother loves to ___travel___. He has ⟨visited⟩ over fifty different ⟨countries⟩.

    travel       shout       buy       play

**132**

### Cathy Uses More Context Clues

When you read, it is important to know about context clues. **Context clues** can help you figure out the meaning of a word, or a missing word, just by looking at the **other words** in the sentence.

**Directions:** Read each sentence below. Circle the context clues.

Write the answer that fits in each blank.

1. I am a very good ___artist___. I love to ⟨draw, paint,⟩ and ⟨sculpt⟩. My art teacher says I have a lot of talent.

    teacher       boss       captain       artist

2. ⟨Playing⟩ the ___piano___ is fun. I like to sit on the bench and press those ⟨black⟩ and ⟨white⟩ ⟨keys⟩.

    violin       piano       rubberband       desk

3. The telephone ⟨rings⟩ so ___loudly___ in my house that I can ⟨never fall asleep⟩.

    softly       beautifully       loudly       ugly

4. Summer is my ___favorite___ ⟨season⟩ because I go to camp and ⟨have fun⟩.

    favorite       hungry       bad       study

5. The eagle ⟨flew⟩ so ___high___ that it looked like a ⟨dot⟩ in the sky.

    middle       low       high       deep

**133**

### Chris's Context Clues

**Context clues** can help you figure out the meaning of a word just by looking at the **other words** in the sentence.

**Directions:** Read each sentence below. Circle the context clues. Choose a word from the word list to replace each word in **bold**. Write it on the line.

| Word List | | |
|---|---|---|
| long | extra | happy |
| weak | hot | limped |

1. I have ⟨lost⟩ my pen. Do you have a **spare** one I could borrow? ___extra___

2. Your ⟨smiling⟩ brother seems so **content** with his new birthday toy. ___happy___

3. The old, old man was so **feeble** that he looked like he would ⟨break⟩! ___weak___

4. Don't touch that ⟨steaming⟩ pot on the stove! It is full of **scalding** water! ___hot___

5. The athlete got ⟨hurt⟩ and **hobbled** off the football field. ___limped___

6. The play was quite **lengthy**. I thought it would never ⟨end⟩! ___long___

**134**

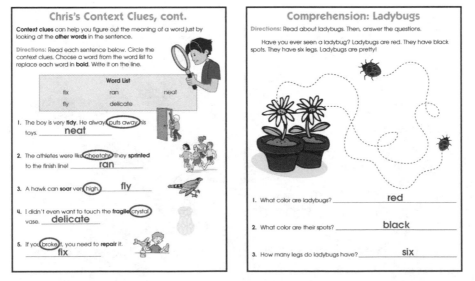

### Chris's Context Clues, cont.

**Context clues** can help you figure out the meaning of a word just by looking at the **other words** in the sentence.

**Directions:** Read each sentence below. Circle the context clues. Choose a word from the word list to replace each word in **bold**. Write it on the line.

| Word List | | |
|---|---|---|
| fix | ran | neat |
| fly | delicate | |

1. The boy is very **tidy**. He always ⟨puts away⟩ his toys. ___neat___

2. The athletes were like ⟨cheetahs⟩. They **sprinted** to the finish line! ___ran___

3. A hawk can **soar** very ⟨high⟩. ___fly___

4. I didn't even want to touch the **fragile** ⟨crystal⟩ vase. ___delicate___

5. If you ⟨broke⟩ it, you need to **repair** it. ___fix___

**135**

### Comprehension: Ladybugs

**Directions:** Read about ladybugs. Then, answer the questions.

Have you ever seen a ladybug? Ladybugs are red. They have black spots. They have six legs. Ladybugs are pretty!

1. What color are ladybugs? ___red___

2. What color are their spots? ___black___

3. How many legs do ladybugs have? ___six___

**136**

## Making History

**Directions:** Read the story and answer the questions about Mark McGwire.

On September 8, 1998, Mark McGwire, #25 of the St. Louis Cardinals, hit his 62nd home run of the season. He set a new record for home runs hit in a single baseball season. On September 27, 1998, McGwire hit home runs 69 and 70 in St. Louis, Missouri, to become baseball's all-time single season "Home Run King."

1. How many home runs did Mark McGwire hit in 1998?
   **62**

2. What team does he play for? **St. Louis Cardinals**

3. What number is on Mark McGwire's jersey? **25**

4. On what date did he hit home run 62?
   **September 8, 1998**

5. Why is Mark McGwire known as the "Home Run King?"
   **Because he hit more home runs in a single season than any other player.**

**137**

## Five Senses, cont.

**Directions:** Draw a line to match the sense to the body part that works with it.

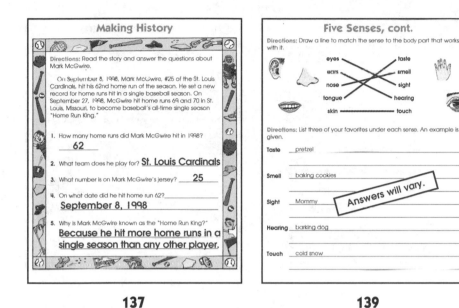

eyes — taste
ears — smell
nose — sight
tongue — hearing
skin — touch

**Directions:** List three of your favorites under each sense. An example is given.

| Taste | pretzel |
| Smell | baking cookies |
| Sight | Mommy |
| Hearing | barking dog |
| Touch | cold snow |

*Answers will vary.*

**139**

## Comprehension: Playing Store

**Directions:** Read about playing store. Then, answer the questions.

Tyson and his friends like to play store. They use boxes and cans. They line them up. Then, they put them in bags.

1. Circle the main idea:
   Tyson and his friends use boxes, cans, and bags to play store.
   You need bags to play store.

2. Circle your answer:
   Who likes to play store?
   all kids      some kids

3. Do you like to play store? **Answers will vary.**

**140**

## Comprehension: Playful Cats

**Directions:** Read about cats. Then, follow the instructions.

Cats make good pets. They like to play. They like to jump. They like to run. Do you?

Answers will vary.

1. Circle your answer:
   Cats make good _____.
   pets.
   friends.

2. Write three things cats like to do:
   **play**
   **jump**
   **run**

3. Think of a good name for a cat. Write it on the cat's tag.

**141**

## Comprehension: Types of Tops

The **main idea** is the most important point or idea in a story.

**Directions:** Read about tops. Then, answer the questions.

Tops come in all sizes. Some tops are made of wood. Some tops are made of tin. All tops do the same thing. They spin! Do you have a top?

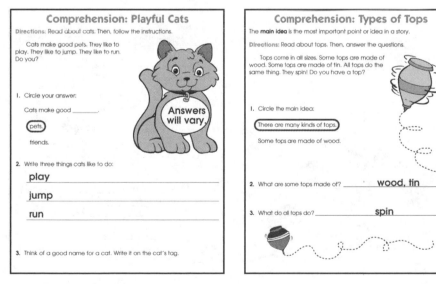

1. Circle the main idea:
   There are many kinds of tops.
   Some tops are made of wood.

2. What are some tops made of? **wood, tin**

3. What do all tops do? **spin**

**142**

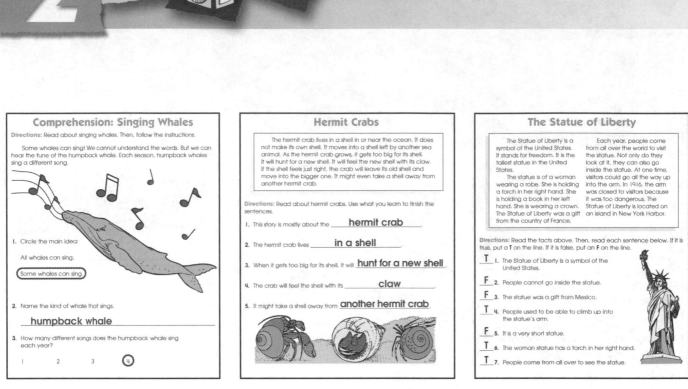
## Comprehension: Singing Whales

**Directions:** Read about singing whales. Then, follow the instructions.

Some whales can sing! We cannot understand the words. But we can hear the tune of the humpback whale. Each season, humpback whales sing a different song.

1. Circle the main idea:

   All whales can sing.

   (Some whales can sing.)

2. Name the kind of whale that sings.

   humpback whale

3. How many different songs does the humpback whale sing each year?

   1        2        3        ④

**143**

## Hermit Crabs

The hermit crab lives in a shell in or near the ocean. It does not make its own shell. It moves into a shell left by another sea animal. As the hermit crab grows, it gets too big for its shell. It will hunt for a new shell. It will feel the new shell with its claw. If the shell feels just right, the crab will leave its old shell and move into the bigger one. It might even take a shell away from another hermit crab.

**Directions:** Read about hermit crabs. Use what you learn to finish the sentences.

1. This story is mostly about the _____ hermit crab _____ .

2. The hermit crab lives _____ in a shell _____ .

3. When it gets too big for its shell, it will _____ hunt for a new shell _____ .

4. The crab will feel the shell with its _____ claw _____ .

5. It might take a shell away from _____ another hermit crab _____

**144**

## The Statue of Liberty

The Statue of Liberty is a symbol of the United States. It stands for freedom. It is the tallest statue in the United States.

The statue is of a woman wearing a robe. She is holding a torch in her right hand. She is holding a book in her left hand. She is wearing a crown. The Statue of Liberty was a gift from the country of France.

Each year, people come from all over the world to visit the statue. Not only do they look at it, they can also go inside the statue. At one time, visitors could go all the way up into the arm. In 1916, the arm was closed to visitors because it was too dangerous. The Statue of Liberty is located on an island in New York Harbor.

**Directions:** Read the facts above. Then, read each sentence below. If it is true, put a **T** on the line. If it is false, put an **F** on the line.

_T_ 1. The Statue of Liberty is a symbol of the United States.

_F_ 2. People cannot go inside the statue.

_F_ 3. The statue was a gift from Mexico.

_T_ 4. People used to be able to climb up into the statue's arm.

_F_ 5. It is a very short statue.

_T_ 6. The woman statue has a torch in her right hand.

_T_ 7. People come from all over to see the statue.

**145**

## Venus Flytraps

Many insects eat plants. There is one kind of plant that eats insects. It is the Venus flytrap. The Venus flytrap works like a trap. Each leaf is shaped like a circle. The circle is in two parts. When the leaf closes, the two parts fold together. The leaf has little spikes all the way around it. Inside the leaf, there are little hairs. If an insect touches the little hairs, the two sides of the Venus flytrap leaf will clap together. The spikes will trap the insect inside. The Venus flytrap will then eat the insect.

**Directions:** Read about the Venus flytrap. Then, read each sentence below. If it is true, circle the sentence. If it is **not** true, draw an **X** on the sentence.

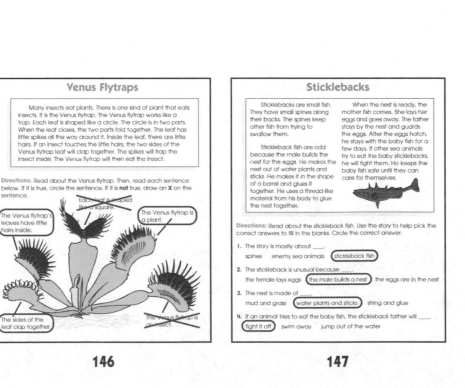

Each leaf is shaped like a square.

The Venus flytrap's leaves have little hairs inside.

The Venus flytrap is a plant.

The sides of the leaf clap together.

The Venus flytrap is an insect.

**146**

## Sticklebacks

Sticklebacks are small fish. They have small spines along their backs. The spines keep other fish from trying to swallow them.

Stickleback fish are odd because the male builds the nest for the eggs. He makes the nest out of water plants and sticks. He makes it in the shape of a barrel and glues it together. He uses a thread-like material from his body to glue the nest together.

When the nest is ready, the mother fish comes. She lays her eggs and goes away. The father stays by the nest and guards the eggs. After the eggs hatch, he stays with the baby fish for a few days. If other sea animals try to eat the baby sticklebacks, he will fight them. He keeps the baby fish safe until they can care for themselves.

**Directions:** Read about the stickleback fish. Use the story to help pick the correct answers to fill in the blanks. Circle the correct answer.

1. The story is mostly about ____.
   spines        enemy sea animals        (stickleback fish)

2. The stickleback is unusual because ____.
   the female lays eggs        (the male builds a nest)        the eggs are in the nest

3. The nest is made of ____.
   mud and grass        (water plants and sticks)        string and glue

4. If an animal tries to eat the baby fish, the stickleback father will ____.
   (fight it off)        swim away        jump out of the water

**147**

## Eagles

Eagles are large birds. They eat small animals such as mice and rabbits. Eagles make their nests in high places such as the tops of trees. Their nests are made of sticks, weeds, and dirt. Eagles can live in the same nest for many years.

The mother eagle lays one or two eggs each year. When she sits on the eggs, the father eagle brings her food. Baby eagles are called eaglets.

**Directions:** Read about eagles. Then, circle the correct ending to each sentence below.

1. Eagles are
   large dogs. (large birds.)

2. Eagles eat
   (small animals.)
   plants and trees.

3. Eagles
   build a nest each year.
   (live in the same nest for many years.)

4. The mother eagle lays
   (one or two eggs.)
   three or four eggs.

5. Baby eagles are called
   igloos. (eaglets.)

**148**

## Seals

Seals live in the oceans and on land. They eat different kinds of sea animals, such as fish, shrimp, squid, and krill. They are very good swimmers. They use their flippers to help them move in the water and on the land. They talk to each other by making barking sounds.

**Directions:** Read the facts above. Then, answer each question using complete sentences.

1. What do seals eat? __fish, shrimp, squid, krill__

2. For what do seals use their flippers? __to help them move in the water and on land__

3. Where do seals live? __in the oceans and on land__

4. How do seals talk? __by making barking sounds__

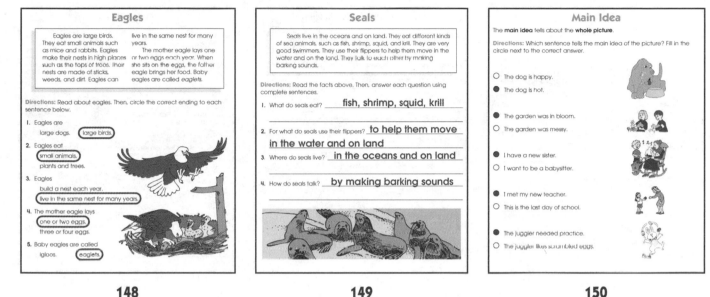

**149**

## Main Idea

The **main idea** tells about the **whole picture**.

**Directions:** Which sentence tells the main idea of the picture? Fill in the circle next to the correct answer.

○ The dog is happy.
● The dog is hot.

● The garden was in bloom.
○ The garden was messy.

● I have a new sister.
○ I want to be a babysitter.

● I met my new teacher.
○ This is the last day of school.

● The juggler needed practice.
○ The juggler likes scrambled eggs.

**150**

## Main Idea

The **main idea** tells about the **whole picture**.

**Directions:** Which sentence tells the main idea of the picture? Fill in the circle next to the correct answer.

● She saw a shooting star.
○ She likes to climb hills.
○ She likes to stay up late.

○ Skateboarding can be done anywhere.
○ Skateboarding is easy.
● Skateboarders should wear helmets.

● Grandpa is a great storyteller.
○ Grandpa is boring.
○ Grandpa is funny.

● Mom made me a birthday cake.
○ We ate ice cream.
○ I opened presents.

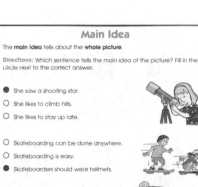

**151**

## What's the Main Idea?

The **main idea** tells about the **whole story**.

**Directions:** Read the story below.

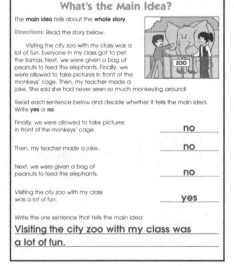

Visiting the city zoo with my class was a lot of fun. Everyone in my class got to pet the llamas. Next, we were given a bag of peanuts to feed the elephants. Finally, we were allowed to take pictures in front of the monkeys' cage. Then, my teacher made a joke. She said she had never seen so much monkeying around!

Read each sentence below and decide whether it tells the main idea. Write **yes** or **no**.

Finally, we were allowed to take pictures in front of the monkeys' cage. __no__

Then, my teacher made a joke. __no__

Next, we were given a bag of peanuts to feed the elephants. __no__

Visiting the city zoo with my class was a lot of fun. __yes__

Write the one sentence that tells the main idea:
__Visiting the city zoo with my class was a lot of fun.__

**152**

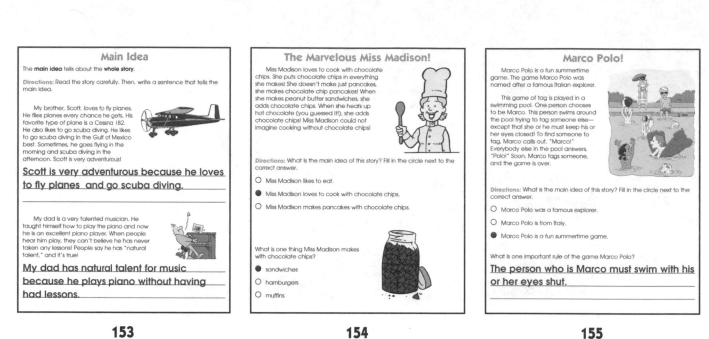

### Main Idea

The **main idea** tells about the **whole story**.

**Directions:** Read the story carefully. Then, write a sentence that tells the main idea.

My brother, Scott, loves to fly planes. He flies planes every chance he gets. His favorite type of plane is a Cessna 182. He also likes to go scuba diving. He likes to go scuba diving in the Gulf of Mexico best. Sometimes, he goes flying in the morning and scuba diving in the afternoon. Scott is very adventurous!

Scott is very adventurous because he loves to fly planes and go scuba diving.

My dad is a very talented musician. He taught himself how to play the piano and now he is an excellent piano player. When people hear him play, they can't believe he has never taken any lessons! People say he has "natural talent," and it's true!

My dad has natural talent for music because he plays piano without having had lessons.

**153**

### The Marvelous Miss Madison!

Miss Madison loves to cook with chocolate chips. She puts chocolate chips in everything she makes! She doesn't make just pancakes, she makes chocolate chip pancakes! When she makes peanut butter sandwiches, she adds chocolate chips. When she heats up hot chocolate (you guessed it!), she adds chocolate chips! Miss Madison could not imagine cooking without chocolate chips!

**Directions:** What is the main idea of this story? Fill in the circle next to the correct answer.

○ Miss Madison likes to eat.

● Miss Madison loves to cook with chocolate chips.

○ Miss Madison makes pancakes with chocolate chips.

What is one thing Miss Madison makes with chocolate chips?

● sandwiches

○ hamburgers

○ muffins

**154**

### Marco Polo!

Marco Polo is a fun summertime game. The game Marco Polo was named after a famous Italian explorer.

This game of tag is played in a swimming pool. One person chooses to be Marco. This person swims around the pool trying to tag someone else—except that she or he must keep his or her eyes closed! To find someone to tag, Marco calls out, "Marco!" Everybody else in the pool answers, "Polo!" Soon, Marco tags someone, and the game is over.

**Directions:** What is the main idea of this story? Fill in the circle next to the correct answer.

○ Marco Polo was a famous explorer.

○ Marco Polo is from Italy.

● Marco Polo is a fun summertime game.

What is one important rule of the game Marco Polo?

The person who is Marco must swim with his or her eyes shut.

**155**

### What's the Big Idea?

The **main idea** is the most important idea in a story. The main idea tells what happens.

**Directions:** Look at the pictures. Read the sentences. Circle **yes** if the sentence tells the main idea of the picture. Circle **no** if it does not. The first one is done for you.

The hat is too small. — no

The bear is afraid of the mouse. — yes

The bear washed three shirts. — yes

The circus is fun. — yes

The bear has two mittens. — no

The bear walks to school. — no

**156**

### Find the Main Idea

**Directions:** Look at the pictures. Read the sentences. In the circle, write the letter of the sentence that tells the main idea.

D   B   F

A   C   E

A. The eggs are ready to hatch.

B. It is a very windy day.

C. The old house looks scary.

D. The popcorn popper is too full.

E. The girl thinks the music is too loud.

F. It is too warm for a snowman.

**157**

# What's the Idea?

**Directions:** Look at the pictures. Read the sentences in the speech balloons. Fill in the circle beside the sentence that tells the main idea.

My tummy hurts.
- ○ The mouse wants more to eat.
- ● The mouse ate too much cheese.

My hat is blowing away.
- ● It is a very windy day.
- ○ He doesn't want a hat.

I am seven years old today.
- ○ The cake is very big.
- ● Today is her birthday.

I can't find my home.
- ● The cat is lost.
- ○ The cat has a new home.

**158**

# Read All About It

**Directions:** Read each part of the paper. Fill in the circle beside the sentence that tells the main idea.

**Hundreds Enjoy Town Carnival**
- ● Many people had fun at the carnival.
- ○ The carnival was not a success.

**Bank Robbers Caught**
- ○ Five bank robbers got away.
- ● Two bank robbers were caught.

**CLASSIFIEDS For Sale** 3 black kittens 2 brown puppies Call 555-4109
- ○ Someone wants to buy kittens and puppies.
- ● Someone wants to sell kittens and puppies.

**Garden Club to Meet** Wednesday and Thursday This Week
- ○ The Garden Club will not meet this week.
- ● The Garden Club will meet two times this week.

**159**

# What Doesn't Belong?

**Directions:** Read the sentences under each title. Cross out the sentence that does **not** tell about the main idea.

**Fun at the Playground**
He runs to the slide.
She plays on the swings.
~~I clean my room.~~
They climb the monkey bars.
We sit on the seesaw.

**Doing My Homework**
I open my book.
~~I take a bath.~~
I read the book.
I write the words.
I add the numbers.

**Going to the Zoo**
The monkeys climb the trees.
The seals eat fish.
The snakes move slowly.
~~The kitten plays with yarn.~~
The zebra runs fast.

**Eating Dinner**
Mother cuts the meat.
Father chews the corn.
Sister drinks the milk.
Brother eats his peas.
~~Grandmother has a big house.~~

**160**

# Main Ideas About Meals

**Directions:** Read each story to find the main idea. Fill in the circle beside the phrase that tells the main idea.

**Open Wide!**
An anteater slowly walked up to a log. Many ants were inside the log. The anteater put on a bib. Then, she laid a plate and a big spoon down on the ground. She began to eat and eat. When she was finished, she had eaten 30,000 ants!
- ○ many ants
- ○ a log on the ground
- ● a hungry anteater

**Bite Down!**
It's a good thing that Rollo Rabbit likes to chew. He nibbles on carrots, lettuce, and cabbage all day long. Every time he chews, he wears down his teeth. If Rollo did not chew so much, his front teeth could grow to be ten feet long!
- ○ good vegetables
- ● wearing down teeth
- ○ a fluffy rabbit

**161**

# Ouch!

**Directions:** Read the story below. Then, complete the activity at the bottom of the page.

Marsha and I went for a bike ride on Sunday morning. The streets weren't crowded so we rode down Main Street. A delivery truck in front of us had just gone over a huge bump. Suddenly, a box labeled NAILS flew off the truck and into the air…

Tell what happens next:

_Answers will vary._

**162**

Answer Key
**335**
Total Reading Grade 2

### What Will Happen Next?

**Directions:** Write what happens next:

**Answers will vary.**

163

### What's Next?

**Directions:** Draw a picture of what will happen next in the boxes below:

Pictures will vary.

164

### What Happens Next?

**Directions:** Read each paragraph. Predict what will happen next by placing an **X** in front of the best answer.

1. Robin went hiking with her friend. It was very hot outside. In the distance, they saw a blue glimmering lake.

___ They turned around and went home.

___ They yelled for help.

**X** They waded into the cool water.

2. Jack and Tina are brother and sister. They love to watch basketball games. They also like to practice basketball in their driveway. Their grandma wants to get them the best birthday present ever. What should she get them?

___ Four pairs of shoes.

**X** Season tickets to see the Los Angeles Lakers.

___ A new video game.

165

### What Will They Do?

**Directions:** Read each sentence. Fill in the circle beside the best prediction. Then, circle the picture that matches your answer.

The boy is putting on his skates.
○ He will go swimming.
● He will go skating.

The girl fills her glass with milk.
● She will drink the milk.
○ She will drink water.

The woman wrote a letter to her friend.
○ She will call her friend on the phone.
● She will put the letter in the mailbox.

The kids gave Sally a birthday gift.
● She will open the gift.
○ She will throw the gift away.

166

### Pup Predictions

**Directions:** Read the story.

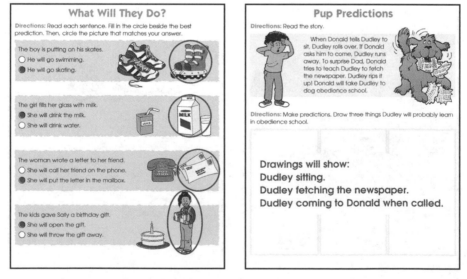

When Donald tells Dudley to sit, Dudley rolls over. If Donald asks him to come, Dudley runs away. To surprise Dad, Donald tries to teach Dudley to fetch the newspaper. Dudley rips it up! Donald will take Dudley to dog obedience school.

**Directions:** Make predictions. Draw three things Dudley will probably learn in obedience school.

Drawings will show:
Dudley sitting.
Dudley fetching the newspaper.
Dudley coming to Donald when called.

167

## How Will It End?

**Directions:** Read each story. Fill in the circle beside the sentence that tells what will happen next.

It is a snowy winter night. The lights flicker once, twice, and then they go out. It is cold and dark. Dad finds the flashlight and matches. He brings logs in from outside. What will Dad do?

● Dad will make a fire.
○ Dad will cook dinner.
○ Dad will clean the fireplace.

Maggie has a garden. She likes fresh, homegrown vegetables. She says they make salads taste better. Maggie is going to make a salad for a picnic. What will Maggie do?

○ Maggie will buy the salad at the store.
○ Maggie will buy the vegetables at the store.
● Maggie will use vegetables from her garden.

The big white goose wakes up. It stands and stretches its wings. It looks all around. It feels very hungry. What will the goose do?

○ The goose will go swimming.
● The goose will look for food.
○ The goose will go back to sleep.

**168**

## Boa Constrictors

Boa constrictors are very big. They may grow up to 14 feet (4.3 meters) long. A boa kills its prey by squeezing it. Then, the prey is swallowed.

Boas do not eat cows or other large animals. They do eat animals that are larger than their own heads. The bones in their jaws stretch so they can swallow small animals such as rodents and birds.

Boa constrictors hunt while hanging from trees. They watch for their prey. Then, they attack. After eating, they may sleep for a week. Boas do not need to eat often. They can live without food for many months.

Boas are not poisonous. They defend themselves by striking and biting with their sharp teeth.

Boa constrictors give birth to live baby snakes. They do not lay eggs. They may have up to fifty baby snakes at one time.

**Directions:** Use facts from the story to help predict what will happen. Fill in the circle next to the correct answer.

1. A boa is hanging from a tree. Suddenly, a bird hops under it. The boa will ___.
   ○ strike and bite it
   ● squeeze it, then swallow it
   ○ poison it, then eat it
   ○ sleep for one week

2. The boa is hungry and hunting for food. Which type of prey will the snake most likely eat?
   ○ cow   ○ panther   ○ horse   ● mouse

3. A boa constrictor is slithering through the grass. Out of the grass comes a hunter walking toward it. The boa will probably ___.
   ● strike the hunter
   ○ slither up a tree to sleep
   ○ squeeze and kill the hunter
   ○ poison the hunter

**171**

## Fact or Opinion?

In sports, there are many facts and opinions. A **fact** is something that is true. An **opinion** is a belief someone has about something.

**Directions:** Read the sports sentences below. Next to each sentence, write **F** if it is a fact and **O** if it is an opinion.

1. __F__ In bowling, a poodle is a ball that rolls down the gutter.
2. __O__ I think poodles are cute.
3. __O__ Julio is my favorite football player.
4. __F__ A football player is a person who plays in a football game.
5. __F__ A catcher's mask protects the catcher's face.
6. __O__ My catcher's mask is too tight.
7. __O__ I had a great putt!
8. __F__ A putt is when a golfer hits the ball into the hole on a green.
9. __F__ A referee is a person who enforces the rules in a game.
10. __O__ Josh thought the referee did a good job.
11. __O__ This silly javelin is really hard to throw!
12. __F__ A metal spear that is thrown for a distance is called a javelin.
13. __O__ Jake said, "The defense tried its best to block the ball."

**172**

## Fact and Opinion: Games!

A **fact** is something that can be proven. An **opinion** is a feeling or belief about something and cannot be proven.

**Directions:** Read these sentences about different games. Then, write **F** next to each fact and **O** next to each opinion.

__O__ 1. Tennis is cool!
__F__ 2. There are red and black markers in a Checkers game.
__F__ 3. In football, a touchdown is worth six points.
__O__ 4. Being a goalie in soccer is easy.
__F__ 5. A yo-yo moves on a string.
__O__ 6. June's sister looks like the queen on the card.
__F__ 7. The six kids need three more players for a baseball team.
__O__ 8. Table tennis is more fun than court tennis.
__F__ 9. Hide-and-Seek is a game that can be played outdoors or indoors.
__F__ 10. Play money is used in many board games.

**173**

## Fact and Opinion: Recycling

**Directions:** Read about recycling. Then, follow the instructions.

What do you throw away every day? What could you do with these things? You could change an old greeting card into a new card. You could make a puppet with an old paper bag. Old buttons make great refrigerator magnets. You can plant seeds in plastic cups. Cardboard tubes make perfect rockets. So, use your imagination!

1. Write **F** next to each fact and **O** next to each opinion.

__O__ Cardboard tubes are ugly.
__F__ Buttons can be made into refrigerator magnets.
__F__ An old greeting card can be changed into a new card.
__O__ Paper-bag puppets are cute.
__F__ Seeds can be planted in plastic cups.
__F__ Rockets can be made from cardboard tubes.

2. What could you do with a cardboard tube? _____
   **Make a rocket.**

**174**

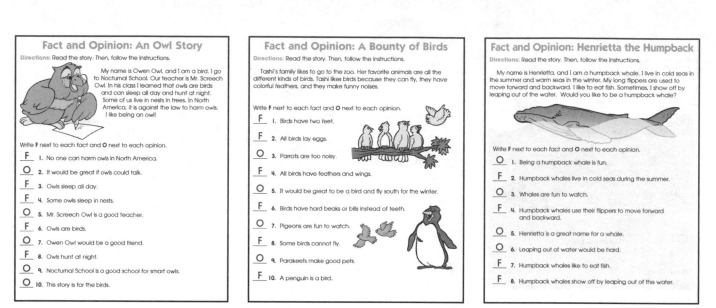

### Fact and Opinion: An Owl Story

**Directions:** Read the story. Then, follow the instructions.

My name is Owen Owl, and I am a bird. I go to Nocturnal School. Our teacher is Mr. Screech Owl. In his class I learned that owls are birds and can sleep all day and hunt at night. Some of us live in nests in trees. In North America, it is against the law to harm owls. I like being an owl!

Write **F** next to each fact and **O** next to each opinion.

**F** 1. No one can harm owls in North America.
**O** 2. It would be great if owls could talk.
**F** 3. Owls sleep all day.
**F** 4. Some owls sleep in nests.
**O** 5. Mr. Screech Owl is a good teacher.
**F** 6. Owls are birds.
**O** 7. Owen Owl would be a good friend.
**F** 8. Owls hunt at night.
**O** 9. Nocturnal School is a good school for smart owls.
**O** 10. This story is for the birds.

**175**

### Fact and Opinion: A Bounty of Birds

**Directions:** Read the story. Then, follow the instructions.

Tashi's family likes to go to the zoo. Her favorite animals are all the different kinds of birds. Tashi likes birds because they can fly, they have colorful feathers, and they make funny noises.

Write **F** next to each fact and **O** next to each opinion.

**F** 1. Birds have two feet.
**F** 2. All birds lay eggs.
**O** 3. Parrots are too noisy.
**F** 4. All birds have feathers and wings.
**O** 5. It would be great to be a bird and fly south for the winter.
**F** 6. Birds have hard beaks or bills instead of teeth.
**O** 7. Pigeons are fun to watch.
**F** 8. Some birds cannot fly.
**O** 9. Parakeets make good pets.
**F** 10. A penguin is a bird.

**176**

### Fact and Opinion: Henrietta the Humpback

**Directions:** Read the story. Then, follow the instructions.

My name is Henrietta, and I am a humpback whale. I live in cold seas in the summer and warm seas in the winter. My long flippers are used to move forward and backward. I like to eat fish. Sometimes, I show off by leaping out of the water. Would you like to be a humpback whale?

Write **F** next to each fact and **O** next to each opinion.

**O** 1. Being a humpback whale is fun.
**F** 2. Humpback whales live in cold seas during the summer.
**O** 3. Whales are fun to watch.
**F** 4. Humpback whales use their flippers to move forward and backward.
**O** 5. Henrietta is a great name for a whale.
**O** 6. Leaping out of water would be hard.
**F** 7. Humpback whales like to eat fish.
**F** 8. Humpback whales show off by leaping out of the water.

**177**

### Strings Attached!

**Directions:** Draw a line to connect each string of words on the left with a string of words on the right to make a complete sentence. Make sure that each sentence you form makes sense.

**Hint:** There are several ways to connect the groups of words. Try out different combinations to find the ones you like best.

The tired mom — the stinky garbage.
We picked apples — had a shaky voice.
I threw out — smelled bad.
The nervous man — and made a pie!
I love to eat — rocked her baby.
The wet cat — vanilla ice cream.

**178**

### Best Guess!

**Directions:** Read each sentence below. Using the information in the first sentence, decide which answer best completes each question. Fill in the circle next to your answer choice.

"Is it cold in here?" asked my grandma as she shivered.

What do you think your grandma would like you to do?

○ Open a window.
● Turn on the heat.
○ Give her a hug.

James' stomach growled really loudly in class today!

What would help James?

○ medicine
○ a new toy
● food

**179**

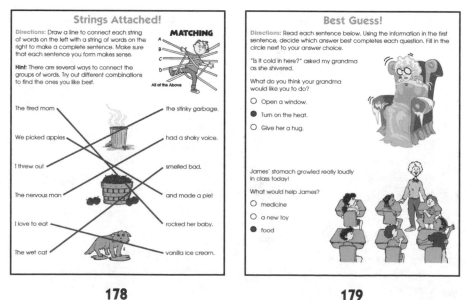

## Who Will Help Me?

**Directions:** Write the best choice from the word list to answer each question.

| Word List | | | |
|---|---|---|---|
| captain | dentist | fireman | doctor |
| plumber | police | teacher | baker |

I think I have a cavity in my tooth. Who can help me?

____ **dentist** ____

My mom needs to order a wedding cake for my uncle. Who can help her?

____ **baker** ____

I hurt my ankle during gym class. Who can help me?

____ **doctor** ____

My pipes are leaking. Who can help me?

____ **plumber** ____

**180**

## What Could I Be?

**Directions:** Write the answer to each riddle. Use a word from the word list.

| Word List |
|---|
| bed   car   stove   umbrella   refrigerator |

I have four wheels.
I have a steering wheel.
I can go very fast or slow. ____ **car**

I protect you from rain.
I open big and close small.
I come in different colors. ____ **umbrella**

I keep food cold.
I usually have two doors.
I have different shelves. ____ **refrigerator**

I am used for sleeping.
I can be soft or hard.
I come in different sizes. ____ **bed**

I am used for cooking food.
I have four burners.
I can heat up soup or fry chicken.
I can burn you if you touch me. Be careful! ____ **stove**

**181**

## It Isn't!

**Directions:** Finish the sentences about the stories.

Something is inside the kitchen cabinet. It isn't a
____ **crocodile** ____

can          vase          crocodile

I smell something delicious in the kitchen. It isn't
____ **dirty socks** ____ .

a cherry pie     dirty socks    a plate of brownies

I touch something soft and fluffy. It isn't
____ **sand paper** ____

sand paper      a kitten      a bath towel

I taste something sour. It isn't a
____ **chocolate bar** ____

lemon          chocolate bar

I hear something making noise. It isn't
____ **a book** ____

a dog          a squirrel          a book

**182**

## Making Inferences

Not every story tells you all the facts. Sometimes you need to put together details to understand what is happening in a story. When you put details together, you **make inferences**.

**Directions:** Read each story. Fill in the circle beside the inference you can make from the details you have.

Everyone on the Pine School baseball team wears a blue shirt on Mondays. It is Monday and Brenda is wearing a blue shirt.

○ Brenda always wears blue clothes.
○ Brenda cannot find her red shirt.
● Brenda is on the baseball team.

My cat has brown and white stripes. It meows when it wants to be fed. My cat is meowing now.

○ The cat wants to go outside.
● The cat is hungry.
○ The cat doesn't like brown and white stripes.

Every afternoon the children run outside when they hear a bell ring. At 2:00, Mr. Chocovan drives by in his ice-cream truck. The children hear a bell ringing. They run outside.

● It is time for ice cream.
○ It is time for the children to go home.
○ It is time for a fire drill.

**183**

## Figure It Out

**Directions:** Read the story.

It is a rainy day. Mom tells Tosh to stay inside until the weather clears up. Tosh lies on his bed and pouts. He sings one song over and over. Now and then, he checks to see if the rain has stopped.

**Directions:** Use details in the story to make inferences. Fill in the circle beside the phrase that completes each sentence.

Tosh probably wants to
● go outside and play.
○ lie in bed all day.

Tosh probably feels
○ happy.
● bored and grumpy.

The song Tosh probably sings is
● "Rain, Rain, Go Away."
○ "Jingle Bells."

**184**

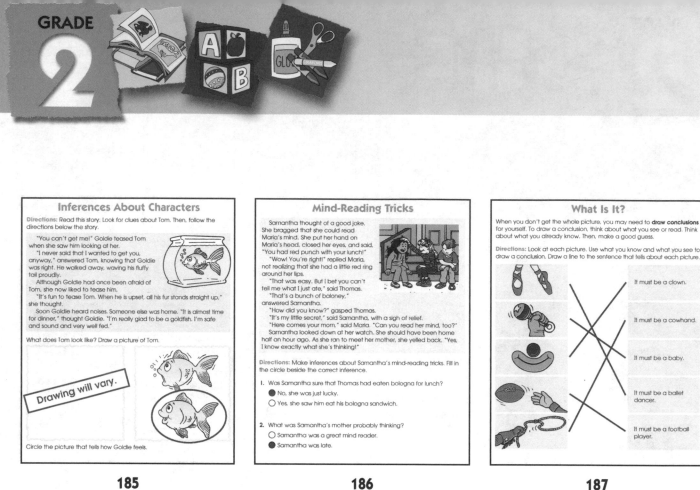

## Inferences About Characters

**Directions:** Read this story. Look for clues about Tom. Then, follow the directions below the story.

"You can't get me!" Goldie teased Tom when she saw him looking at her.

"I never said that I wanted to get you, anyway," answered Tom, knowing that Goldie was right. He walked away, waving his fluffy tail proudly.

Although Goldie had once been afraid of Tom, she now liked to tease him.

"It's fun to tease Tom. When he is upset, all his fur stands straight up," she thought.

Soon Goldie heard noises. Someone else was home. "It is almost time for dinner," thought Goldie. "I'm really glad to be a goldfish. I'm safe and sound and very well fed."

What does Tom look like? Draw a picture of Tom.

Drawing will vary.

Circle the picture that tells how Goldie feels.

## Mind-Reading Tricks

Samantha thought of a good joke. She bragged that she could read Maria's mind. She put her hand on Maria's head, closed her eyes, and said, "You had red punch with your lunch!"

"Wow! You're right!" replied Maria, not realizing that she had a little red ring around her lips.

"That was easy. But I bet you can't tell me what I just ate," said Thomas.

"That's a bunch of baloney," answered Samantha.

"How did you know?" gasped Thomas.

"It's my little secret," said Samantha, with a sigh of relief.

"Here comes your mom," said Maria. "Can you read her mind, too?" Samantha looked down at her watch. She should have been home half an hour ago. As she ran to meet her mother, she yelled back, "Yes, I know exactly what she's thinking!"

**Directions:** Make inferences about Samantha's mind-reading tricks. Fill in the circle beside the correct inference.

1. Was Samantha sure that Thomas had eaten bologna for lunch?
   - ● No, she was just lucky.
   - ○ Yes, she saw him eat his bologna sandwich.

2. What was Samantha's mother probably thinking?
   - ○ Samantha was a great mind reader.
   - ● Samantha was late.

## What Is It?

When you don't get the whole picture, you may need to **draw conclusions** for yourself. To draw a conclusion, think about what you see or read. Think about what you already know. Then, make a good guess.

**Directions:** Look at each picture. Use what you know and what you see to draw a conclusion. Draw a line to the sentence that tells about each picture.

It must be a clown.

It must be a cowhand.

It must be a baby.

It must be a ballet dancer.

It must be a football player.

185                    186                    187

## Who Said It?

**Directions:** Use what you see, what you read, and what you know to draw conclusions. Draw a line from the animal to what it might say.

"I save lots of bones and bury them in the yard."

"I live in the ocean and have sharp teeth."

"I love to walk in the snow and slide on the ice."

"I hop on lily pads in a pond with my webbed feet."

"I slither on the ground because I have no arms or legs."

## What Happened?

**Directions:** Look at the pictures. Fill in the circle beside the sentence that tells what happened in the missing picture. Draw a picture that shows what happened.

What happened?

Drawings will vary.

- ● The boy dropped the string.
- ○ The boy took his kite home.

What happened?

Drawings will vary.

- ○ The angry baby played in its bed.
- ● The hungry baby drank the milk.

188                    189

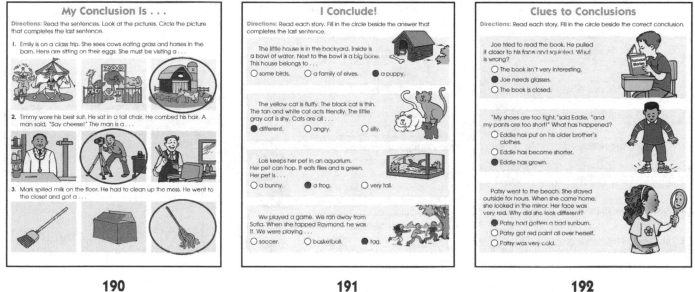

## My Conclusion Is . . .

**Directions:** Read the sentences. Look at the pictures. Circle the picture that completes the last sentence.

1. Emily is on a class trip. She sees cows eating grass and horses in the barn. Hens are sitting on their eggs. She must be visiting a . . .

2. Timmy wore his best suit. He sat in a tall chair. He combed his hair. A man said, "Say cheese!" The man is a . . .

3. Mark spilled milk on the floor. He had to clean up the mess. He went to the closet and got a . . .

**190**

## I Conclude!

**Directions:** Read each story. Fill in the circle beside the answer that completes the last sentence.

The little house is in the backyard. Inside is a bowl of water. Next to the bowl is a big bone. This house belongs to . . .
- ○ some birds.
- ○ a family of elves.
- ● a puppy.

The yellow cat is fluffy. The black cat is thin. The tan and white cat acts friendly. The little gray cat is shy. Cats are all . . .
- ● different.
- ○ angry.
- ○ silly.

Lois keeps her pet in an aquarium. Her pet can hop. It eats flies and is green. Her pet is . . .
- ○ a bunny.
- ● a frog.
- ○ very tall.

We played a game. We ran away from Sofia. When she tapped Raymond, he was it. We were playing . . .
- ○ soccer.
- ○ basketball.
- ● tag.

**191**

## Clues to Conclusions

**Directions:** Read each story. Fill in the circle beside the correct conclusion.

Joe tried to read the book. He pulled it closer to his face and squinted. What is wrong?
- ○ The book isn't very interesting.
- ● Joe needs glasses.
- ○ The book is closed.

"My shoes are too tight," said Eddie, "and my pants are too short!" What has happened?
- ○ Eddie has put on his older brother's clothes.
- ○ Eddie has become shorter.
- ● Eddie has grown.

Patsy went to the beach. She stayed outside for hours. When she came home, she looked in the mirror. Her face was very red. Why did she look different?
- ● Patsy had gotten a bad sunburn.
- ○ Patsy got red paint all over herself.
- ○ Patsy was very cold.

**192**

## Cause and Effect

**Cause:** An action or act that makes something happen.

**Effect:** Something that happens because of an action or cause.

Look at the following example of cause and effect.

We forgot to put the lid on the trash can.  The raccoons ate the trash.

**Directions:** Now, draw a line connecting each cause on the left side of the page to its effect on the right side of the page.

**193**

## How Did It Happen?

**Directions:** Read the stories below. Then, write the missing cause or effect.

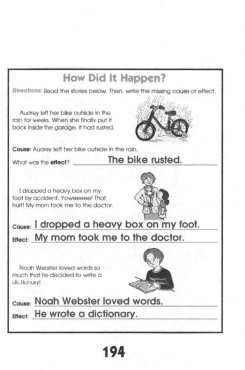

Audrey left her bike outside in the rain for weeks. When she finally put it back inside the garage, it had rusted.

**Cause:** Audrey left her bike outside in the rain.
What was the **effect?** _The bike rusted._

I dropped a heavy box on my foot by accident. Yoweeeee! That hurt! My mom took me to the doctor.

**Cause:** I dropped a heavy box on my foot.
**Effect:** My mom took me to the doctor.

Noah Webster loved words so much that he decided to write a dictionary!

**Cause:** Noah Webster loved words.
**Effect:** He wrote a dictionary.

**194**

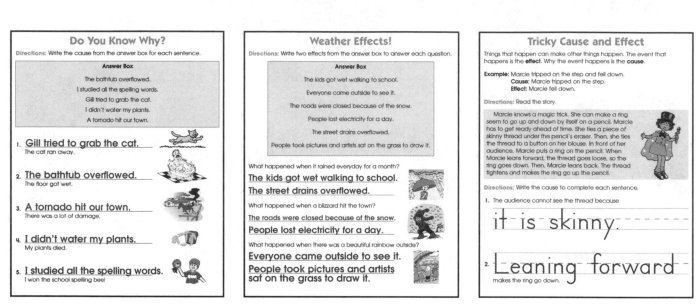

### Do You Know Why?

**Directions:** Write the cause from the answer box for each sentence.

**Answer Box**

The bathtub overflowed.
I studied all the spelling words.
Gill tried to grab the cat.
I didn't water my plants.
A tornado hit our town.

1. Gill tried to grab the cat.
   The cat ran away.

2. The bathtub overflowed.
   The floor got wet.

3. A tornado hit our town.
   There was a lot of damage.

4. I didn't water my plants.
   My plants died.

5. I studied all the spelling words.
   I won the school spelling bee!

**195**

### Weather Effects!

**Directions:** Write two effects from the answer box to answer each question.

**Answer Box**

The kids got wet walking to school.
Everyone came outside to see it.
The roads were closed because of the snow.
People lost electricity for a day.
The street drains overflowed.
People took pictures and artists sat on the grass to draw it.

What happened when it rained everyday for a month?
The kids got wet walking to school.
The street drains overflowed.

What happened when a blizzard hit the town?
The roads were closed because of the snow.
People lost electricity for a day.

What happened when there was a beautiful rainbow outside?
Everyone came outside to see it.
People took pictures and artists sat on the grass to draw it.

**196**

### Tricky Cause and Effect

Things that happen can make other things happen. The event that happens is the **effect**. Why the event happens is the **cause**.

**Example:** Marcie tripped on the step and fell down.
   **Cause:** Marcie tripped on the step.
   **Effect:** Marcie fell down.

**Directions:** Read the story.

Marcie knows a magic trick. She can make a ring seem to go up and down by itself on a pencil. Marcie has to get ready ahead of time. She ties a piece of skinny thread under the pencil's eraser. Then, she ties the thread to a button on her blouse. In front of her audience, Marcie puts a ring on the pencil. When Marcie leans forward, the thread goes loose, so the ring goes down. Then, Marcie leans back. The thread tightens and makes the ring go up the pencil.

**Directions:** Write the cause to complete each sentence.

1. The audience cannot see the thread because
   it is skinny.

2. Leaning forward
   makes the ring go down.

**197**

### Why Did It Happen?

**Directions:** Read the effects. Fill in the circle beside the sentence that tells what caused the effect.

The soccer coach is cheering.
○ Her team lost the game.
● Her team won the game.

Patty found only one cookie in the cookie jar.
● Someone ate all the other cookies.
○ It was a brand new cookie jar.

Fred has a new pair of glasses.
● Fred was having trouble seeing the chalkboard.
○ There was a sale on glasses.

Lynn turned the fan to high.
○ It was a very cold day.
● It was a very hot day.

Jason took his umbrella to school.
● The sky was cloudy.
○ The sun was shining.

**198**

### Chain of Effects

**Directions:** Read the story.

At night, Tran set his alarm clock for seven o'clock. When it rang the next morning, he was so tired he turned the alarm off. Then, he went back to sleep. Tran finally woke up at eight o'clock. Tran had missed the school bus. He had to walk to school. It was a long walk. Tran was very late!

**Directions:** Draw a line to match a cause to an effect.

| Cause | Effect |
|---|---|
| Because he was tired, | Tran missed the school bus. |
| Because Tran turned off the alarm, | he had to walk to school. |
| Because he woke up at eight o'clock, | Tran turned off the alarm. |
| Because Tran missed the bus, | Tran was late for school. |
| Because he had a long walk, | he overslept. |

**199**

## A Cause-and-Effect Fable

**Directions:** Read the story.

Four animals caught a talking fish. "If you let me go, I will grant each of you a wish," announced the fish.

"Make my trunk smaller!" demanded the vain elephant. "I wish to be the most beautiful elephant that ever lived."

"Make my legs longer!" commanded the alligator. "I want to be taller than all my alligator friends."

"Make my neck shorter!" ordered the giraffe. "I am tired of always staring at the tops of trees."

"Dear Fish, please make me be satisfied with who-o-o-o I am," whispered the wise old owl.

Poof! Kazaam! Their wishes were granted. However, soon after, only one of these animals was happy. Can you guess who-o-o-o?

**Directions:** Draw a line to match a cause to an effect.

| | |
|---|---|
| Because of its short trunk, | the giraffe could no longer eat leaves from treetops. |
| Because of its long legs, | the elephant could no longer spray water on its back. |
| Because of its short neck, | the owl was happy about his wish. |
| Because he could still do all the things he needed, | the alligator could no longer hide in shallow water. |

**200**

## Fiction or Nonfiction?

Some stories are made up and some are true. **Fiction** stories are made up, and **nonfiction** stories are true.

**Directions:** Read the passages below. Then, write if they are **fiction** or **nonfiction**.

Following a balanced diet is important for good health. Your body needs many kinds of vitamins and minerals found in different types of food. For example, oranges provide vitamin C, and bananas are a good source of the mineral potassium.

**nonfiction**

We call my dog the alphabet dog. Why? Because my dog can sing the alphabet! That's right! My dog, Smarty Pants, is a dog genius! Smarty Pants can sing the entire alphabet! "S.P.," as we sometimes call her, is also starting her own dog academy to teach other dogs how to sing the alphabet! You should sign up your dog for classes with Smarty Pants today!

**fiction**

**201**

## Fiction/Nonfiction: Heavy Hitters

**Fiction** is a make-believe story. **Nonfiction** is a true story.

**Directions:** Read the stories about two famous baseball players. Then, write **fiction** or **nonfiction** in the baseball bats.

In 1998, Mark McGwire played for the St. Louis Cardinals. He liked to hit home runs. On September 27, 1998, he hit home run number 70, to set a new record for the most home runs hit in one season. The old record was set in 1961 by Roger Maris, who later played for the St. Louis Cardinals (1967 to 1968), when he hit 61 home runs.

**nonfiction**

The Mighty Casey played baseball for the Mudville Nine and was the greatest of all baseball players. He could hit the cover off the ball with the power of a hurricane. But, when the Mudville Nine was behind 4 to 2 in the championship game, Mighty Casey struck out with the bases loaded. There was no joy in Mudville that day, because the Mudville Nine had lost the game.

**fiction**

**202**

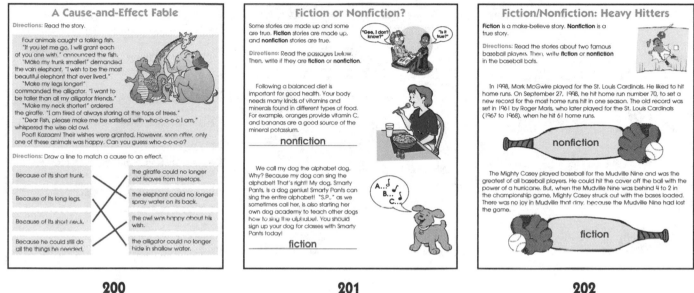

## Nonfiction: Tornado Tips

**Directions:** Read about tornadoes. Then, follow the instructions.

A tornado begins over land with strong winds and thunderstorms. The spinning air becomes a funnel. It can cause damage. If you are inside, go to the lowest floor of the building. A basement is a safe place. A bathroom or closet in the middle of a building can be a safe place, too. If you are outside, lie in a ditch. Remember, tornadoes are dangerous.

Write five facts about tornadoes.

1. **A tornado begins over land.**

2. **Spinning air becomes a funnel.**

3. **Tornadoes can cause damage.**

4. **A basement is a safe place to be in a tornado.**

5. **If you are outside during a tornado, you should lie in a ditch.**

**203**

## Fiction: Hercules

The **setting** is where a story takes place. The **characters** are the people in a story or play.

**Directions:** Read about Hercules. Then, answer the questions.

Hercules was born in the warm Atlantic Ocean. He was a very small and weak baby. He wanted to be the strongest hurricane in the world. But he had one problem. He couldn't blow 75-mile-per-hour winds. Hercules blew and blew in the ocean, until one day, his sister, Hola, told him it would be more fun to be a breeze than a hurricane. Hercules agreed. It was a breeze to be a breeze!

1. What is the setting of the story? **Atlantic Ocean**

2. Who are the characters? **Hercules, Hola**

3. What is the problem? **Hercules couldn't blow 75 mile-per-hour winds.**

4. How does Hercules solve his problem? **He decides that it is more fun to be a breeze than a hurricane.**

**204**

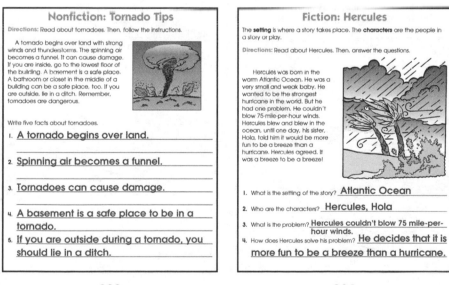

## Fiction/Nonfiction: The Fourth of July

**Directions:** Read each story. Then, write whether it is fiction or nonfiction.

One sunny day in July, a dog named Stan ran away from home. He went up one street and down the other looking for fun, but all the yards were empty. Where was everybody? Stan kept walking until he heard the sound of band music and happy people. Stan walked faster until he got to Central Street. There he saw men, women, children, and dogs getting ready to walk in a parade. It was the Fourth of July!

Fiction or nonfiction? **Fiction**

Americans celebrate the Fourth of July every year, because it is the birthday of the United States of America. On July 4, 1776, the United States got its independence from Great Britain. Today, Americans celebrate this holiday with parades, picnics, and fireworks as they proudly wave the red, white, and blue American flag.

Fiction or nonfiction? **Nonfiction**

**205**

## Fiction and Nonfiction: Which Is It?

**Directions:** Read about fiction and nonfiction books. Then, follow the instructions.

There are many kinds of books. Some books have make-believe stories about princesses and dragons. Some books contain poetry and rhymes, like Mother Goose. These are fiction.

Some books contain facts about space and plants. And still other books have stories about famous people in history like Abraham Lincoln. These are nonfiction.

Write **F** for **fiction** and **NF** for **nonfiction**.

- F  1. nursery rhyme
- F  2. fairy tale
- NF  3. true life story of a famous athlete
- F  4. Aesop's fables
- NF  5. dictionary entry about foxes
- NF  6. weather report
- F  7. story about a talking tree
- NF  8. story about how a tadpole becomes a frog
- NF  9. story about animal habitats
- F  10. riddles and jokes

**206**

## Character, cont.

First, authors must decide who their main character is going to be. Next, they decide what their main character looks like. Then, they reveal the character's personality by:

**what the character does**

**what the character says**

**Directions:** Answer the questions about the story you just read.

Who is the main character in "Adventurous Alenna!"?

**Alenna is the main character.**

What does Alenna look like? Describe her appearance on the line below:

**Alenna had long, blond hair and sea-green eyes.**

Give two examples of what Alenna **does** that shows that she is adventurous:

1. **She goes on long bike rides.**
2. **She water-skis.**

Give an example of what Alenna **says** that reveals she is adventurous.

**She wants to go snorkeling.**

**208**

## Character Interview—Lights! Camera! Action!

An **interview** takes place between two people, usually a reporter and another person. The interviewer asks questions for the person to answer.

**Directions:** Pretend that you are a reporter. Choose a character from a book you read. If you could ask the character anything you wanted to, what would you ask?

Make a **list of questions** you would like to ask your character:

1. _____
2. _____ **Answers will vary.**
3. _____
4. _____

Now, pretend your character has come to life and could **answer your questions**. Write what you think he, she, or it would say:

1. _____
2. _____ **Answers will vary.**
3. _____
4. _____

**209**

## Setting—Place

Every story has a **setting**. The setting is the **place** where the story happens. Think of a place that you know well. It could be your room, your kitchen, your backyard, your classroom, or an imaginary place.

**Directions:** Brainstorm some words and ideas about that place. Think about what you see, hear, smell, taste, or feel in that place.

Brainstorm your ideas for a setting below:

see   hear   smell

taste   touch

**Answers will vary.**

Where are we? _____

**210**

## Setting—Place

**Directions:** Read the story below and answer the questions about the setting.

### The Amazing Amazon

The Amazon jungle is a huge rain forest in South America. It is full of gigantic green trees, thick jungle vines, and many species of dangerous animals. It is very humid in the jungle.

What is the temperature like in the Amazon jungle?

**It is very humid.**

Where is the Amazon jungle located?

**The Amazon jungle is located in South America.**

Would it be easy to travel in the Amazon jungle? Why or why not?

**It would not be easy to travel because of the gigantic green trees, thick jungle vines, and the many species of dangerous animals.**

Does it rain a lot in the Amazon jungle?

**It rains a lot because it is a rain forest.**

**211**

## Setting—Time

The **setting** is the **place** where the story happens. The setting is also the **time** in which the story happens. A reader needs to know **when** the story is happening. Does it take place at night? On a sunny day? In the future? During the winter?

**Time** can be:

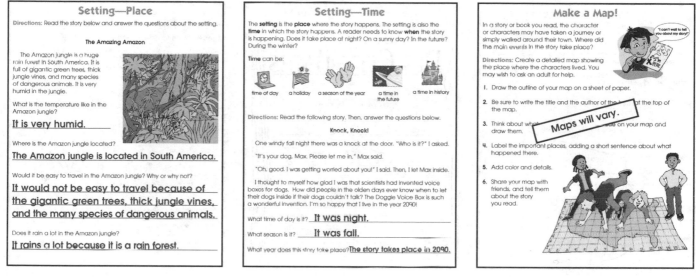

time of day    a holiday    a season of the year    a time in the future    a time in history

**Directions:** Read the following story. Then, answer the questions below.

### Knock, Knock!

One windy fall night there was a knock at the door. "Who is it?" I asked.

"It's your dog, Max. Please let me in," Max said.

"Oh, good. I was getting worried about you!" I said. Then, I let Max inside.

I thought to myself how glad I was that scientists had invented voice boxes for dogs. How did people in the olden days ever know when to let their dogs inside if their dogs couldn't talk? The Doggie Voice Box is such a wonderful invention. I'm so happy that I live in the year 2090!

What time of day is it? **It was night.**

What season is it? **It was fall.**

What year does this story take place? **The story takes place in 2090.**

**212**

## Make a Map!

In a story or book you read, the character or characters may have taken a journey or simply walked around their town. Where did the main events in the story take place?

**Directions:** Create a detailed map showing the place where the characters lived. You may wish to ask an adult for help.

1. Draw the outline of your map on a sheet of paper.

2. Be sure to write the title and the author of the book at the top of the map.

3. Think about what ~~places you want~~ to make on your map and draw them.

4. Label the important places, adding a short sentence about what happened there.

5. Add color and details.

6. Share your map with friends, and tell them about the story you read.

*Maps will vary.*

**213**

## Travel Brochure

A travel brochure gives information about interesting places to visit. Travel brochures usually include beautiful color pictures and descriptive sentences that make people want to visit that place. They also give useful facts about a place.

**Directions:** Plan a travel brochure for the **setting** of a book you have read.

First, brainstorm and write down some ideas about the setting in your book. What would you want to talk about the ~~setting~~ there: What it looked like? local plants and animals? other interesting places to visit there?

Take a sheet of paper and fold it into three sections. You can write on both the front and back sides.

Color your brochure with crayons or markers.

Share your brochure with friends, and tell them about the setting of the book you read.

*Brochures will vary.*

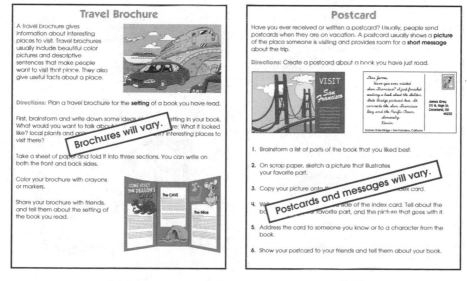

**214**

## Postcard

Have you ever received or written a postcard? Usually, people send postcards when they are on vacation. A postcard usually shows a **picture** of the place someone is visiting and provides room for a **short message** about the trip.

**Directions:** Create a postcard about a book you have just read.

1. Brainstorm a list of parts of the book that you liked best.

2. On scrap paper, sketch a picture that illustrates your favorite part.

3. Copy your picture onto ~~one side of the~~ index card.

4. Write ~~on the other~~ side of the index card. Tell about the bo~~ok~~ your favorite part, and the picture that goes with it.

5. Address the card to someone you know or to a character from the book.

6. Show your postcard to your friends and tell them about your book.

*Postcards and messages will vary.*

**215**

## Extra! Extra! Read All About It!

Newspaper reporters have very important jobs. They have to catch a reader's attention and, at the same time, **tell the facts.**

Newspaper reporters write their stories by answering **who, what, where, when, why,** and **how.**

**Directions:** Think about a book you just read and answer the questions below.

**Who:**   Who is the story about?
_____

**What:**   What happened to the main character?
_____

**Where:**   Where do**Answers will vary.**
_____

**When:**   When does the story take place?
_____

**Why:**   Why do these story events happen?
_____

**How:**   How do these events happen?
_____

**216**

## Extra! Extra! Read All About It!

**Directions:** Use your answers on page 216 to write a newspaper article about the book you read.

### BIG CITY TIMES

Title

(Write a catchy title for your article.)

**Articles will vary.**

**217**

## Common Nouns

A **common noun** names a person, place, or thing.

**Example:** The **boy** had several **chores** to do.

**Directions:** Fill in the circle below each common noun.

1. First, the **boy** had to feed his **puppy.**
2. He got fresh **water** for his **pet.**
3. Next, the **boy** poured some dry **food** into a **bowl.**
4. He set the **dish** on the **floor** in the **kitchen.**
5. Then, he called his **dog** to come to **dinner.**
6. The **boy** and his **dad** worked in the **garden.**
7. The **father** turned the **dirt** with a **shovel.**
8. The **boy** carefully dropped **seeds** into little **holes.**
9. Soon, tiny **plants** would sprout from the **soil.**
10. **Sunshine** and **showers** would help the **radishes** grow.

**218**

## Proper Nouns

A **proper noun** names a specific or certain person, place, or thing. A proper noun always begins with a capital letter.

**Example: Becky** flew to **St. Louis** in a **Boeing 747.**

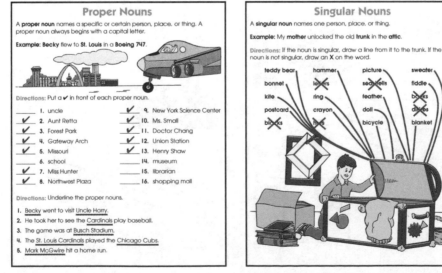

**Directions:** Put a ✔ in front of each proper noun.

| | | | |
|---|---|---|---|
| ___ | 1. uncle | ✔ | 9. New York Science Center |
| ✔ | 2. Aunt Retta | ✔ | 10. Ms. Small |
| ✔ | 3. Forest Park | ✔ | 11. Doctor Chang |
| ✔ | 4. Gateway Arch | ✔ | 12. Union Station |
| ✔ | 5. Missouri | ✔ | 13. Henry Shaw |
| ___ | 6. school | ___ | 14. museum |
| ✔ | 7. Miss Hunter | ___ | 15. librarian |
| ✔ | 8. Northwest Plaza | ___ | 16. shopping mall |

**Directions:** Underline the proper nouns.

1. <u>Becky</u> went to visit <u>Uncle Harry.</u>
2. He took her to see the <u>Cardinals</u> play baseball.
3. The game was at <u>Busch Stadium.</u>
4. The <u>St. Louis Cardinals</u> played the <u>Chicago Cubs.</u>
5. <u>Mark McGwire</u> hit a home run.

**219**

## Singular Nouns

A **singular noun** names one person, place, or thing.

**Example:** My **mother** unlocked the old **trunk** in the **attic.**

**Directions:** If the noun is singular, draw a line from it to the trunk. If the noun is not singular, draw an **X** on the word.

teddy bear    hammer    picture    sweater
bonnet    le~~tters~~    sea~~shells~~    fiddle
kite    ring    feather    bo~~oks~~
postcard    crayon    doll    di~~shes~~
blo~~cks~~    ha~~ts~~    bicycle    blanket

**220**

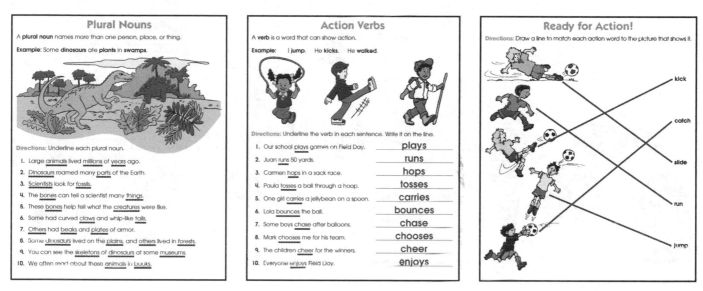

## Plural Nouns

A **plural noun** names more than one person, place, or thing.

**Example:** Some **dinosaurs** ate **plants** in swamps.

**Directions:** Underline each plural noun.

1. Large animals lived millions of years ago.
2. Dinosaurs roamed many parts of the Earth.
3. Scientists look for fossils.
4. The bones can tell a scientist many things.
5. These bones help tell what the creatures were like.
6. Some had curved claws and whip-like tails.
7. Others had beaks and plates of armor.
8. Some dinosaurs lived on the plains, and others lived in forests.
9. You can see the skeletons of dinosaurs at some museums.
10. We often read about these animals in books.

**221**

## Action Verbs

A **verb** is a word that can show action.

**Example:** I **jump**.  He **kicks**.  He **walked**.

**Directions:** Underline the verb in each sentence. Write it on the line.

1. Our school plays games on Field Day.  plays
2. Juan runs 50 yards.  runs
3. Carmen hops in a sack race.  hops
4. Paula tosses a ball through a hoop.  tosses
5. One girl carries a jellybean on a spoon.  carries
6. Lola bounces the ball.  bounces
7. Some boys chase after balloons.  chase
8. Mark chooses me for his team.  chooses
9. The children cheer for the winners.  cheer
10. Everyone enjoys Field Day.  enjoys

**222**

## Ready for Action!

**Directions:** Draw a line to match each action word to the picture that shows it.

kick
catch
slide
run
jump

**223**

## Irregular Verbs

Verbs that do not add **ed** to show what happened in the past are called **irregular verbs**.

**Example: Present    Past**
run, runs    ran
fall, falls    fell

Jim **ran** past our house yesterday.
He **fell** over a wagon on the sidewalk.

**Directions:** Fill in the verbs that tell what happened in the past in the chart. The first one is done for you.

| Present | Past |
| --- | --- |
| hear, hears | heard |
| draw, draws | drew |
| do, does | did |
| give, gives | gave |
| sell, sells | sold |
| come, comes | came |
| fly, flies | flew |
| build, builds | built |
| know, knows | knew |
| bring, brings | brought |

**224**

## Linking Verbs

A **linking verb** does not show action. Instead, it links the subject with a word in the predicate. **Am, is, are, was,** and **were** are **linking verbs**.

**Example:** Many people **are** collectors.
(**Are** connects **people** and **collectors**.)
The collection **was** large.
(**Was** connects **collection** and **large**.)

**Directions:** Underline the linking verb in each sentence.

1. I am happy.
2. Toy collecting is a nice hobby.
3. Mom and Dad are helpful.
4. The rabbit is beautiful.
5. Itsy and Bitsy are stuffed mice.
6. Monday was special.
7. I was excited.
8. The class was impressed.
9. The elephants were gray.
10. My friends were a good audience.

**225**

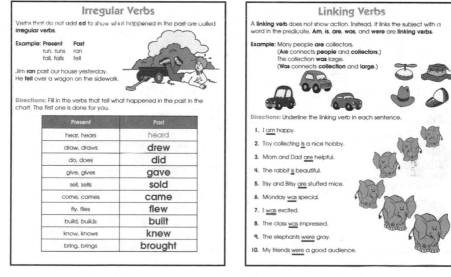

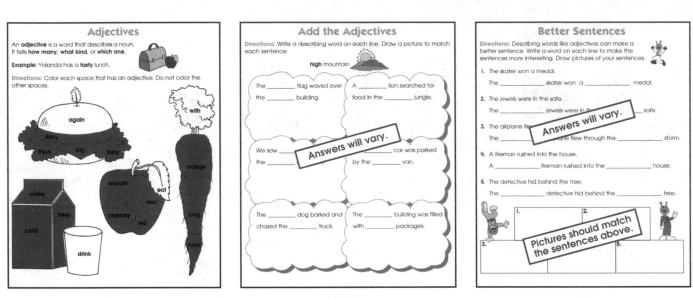

**Adjectives**

An **adjective** is a word that describes a noun. It tells **how many**, **what kind**, or **which one**.

**Example:** Yolanda has a **tasty** lunch.

**Directions:** Color each space that has an adjective. Do not color the other spaces.

again
juicy
thick    big    tasty
white
fresh
cold
drink
with
smooth
eat
sour
crunchy    long
red
hard
orange

**226**

**Add the Adjectives**

**Directions:** Write a describing word on each line. Draw a picture to match each sentence.

**high** mountain

The _____ flag waved over the _____ building.

A _____ lion searched for food in the _____ jungle.

We saw the _____ _____ car was parked by the _____ van.

*Answers will vary.*

The _____ dog barked and chased the _____ truck.

The _____ building was filled with _____ packages.

**227**

**Better Sentences**

**Directions:** Describing words like adjectives can make a better sentence. Write a word on each line to make the sentences more interesting. Draw pictures of your sentences.

1. The skater won a medal.
   The _____ skater won a _____ medal.

2. The jewels were in the safe.
   The _____ jewels were in the _____ safe.

3. The airplane flew through the storm.
   The _____ plane flew through the _____ storm.

4. A fireman rushed into the house.
   A _____ fireman rushed into the _____ house.

5. The detective hid behind the tree.
   The _____ detective hid behind the _____ tree.

*Answers will vary.*

*Pictures should match the sentences above.*

1.    2.
3.    5.

**228**

**Describing People**

**Directions:** Choose two words from the box that describe each character. Then, complete each sentence to tell why you chose those words.

| understanding | spoiled | responsible | lazy | helpful | upset | happy |
| busy | caring | kind | mean | confused | unhappy | patient | nice |

*Answer may include:* _happy_ and _kind_ she likes to help people and makes a lot of friends that way.

Mother is _____ and _____ because she _____

Father _____ and _____ because he _____

*Answers will vary.*

**229**

**Using Exact Adjectives**

Use an **adjective** that best describes the noun or pronoun. Be specific.

**Example:** David had a nice birthday.
David had a **fun** birthday.

**Directions:** Rewrite each sentence, replacing **nice** or **good** with a better adjective from the box or one of your own.

| sturdy | new | great | chocolate | delicious | special |

1. David bought a nice pair of in-line skates.
   **David bought a new pair of in-line skates.**

2. He received a nice helmet.
   **He received a great helmet.**

3. He got nice knee pads.
   **He got sturdy knee pads.**

4. Father baked a good cake.
   **Father baked a delicious cake.**

5. David made a good wish.
   **David made a special wish.**

6. Mom served good ice cream.
   **Mom served chocolate ice cream.**

**230**

GRADE 2

## Subjects of Sentences

The **subject** of a sentence tells **who** or **what** does something.

**Example: Some people** eat foods that may seem strange to you.

**Directions:** Underline the subject of each sentence.

1. Some people like crocodile steak.
2. The meat tastes like fish.
3. Australians eat kangaroo meat.
4. Kangaroo meat tastes like beef.
5. People in the Southwest eat rattlesnake meat.
6. Snails make a delicious treat for some people.
7. Some Africans think roasted termites are tasty.
8. Bird's-nest soup is a famous Chinese dish.
9. People in Florida serve alligator meat.
10. Almost everyone treats themselves with ice cream.

**231**

## Predicates of Sentences

The **predicate** of a sentence tells what the subject is or does. It is the verb part of the sentence.

**Examples:** Sally Ride **flew in a space shuttle.**

She **was an astronaut.**

**Directions:** Underline the predicate in each sentence.

1. She was the first American woman astronaut in space.
2. Sally worked hard for many years to become an astronaut.
3. She studied math and science in college.
4. Ms. Ride passed many tests.
5. She learned things quickly.
6. Sally trained to become a jet pilot.
7. This astronaut practiced using a robot arm.
8. Ms. Ride used the robot arm on two space missions.
9. She conducted experiments with it.
10. The robot arm is called a remote manipulator.

**232**

## Compound Subjects

A **compound subject** has two or more subjects joined by the word **and**.

**Example: Owls** are predators. **Wolves** are predators.
**Owls and wolves** are predators. (compound subject)

**Directions:** If the sentence has a compound subject, write **CS**. If it does not, write **No**.

_No_ 1. A predator is an animal that eats other animals.
_No_ 2. Prey is eaten by predators.
_CS_ 3. Robins and bluejays are predators.
_No_ 4. Some predators eat only meat.
_CS_ 5. Crocodiles and hawks eat meat only.
_CS_ 6. Raccoons and foxes eat both meat and plants.

**Directions:** Combine the subjects of the two sentences to make a compound subject. Write the new sentence on the line.

1. Snakes are predators. Spiders are predators.
**Snakes and spiders are predators.**
2. Frogs prey on insects. Chameleons prey on insects.
**Frogs and chameleons prey on insects.**

**235**

## Compound Predicates

A **compound predicate** has two or more predicates joined by the word **and**.

**Example:** Abe Lincoln was born in Kentucky. Abe Lincoln lived in a log cabin there.
Abe Lincoln **was born in Kentucky and lived in a log cabin there.**

**Directions:** If the sentence has a compound predicate, write **CP**. If it does not, write **No**.

_CP_ 1. Abe Lincoln cut trees and chopped wood.
_No_ 2. Abe and his sister walked to a spring for water.
_CP_ 3. Abe's family packed up and left Kentucky.
_No_ 4. They crossed the Ohio River to Indiana.
_No_ 5. Abe's father built a new home.
_CP_ 6. Abe's mother became sick and died.
_No_ 7. Mr. Lincoln married again.
_CP_ 8. Abe's new mother loved Abe and his sister and cared for them.

**236**

## Complete Sentences

A **sentence** is a group of words that tells a whole idea. It has a subject and a predicate.

**Examples:** Some animals have stripes.
(sentence)
Help to protect.
(not a sentence)

**Directions:** Write **S** in front of each sentence. Write **No** if it is **not** a sentence.

_S_ 1. There are different kinds of chipmunks.
_No_ 2. They all have.
_S_ 3. They all have stripes to help protect them.
_S_ 4. The stripes make them hard to see in the forest.
_S_ 5. Zebras have stripes, too.
_No_ 6. Some caterpillars also.
_S_ 7. Other animals have spots.
_S_ 8. Some dogs have spots.
_No_ 9. Beautiful, little fawns.
_S_ 10. Their spots help to hide them in the woods.

**237**

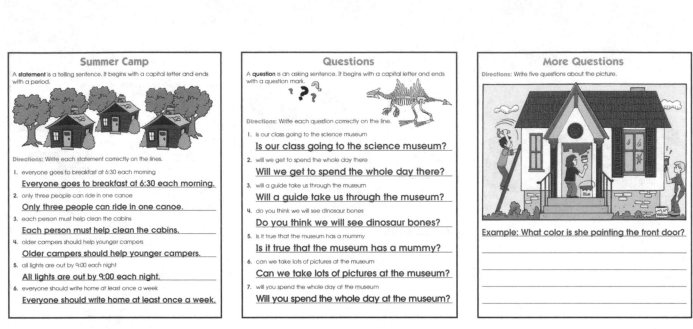

## Summer Camp

A **statement** is a telling sentence. It begins with a capital letter and ends with a period.

**Directions:** Write each statement correctly on the lines.

1. everyone goes to breakfast at 6:30 each morning

   Everyone goes to breakfast at 6:30 each morning.

2. only three people can ride in one canoe

   Only three people can ride in one canoe.

3. each person must help clean the cabins

   Each person must help clean the cabins.

4. older campers should help younger campers

   Older campers should help younger campers.

5. all lights are out by 9:00 each night

   All lights are out by 9:00 each night.

6. everyone should write home at least once a week

   Everyone should write home at least once a week.

**238**

## Questions

A **question** is an asking sentence. It begins with a capital letter and ends with a question mark.

**Directions:** Write each question correctly on the line.

1. is our class going to the science museum

   Is our class going to the science museum?

2. will we get to spend the whole day there

   Will we get to spend the whole day there?

3. will a guide take us through the museum

   Will a guide take us through the museum?

4. do you think we will see dinosaur bones

   Do you think we will see dinosaur bones?

5. is it true that the museum has a mummy

   Is it true that the museum has a mummy?

6. can we take lots of pictures at the museum

   Can we take lots of pictures at the museum?

7. will you spend the whole day at the museum

   Will you spend the whole day at the museum?

**239**

## More Questions

**Directions:** Write five questions about the picture.

Example: What color is she painting the front door?

**240**

## Kinds of Sentences

A **statement** ends with a period. **.** A **question** ends with a question mark. **?**

**Directions:** Write the correct mark in each box.

1. Would you like to help me make an aquarium **?**
2. We can use my brother's big fish tank **.**
3. Will you put this colored sand in the bottom **?**
4. I have three shells to put on the sand **.**
5. Can we use your little toy boat, too **?**
6. Let's go buy some fish for our aquarium **.**
7. Will twelve fish be enough **?**
8. Look, they seem to like their new home **.**
9. How often do we give them fish food **?**
10. Let's tell our friends about our new aquarium **.**

**241**

## Writing Sentences

Every sentence begins with a capital letter.

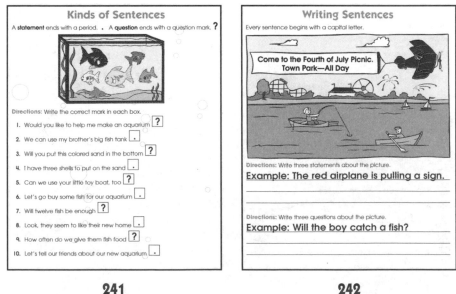

Come to the Fourth of July Picnic.
Town Park—All Day

**Directions:** Write three statements about the picture.

Example: The red airplane is pulling a sign.

**Directions:** Write three questions about the picture.

Example: Will the boy catch a fish?

**242**

# GRADE 2

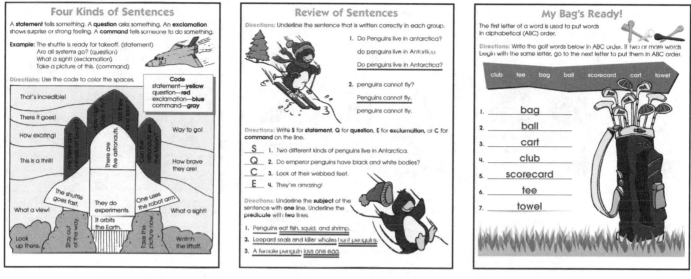

## Four Kinds of Sentences

A **statement** tells something. A **question** asks something. An **exclamation** shows surprise or strong feeling. A **command** tells someone to do something.

**Example:** The shuttle is ready for takeoff. (statement)
Are all systems go? (question)
What a sight! (exclamation)
Take a picture of this. (command)

**Directions:** Use the code to color the spaces.

**Code**
statement—**yellow**
question—**red**
exclamation—**blue**
command—**gray**

That's incredible!
There it goes!
How exciting!
This is a thrill!
What a view!
Look up there.
Way to go!
How brave they are!
What a sight!
The shuttle goes fast.
They do experiments.
One uses the robot arm.
It orbits the Earth.
Watch the liftoff.

**243**

## Review of Sentences

**Directions:** Underline the sentence that is written correctly in each group.

1. Do Penguins live in antarctica?
   do penguins live in Antarctica
   <u>Do penguins live in Antarctica?</u>

2. penguins cannot fly?
   <u>Penguins cannot fly.</u>
   penguins cannot fly.

**Directions:** Write **S** for **statement**, **Q** for **question**, **E** for **exclamation**, or **C** for **command** on the line.

S 1. Two different kinds of penguins live in Antarctica.
Q 2. Do emperor penguins have black and white bodies?
C 3. Look at their webbed feet.
E 4. They're amazing!

**Directions:** Underline the **subject** of the sentence with **one** line. Underline the **predicate** with **two** lines.

1. <u>Penguins</u> eat fish, squid, and shrimp.
2. <u>Leopard seals and killer whales</u> hunt penguins.
3. <u>A female penguin</u> lays one egg.

**244**

## My Bag's Ready!

The first letter of a word is used to put words in alphabetical (ABC) order.

**Directions:** Write the golf words below in ABC order. If two or more words begin with the same letter, go to the next letter to put them in ABC order.

club  tee  bag  ball  scorecard  cart  towel

1. bag
2. ball
3. cart
4. club
5. scorecard
6. tee
7. towel

**245**

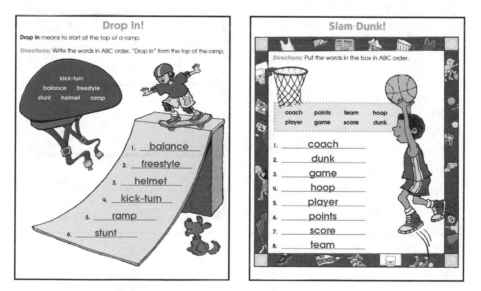

## Drop In!

**Drop in** means to start at the top of a ramp.

**Directions:** Write the words in ABC order. "Drop in" from the top of the ramp.

kick-turn  balance  freestyle  stunt  helmet  ramp

1. balance
2. freestyle
3. helmet
4. kick-turn
5. ramp
6. stunt

**246**

## Slam Dunk!

**Directions:** Put the words in the box in ABC order.

coach  points  team  hoop  player  game  score  dunk

1. coach
2. dunk
3. game
4. hoop
5. player
6. points
7. score
8. team

**247**

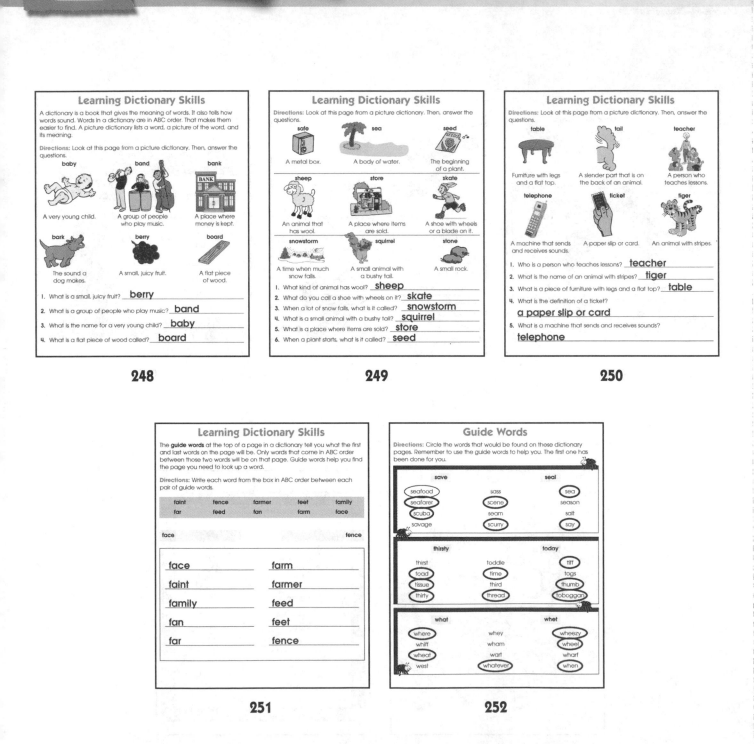

## Learning Dictionary Skills

A dictionary is a book that gives the meaning of words. It also tells how words sound. Words in a dictionary are in ABC order. That makes them easier to find. A picture dictionary lists a word, a picture of the word, and its meaning.

**Directions:** Look at this page from a picture dictionary. Then, answer the questions.

**baby** — A very young child.
**band** — A group of people who play music.
**bank** — A place where money is kept.
**bark** — The sound a dog makes.
**berry** — A small, juicy fruit.
**board** — A flat piece of wood.

1. What is a small, juicy fruit? **berry**
2. What is a group of people who play music? **band**
3. What is the name for a very young child? **baby**
4. What is a flat piece of wood called? **board**

**248**

## Learning Dictionary Skills

**Directions:** Look at this page from a picture dictionary. Then, answer the questions.

**safe** — A metal box.
**sea** — A body of water.
**seed** — The beginning of a plant.
**sheep** — An animal that has wool.
**store** — A place where items are sold.
**skate** — A shoe with wheels or a blade on it.
**snowstorm** — A time when much snow falls.
**squirrel** — A small animal with a bushy tail.
**stone** — A small rock.

1. What kind of animal has wool? **sheep**
2. What do you call a shoe with wheels on it? **skate**
3. When a lot of snow falls, what is it called? **snowstorm**
4. What is a small animal with a bushy tail? **squirrel**
5. What is a place where items are sold? **store**
6. When a plant starts, what is it called? **seed**

**249**

## Learning Dictionary Skills

**Directions:** Look at this page from a picture dictionary. Then, answer the questions.

**table** — Furniture with legs and a flat top.
**tail** — A slender part that is on the back of an animal.
**teacher** — A person who teaches lessons.
**telephone** — A machine that sends and receives sounds.
**ticket** — A paper slip or card.
**tiger** — An animal with stripes.

1. Who is a person who teaches lessons? **teacher**
2. What is the name of an animal with stripes? **tiger**
3. What is a piece of furniture with legs and a flat top? **table**
4. What is the definition of a ticket?
**a paper slip or card**
5. What is a machine that sends and receives sounds?
**telephone**

**250**

## Learning Dictionary Skills

The **guide words** at the top of a page in a dictionary tell you what the first and last words on the page will be. Only words that come in ABC order between those two words will be on that page. Guide words help you find the page you need to look up a word.

**Directions:** Write each word from the box in ABC order between each pair of guide words.

| faint | fence | farmer | feet | family |
|-------|-------|--------|------|--------|
| far | feed | fan | farm | face |

face _____ fence

| face | farm |
|------|------|
| faint | farmer |
| family | feed |
| fan | feet |
| far | fence |

**251**

## Guide Words

**Directions:** Circle the words that would be found on these dictionary pages. Remember to use the guide words to help you. The first one has been done for you.

**save** — **seal**
(seafood) sass (sea)
(seafarer) scene season
(scuba) seam salt
savage (scurry) (say)

**thirsty** — **today**
thirst toddle (tiff)
(toad) time togs
(tissue) third (thumb)
(thirty) (thread) (toboggan)

**what** — **whet**
(where) whey (wheezy)
whiff wham (wheel)
(wheat) wart wharf
west (whatever) (when)

**252**

Make your own book called "Friends" with the cardboard pages attached to the back of this workbook. Have fun drawing and coloring the pictures!

Friends share. Friends care.

When you need them, friends are there.     8

FRIENDS

1

Friends share.
Friends care.

2

when things go wrong.

7

Friends say, "I'm sorry"          6

When you need them,
friends are there.          3

Friends can play                    4

the whole day long.                5